"I got into bed a few nights a̲g̲o̲, ...
before dozing off. The text got my adrenaline running, and I finally
closed the covers two-and-a-half hours later."

—Ted Hechtman, "Smart Money," columnist
Welcomat, Philadelphia

"A fascinating book—the kind of book that agree or disagree,
you're gonna pick it up and throw it against the wall at least twice."

—Buzz Schwartz, Investor's Club of the Air
KMNY Radio, Los Angeles

"Robert Czeschin may be on his way to becoming the Robert
Ludlum of financial advisors.

The Last Wave is ostensibly about how to invest your money. But
it's got all the fixings of potboiling fiction—nuclear terrorists,
international intrigue, Presidents going eyeball to eyeball with the
Soviets over the oil fields of the Mideast, and natural catastrophes
bringing the world to its knees."

—John Strausbaugh
City Paper, Baltimore

"The great bull market that ended in October 1987 was the last
wave of investment prosperity before a new era in which practically
everything—your investments, your livelihood, the future of those
you love—will be at risk. It will be a poor time to be ill advised. But
where upheavals threaten, opportunities also abound."

—Robert W. Czeschin
The Last Wave

This is an unusual book for an unusual time. Czeschin offers both
an understanding of the crisis facing investors in today's financial
markets and a prescription for using this insight to your investment
advantage.

In *The Last Wave*, you will find out what may be the greatest
single profit opportunity in mankind's history. You'll learn how to
profit from the history of markets. Best of all, you'll also benefit from
the ultimate investment leverage—knowledge of the future, and how
to apply it to your own situation...right now!

The Last Wave

Oil, War, and Financial Upheaval in the 1990s

by Robert W. Czeschin

Agora Books
824 E. Baltimore Street
Baltimore, Maryland 21202
USA

Publisher: William Bonner
Managing Editor: Jane Lears
Copy Editors: Dianne R. McCann and Kathie Peddicord
Graphic Designer and Map Illustrations: Becky Mangus
Production: Becky Mangus and Wilma Vinck
Typesetter: Denise Plowman
Research and Computer Graphics: Adrienne C. Locke
Cover Design: Jack French

Fourth Edition

Table of Contents

Foreword

There is a tide in the affairs of men,
Which, taken at the flood, leads on to fortune;
Omitted, all the voyage of their life
Is bound in shallows and in miseries.
　　　　　　　　　　　　—Shakespeare, *Julius Caesar*

　　　The great bull market that ended in the crash of 1987 was the last wave of investment prosperity before the dawning of a new era in which Americans will find themselves increasingly under attack. We stand on the threshold of a decade in which practically everything— your investments, your livelihood, the future of those you love—will be at risk. It will be a bad time to be ill-advised. But when upheavals threaten, opportunities also abound. During the Great Depression of the 1930s, for example, the foundations were laid for some of the great fortunes of the 20th century. This is a book about being prepared for the future.

　　　To a fertile imagination, the notion of a final wave immediately conjures up a formidable array of images. One is a vision of a tropical typhoon spreading destruction in its wake, or a crashing assault from the sea, itself a symbol of the domain of chaos. Another image calls to mind the regular ebb and flow of seasons and tides, which come and go with the reassuring certainty of a known and immutable time schedule. Both are profound, and both describe important aspects of the tough times and dangerous days ahead.

　　　As inheritors of a great tradition of political stability and orderly financial markets, Americans are unprepared by either history or temperament for the tide of accelerating chaos that looms ahead. As a nation unfamiliar with military defeat, we are likely to be both frightened and appalled by increasing vulnerability to events beyond our shores.

　　　This stomach-churning state of affairs did not happen overnight. On the contrary, it has been a long time coming. The problem for

i

most people who end up the victim of events is failure to properly understand the obvious. One can scarcely complain about being carried off by the flood when the river has been plainly rising for more than a decade. In the decade ahead, Americans will find themselves the victims of events on a scale not seen in more than 150 years. Much of this will occur because of the loss of self-sufficiency in two key areas—energy and capital.

Fuel sufficiency

When wood fueled the world's economies, the great coniferous, broadleaf, and roundwood forests of North America assured American self-sufficiency. When coal became the principal source of fuel for home and industry, the presence of the world's largest reserves within the continental borders of the United States was more than enough to ensure self-sufficiency.

We have not seen the last wave of the coal-fired economy. But what displaced coal from its ascendancy as the world's premier fuel was oil—which weighed 30% less and took up only half as much space in storage. Not only did oil burn hotter than coal, but it required little or no ash removal. It did not take long for the military advantages of oil-fired technology to be widely recognized. Soon a wave of competition for reserves began that persists to the present day. As French Senator Henry Berenger observed in 1925:

> *He who owns the oil will own the world, for he will rule the sea by means of the heavy oils, the air by means of the ultra-refined oils, and the land by means of petrol...he will rule his fellow men...by reason of the fantastic wealth he will derive from oil—the wonderful substance which is more sought after and precious today than gold itself.*[1]

As with wood and coal, the United States was blessed with abundant supplies of oil. For most of the 1930s, 40s, and 50s, American wells accounted for nearly two out of every three barrels of world production. OPEC was not the first to realize the political advantages of being a major oil exporter. It was Presidents Franklin Roosevelt and Dwight Eisenhower who pioneered the use of oil as a political weapon.

At the end of World War II, the United States accounted for over 70% of world production. Forty years later, that fraction has fallen to only 16%. In 1970, America crossed the fateful threshold of energy dependence. Today, the United States is the victim of the very weapon it once wielded with impunity.

Political and financial fallout

It is difficult to overestimate the financial and political implications of these developments. The bear market of 1973-74 and the debt crisis that today threatens a new depression on a scale not seen since the 1930s are both products of the OPEC-induced oil shocks of the 1970s. Other implications go far beyond the merely economic. Oil-related conflicts lie at the heart of the wave of terrorism sweeping the globe today. And at least twice, the United States has been on the verge of launching a nuclear attack to preserve access to oil for itself and its allies.

Capital dependency

The loss of energy self-sufficiency in 1970 was only one symptom of the decline of American power. In 1985, the United States surrendered self-sufficiency in capital as well. For the first time in more than 70 years, we became a debtor nation.

Today, the United States is utterly dependent on a continuous supply of foreign capital to finance the federal budget deficit. Foreign holdings of U.S. Treasury securities increased nearly 19% in 1988 alone.[2] If foreigners suddenly stopped buying U.S. Treasury bills and notes, the government's appetite for borrowing would rapidly overwhelm domestic capital markets. The ensuing rise in interest rates would do more than send the stock market into another tailspin. It would likely push the economy into a depression from which it might take years to emerge.

Foreigners—especially the Japanese—are buying up American companies and real estate at a prodigious rate. Foreign ownership of U.S. assets now dwarfs U.S. ownership of assets abroad. Foreign purchases of U.S. common stocks have also been one of the major engines of the greatest bull market since 1929.

Today, the United States can no longer lay claim to the world's largest stock market. Early in 1987, we were overtaken by Japan. In 1929, a U.S. stock market crash pulled the world into the Great Depression. In the months ahead, a crash in the Japanese market could do the same.

(We have been overtaken in other ways as well. At current exchange rates, the value of all the real estate in the tiny Japanese home islands is worth more than all the real estate in the continental vastness of the United States. On a recent visit to the Far East, one analyst confided to me that the Japanese emperor's imperial palace was worth more than all of California.)

The Japanese are also dependent on imported oil for virtually 100% of their petroleum needs. It was the need to secure its oil supplies that led Japan into World War II. The same concern fuels the debate over Japanese rearmament in the 1980s.

The Japanese are world leaders in both anti-submarine technology and computer-based artificial intelligence, on which the newest generation of weapons systems depend. If they decided again on a course of conquest, few countries in East Asia would be able to stand in their way. As in World War II, such a development would put them on a collision course with the United States. This time, however, the outcome is likely to be different.

As citizens of a once-dominant power, it may be difficult not to regard the decline of American power as something of a catastrophe. A number of authors have written popular books that both exacerbate and take advantage of these fears. James Davidson and William Rees-Mogg, in their book *Blood in the Streets,* suggest that a 1930s-style depression lies ahead. The title of Dr. Ravi Batra's best-selling volume, *The Crash of 1990,* is self-explanatory.

Even newsletter publishers have jumped on the bandwagon. Robert Prechter, the well-known editor of the noted stock-market advisory, *The Elliott Wave Theorist,* for example, has for several years been predicting that the Dow Jones Industrial Average would peak around 3,500—and then plummet as low as 100. (After the crash of 1987, of course, these forecasts had to be revised. In his more recent public appearances, Prechter has been saying the Dow could go as low as 41.)[3]

But there is a sense in which this view of the current state of affairs is inappropriate. Cataclysms do occur. Rome fell. Noah's flood, if you accept the biblical accounts, was an epochal deluge that changed the face of human destiny forever. But rarely has there ever been a catastrophe on such a scale that none survived—or even that none managed somehow to make a buck.

In this sense, the last wave is something of a misnomer. It is true that fearful events threaten. But the next deluge will not be the end of waves, markets, or those with sufficiently long-range vision to prepare for what takes everyone else by surprise. As far as economics is concerned, virtually everything that happens is bad news for someone. But it is also good news for someone else. Successful investing is knowing how to find the good news—even when you must look beneath the surface of seemingly forbidding waters.

The loss of American self-sufficiency in energy and capital is certain to result in further political and financial upheavals in the next few years. But unlike most people, who live without interest or awareness of history's great turning points, you need not be taken by surprise. In fact, I hope to show you ways to turn these seemingly ominous currents of events to your advantage.

To this end, you will find the remainder of this book divided into three sections. The first section focuses on the struggle for control of the world's supplies of oil as one of the major threats to peace and prosperity. The second section covers the possibility that Japan could trigger the next worldwide economic collapse. The third section is devoted to explaining how you can turn these two currents of history to your investment advantage.

Oil and war

This book is based on the premise that the lessons of the past can not only illuminate the present, but adumbrate the future as well. Accordingly, **Chapter 1** begins the story of oil and war with the history of oil's emergence as a strategic objective in World War I.

In **Chapter 2**, you'll learn how Hitler's nearly invincible war machine ground to a halt because of the lack of gasoline, and how the attack of Pearl Harbor would probably never have occurred had President Roosevelt not cut off U.S. oil exports to the Japanese.

Chapter 3 tells the dramatic story of the first use of Mideast oil as a political weapon—the Suez crisis of 1956. You'll find out how President Eisenhower skillfully wielded the oil weapon to project American power and ensure his own re-election. You'll also read about how the first battle for control of the canal—and its vital oil cargos—unfolded nearly a decade earlier in the arid sands of the Egyptian desert.

In **Chapter 4**, you will read the story of how the United States twice went to the nuclear brink to deter a Soviet assault on the oil lifeline of the Western world. You'll learn how the Russians, flush with the initial success of their invasion of Afghanistan, began to amass troops just on the other side of Iran's northern frontier—and how U.S. military weakness left President Carter no choice but to contemplate the use of nuclear weapons.

Chapter 5 examines oil and the war against civilians—or, the

terrorist threat. You will explore the roots of terrorism in the 1980s—
which go back to the seventh century A.D. In recent years, successes
in the war against the rising tide of international hostage-taking have
been few and far between. You'll learn what you can do as an individual—to avoid becoming a hostage, or to survive if you are unlucky
enough to become one.

Chapter 6 brings you right up to the present oil-related conflict
in the Persian Gulf. You'll read the inside story of the rise and fall of
OPEC, how bungling in the early days of the Gulf War cost Iraq all
hope of ultimate victory. You'll find out why the government in
Tehran defies analysis by Western political science. Finally, you'll get
fresh insight on some of the investment implications of the most
likely course of future events in that turbulent, terrifying part of the
world.

Pearl Harbor II

It is one of the great ironies of history that, once set in motion,
events tend to assume a life of their own. Sometimes these currents
flow back to their origins and unexpectedly inundate the ones responsible for starting them in motion. Something very much like what
happened when American occupation authorities unleashed forces in
postwar Japan and how that came back to haunt them a couple of generations later.

Chapter 7 begins with the story of the Japanese postwar economic miracle—how the country went from ruins to riches in a few
short years, how policy decisions made by the American occupation
authorities in the 1940s unwittingly sowed the seeds of Japanese-
American conflict in the 1980s and beyond.

Chapter 8 covers the Japanese shopping spree in the United
States. You'll find out what's driving the Japanese to buy up huge
chunks of the United States, and the extent to which that leaves us
vulnerable to economic developments far beyond our own shores.

Chapter 9 is about the rearmament of Japan. You'll learn how a
wave of protectionism in the 1930s plunged Japan into depression and
civil disorder—out of which new military rulers emerged whose lust
for empire led directly to World War II. Nowadays, American
politicians are again campaigning for protectionism against the
Japanese—without the slightest understanding of how they could be
putting civilian rule at risk for a second time.

Chapter 10 covers the Japanese stock market. In it, you'll read
about the forces behind the most extraordinary bull market of modern

times. You'll get an up-to-date assessment of the likelihood of a crash—including a discussion of an unfamiliar threat that is almost never discussed in the financial press.

Finally, you'll read about the devastating effects such a crash could have on the stock market in the United States.

Preparing for financial upheaval

The possibility that a crash in Japan could shake markets as far away as the United States leads quite nicely into the theme of the final section, which addresses the topic of investment survival in the decade ahead.

Chapter 11 takes up the question of what lies ahead in the aftermath of the crash of 1987. You'll read about the various long-wave theories of depression, and how the banking crisis could knock both the economy and the stock market into the financial equivalent of a black hole. At a time when bank failures are approaching an all-time high, you'll also learn how to find out how safe your bank is.

Chapter 12 warns you about the most serious threat facing the average investor today—the approaching debacle in mutual funds. You'll find out why bear markets hurt mutual fund investors worse than any other class of investor. In the 1930s, a run on the nation's banks plunged the nation into a depression. In the 1980s, a run on open-end mutual funds could result in similar investment devastation. You'll also find out what you can do to head off this and other threats to your mutual fund portfolio.

Chapter 13 attempts to pull all these various themes and threads together. It is a manual for riding the last wave to prosperity and profit, for finding the good news that lies beneath the surface of what seem to be rather grim and forbidding waters.

Inevitably, perhaps, a book about money and history is a book about tempest and turmoil. I hope you will find it full of high adventure as both a reader and an investor. That great upheavals lie ahead, however, does not mean that the last wave of investment prosperity must end in despair. For those with vision and courage, the future is never dark.

---

1. Quoted by Anton Mohr, *The Oil War,* Harcourt Brace, New York, 1926, p. 35-36.

2. Wessel, D., "U.S. Debt to Rest of World Increased by 40% to $532.5 billion Last Year," *Wall Street Journal,* June 30, 1989, p. 2.

3.Speech delivered by Robert Prechter before the Market Technicians Association Annual Meeting, Hilton Head, South Carolina, May 1985. See also *Wall Street Journal,* Jan. 2, 1987, p. 1; and "The Doomsday Vision of Bob Prechter," *Barron's*, May 1989.

Section I

Oil and War

Chapter I

Oil-fired Engines of War

The History of Oil in World War I

No matter how well-fed, equipped, or officered, without oil and gasoline the modern army is a hopeless monster, mired and marked for destruction.

—T.H. Vail Motter, U.S. Army Historian

World War I marked the beginning of large-scale military use of oil-related technologies. During World War I, oil became a military objective for the first time. It was also the first time an oil strategy—securing one's own supplies while denying them to an adversary—had a measurable impact on victory.

For centuries the world had known about naturally occurring deposits of oil. It was something that seeped into and ruined drinking wells and rendered land unfit for farming. But in 1859, when Edwin Drake struck a gusher in Pennsylvania, oil, for the first time, became available in commercial quantities.

As a fuel, it enjoyed considerable advantages over coal and wood. It was more efficient, giving a greater volume of heat per unit of weight. Because it was a liquid it could be transported through pipelines. This made it a lot easier to handle than solid fuel—and a lot safer to handle than combustible gases, such as hydrogen (at the time used to power lighter-than-air balloons). But it also made possible a further development that was to prove even more revolutionary—the internal combustion engine.

In 1862, Alphonse Beau de Rochas constructed the first oil-powered piston engine. Building on de Rochas' work, the German

1

firm of Nikolaus Otto and E. Langen in 1876 built a version that incorporated an electric spark ignition.

By 1883, another German, Gottlieb Daimler, had constructed an engine-powered bicycle. His engine was the first ever to use a refined by-product of oil—gasoline. In 1892 Rudolf Diesel invented the compression-ignition engine that bears his name to the present century.

The most important thing about the oil-burning internal combustion engine was that it delivered hitherto unachieved amounts of power for an engine of its weight. This new higher power-to-weight ratio, made possible by the new technology, was soon to produce a corresponding revolution in the art of war—in the air, on land, and at sea.

Military aviation

At the turn of the century, military aviation was confined to the use of lighter-than-air balloons. As early as the American Civil War, these balloons were used as fixed observation posts for artillery. But the oil-fired technology offered a new and previously unheard of mobility. No longer would balloon operators have to choose between the tether and the random currents of the wind.

Brigadier Count Ferdinand von Zeppelin was one of the first to conceive a new kind of airship. Using a newly discovered metal— lightweight aluminum—he constructed the world's first metal-framed rigid airship. In 1900, he launched the LZ1, a 420-foot-long cigar-shaped airship powered by two Daimler engines. It was capable of speeds of up to 17 miles per hour.

Heavier-than-air fighters

Of course the real oil-powered revolution in military aviation concerned not improvements to balloons, but the invention of the airplane. In 1903, the Wright brothers made their successful flight at Kitty Hawk, and four years later, the U.S. Army issued the world's first specifications for a military airplane.

In 1910, the U.S. Army conducted a series of tests that included dropping a dummy bomb on a target shaped like a battleship and launching a plane from the deck of a ship. The same year, the Italian army dropped the first airborne torpedo.

Admittedly, these events are more noteworthy for the way they foreshadowed the future than for the way they influenced the outcome of World War I. Some strategic bombing was attempted by Zeppelins and biplanes, but rarely did these bombs hit their targets. So as bombers, aircraft were fit only as weapons of terror that could be used to demoralize and unnerve civilian populations. Pioneering attempts were also made to use aircraft to strafe enemy positions in support of infantry. But by and large, World War I aviation was confined to reconnaissance and range finding for artillery.

Oil and the birth of armored warfare

As early as 1899, F.R. Simms, a British engineer, imagined the advantages a mechanized armored cavalry would have over the traditional horse-borne variety. First, he mounted one of Daimler's engines on a four-wheeled motor bike. Then he armed it with a Maxim machine gun mounted behind a shield on the handle bars.

Encouraged by his early successes, Simms next built a prototype of what he called the War Car, armed with a 1 1/2-pound cannon and a pair of machine guns. He successfully demonstrated it in a series of tests before British army brass, where he achieved speeds in excess of 9 mph. As is so often the case, however, the generals were preparing to fight the last war instead of the next one. He didn't get a single order.

It was the farsighted Winston Churchill who ultimately saved the idea from military oblivion. As first lord of the admiralty, he formed a Land Ships Committee to consider development of the craft. Because the early models had to travel by flat-bed rail car from the factory to the proving ground, there was always a chance they might be spotted by enemy agents. So to ensure secrecy they were routinely covered with tarpaulins stamped with the legend "WATER TANK." In due course, tank became the code word for the new armored fighting vehicle, and later, the vernacular.

Not until much later did the real virtues of armored vehicles finally dawn upon the rest of the British military. But before I tell the story, let me first set the stage.

Before the stalemate

Popular histories of World War I often dwell on the military stalemate that resulted from the network of trenches and barbed wire that stretched across Europe. But in the early days of the campaign, it was a war of feint and thrust, of tactical maneuvers on a grander scale than the world had ever seen.

In the opening weeks of the campaign, German armies, following the battle plan of General von Schlieffen, swept westward through Belgium to open a front from which to descend upon France from the north. As the Allied powers struggled to marshal a counterattack, it seemed that the best chance for disrupting the German advance lay in a flanking maneuver to the west. If only Allied armies could get around the forward elements of the German army, they could fall upon the enemy's rear.

Of course, the Germans soon discovered the Allied intentions and kept trying to extend their line of advance—before the Allies could get around it. These mutual attempts at an outflanking maneuver sent both armies in a headlong rush westward to the sea.

In 1914, some of Winston Churchill's sailors, sent over to assist the hard-pressed Belgians, witnessed a startling innovation. The Belgians, forever outnumbered and outgunned by the Germans, were forced to improvise under pressure to stave off catastrophe on the Plain of Flanders. In a desperate attempt to increase the mobility of

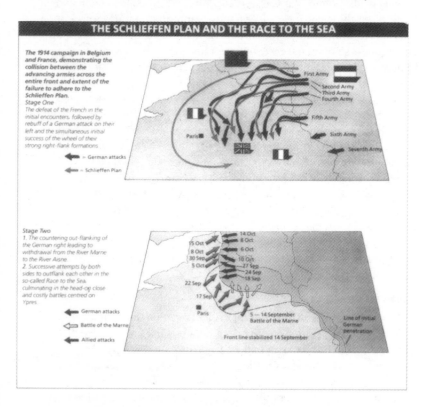

THE SCHLIEFFEN PLAN AND THE RACE TO THE SEA

The 1914 campaign in Belgium and France, demonstrating the collision between the advancing armies across the entire front and extent of the failure to adhere to the Schlieffen Plan.
Stage One
The defeat of the French in the initial encounters, followed by rebuff of a German attack on their left and the simultaneous initial success of the wheel of their strong right-flank formations.

First Army
Second Army
Third Army
Fourth Army
Fifth Army
Sixth Army
Seventh Army
Paris

= German attacks
= Schlieffen Plan

Stage Two
1. The countering out-flanking of the German right leading to withdrawal from the River Marne to the River Aisne.
2. Successive attempts by both sides to outflank each other in the so-called Race to the Sea, culminating in the head-on close and costly battles centred on Ypres.

14 Oct
8 Oct
15 Oct
8 Oct
6 Oct
30 Sep
10 Oct
5 Oct
27 Sep
24 Sep
18 Sep
22 Sep
17 Sep
Paris
5 — 14 September
Battle of the Marne
Line of initial German penetration
Front line stabilized 14 September

= German attacks
= Battle of the Marne
= Allied attacks

Map of von Schlieffen's invasion routes from *Technology and War: The Impact of Science on Weapon Development and Modern Battle,* by Kenneth Macksey, Prentice-Hall Press, New York, 1986, p. 68.

their troops, they put 6-millimeter and later 8-millimeter armor on all the motorized vehicles they could manage to commandeer.

Much to the Germans' consternation, they found that nothing in their arsenal could penetrate 8-millimeter steel plates—except their huge fort-busting artillery. But these big guns were slow-moving and difficult to aim. And such was the state of gunnery at the time that one hit out of 30 at 100 yards was very good shooting. So against fast-moving vehicles, the big guns were useless.

At length, the Germans found the only way they could stop the four-wheeled armored trucks was to dig ditches too deep for them to cross. But before a network of trenches extended across the entire

British Mark I tank from *Tank: A History of the Armored Fighting Vehicle,* by Kenneth Macksey and John H. Batchelor, Ballantine Books, a division of Random House, Inc., New York, 1970, p. 144.

Western front and both sides settled down to a war of attrition, the armored car was estimated by both sides to be the military equivalent of an entire company of infantry.

This early success of the vehicles stimulated a wealth of mechanized armor building. But it was only much later, as the British grew desperate for a way to break the stalemate, that the precursor of the modern battle tank really came into its own.

In 1916, a Royal army engineer, Col. Ernest Swinton, proposed an attack using steel armored tracked vehicles, powered by an internal combustion engine and armed with cannon and machine guns, as a way to break through the heavily fortified Hindenberg line at Cambrai. The tanks that faced the Germans that fateful day were slow-moving and cumbersome affairs, hastily improvised out of available components. The tracks and drive trains were taken from early tractors. Guns and armor were taken from the navy—which, true to the oldest traditions of inter-service rivalry, tried its best to kill the project.

The world's first tank battle—Cambrai

The plan of attack called for 476 tanks, which had to be brought to the front by railroad. In those days, a tank's tracks and sprockets wore out after only 20 miles! Transport by rail also served another purpose. It ensured that the Germans were not tipped off in advance by the distinctive rumbling and clanking sounds of armor on the move.

Each tank carried huge bundles of wood called fascines to dump in ditches that blocked its path. As the trenches were crossed and the barbed wire crushed down, infantry would follow. Once the defensive perimeter was pierced, cavalry would debouch into the open ground beyond, fall upon the German rear, and, so it was hoped, force Germany's withdrawal from northern France.

At 6:10 a.m. on Nov. 19, 1917, the startled German defenders awoke to the ominous rumble of approaching armor. Ten minutes later, suppressive fire from 1,003 Allied artillery engulfed the enemy's forward battery positions. Smoke, fired at enemy observation posts, combined with the morning fog and prevented early discovery of the Allied battle plan.

Breached defenses

The Germans promptly dived into their underground bunkers, content to wait until the big guns exhausted their supplies of ammunition. The enemy high command, believing in the invulnerability of the earthworks that constituted the Hindenberg line, reached a similar conclusion. In the underground comfort of their command bunkers, they never dreamed an invasion was possible, let alone imminent. And so they planned no counterattacks. As a result, the Allied action achieved complete and utter tactical surprise.

On the right flank, the tanks broke through almost without resistance. Grenade and rifle fire from advancing Allied infantry completely routed the terrified defenders. With speedy capture of the front-line positions thus assured, the tanks lunged ahead—at the unheard of speed of 4 mph!—down the long slope toward the vital bridges that spanned the Escaut Canal at Masnieres and Marcoing. But when the first bridge collapsed under the weight of a single tank, the Allies knew they had a problem. Tanks were not waterproof, and portable pontoon bridges had not yet been invented.

On the left flank, the few surviving German gunners made a fortuitous discovery. In the heat of battle, their stocks of explosive artillery shells had been rapidly depleted. In desperation they resorted to solid shot, ample supplies of which were available. Although it came too late to save the German positions on the left, solid shot soon proved to be an excellent armor-piercing weapon.

Nonetheless, Allied tanks swept forward and soon outdistanced the infantry and cavalry, which were supposed to follow in close support. Just as the advance on the right was stopped by an unbridgeable canal, on the left it dissipated as effective coordination was lost between forward elements of the battle. In those days, communication depended on the laying of vulnerable telephone cables and horse-borne messengers. And it often took hours to respond to rapidly changing battlefield conditions.

Still, for the Allies, it was a tactical success, if not a strategic triumph. In exchange for 4,000 dead and 65 tanks destroyed, they captured 10,000 of the enemy, 123 artillery pieces, 179 mortars, and 281 machine guns. And, of course, mechanized armor, driven by the oil-fired engines of war, changed the face of battle forever.

Oil technology afloat

The application of the oil-burning engine to ships changed the nature of surface warfare and opened new avenues of military advantage. And Winston Churchill, Britain's first lord of the admiralty, was among the first to appreciate the advantages of an oil-fired navy.

Because of their superior thermal efficiency, oil-burning boilers delivered more power than their coal-fired predecessors. As a result, the new oil-fired ships were much faster than anything else afloat. Furthermore, oil was much easier than solid fuel to load and store. A liquid, it could be held in the numerous cavities within a ship's hull, which previously had been inaccessible and useless.

The ability to load more fuel on a ship meant a corresponding increase in operational radius. Oil-fired boats were able to steam as much as 40% farther between refuelings than their coal-fired counterparts. In addition, liquid fuel made it possible to supply the boiler by means of mechanical pumps. This freed up a significant amount of manpower that formerly had been used merely to stoke the furnace!

Finally, construction of an oceangoing fleet of tankers raised the possibility of resupply at sea—effectively extending the operational range of the fleet. As commander of the navy, Churchill ordered the conversion of the entire British fleet beginning in 1912.

The war beneath the surface

Another oil-related development at sea, however, took place not above the surface, but below. The idea of the submarine, like that of the piston engine, had been around for centuries. Sketches of a submersible craft, for example, survive among the 15th-century drawings of Leonardo da Vinci.

During the American Revolution, David Bushnell built a man-powered submersible, which he launched against the flagship of the British fleet blockading New York. Driven by the muscle power of its

HMS Dreadnought, 1906, the first oil-fired big-gun battleship, from the National Maritime Museum collection, Greenwich, London.

single crewman, it made its way down the Hudson River and successfully attached a bomb to the underside of the British dreadnought. The attack failed when the timed fuse failed to explode. But the news of the attempt was so convulsive that the target vessel was compelled to shift its berth, and in so doing, the blockade was eventually relaxed.

Development of a proper oceangoing craft, however, had to wait upon advances in materials and engine technology. But by 1900, all the pieces were in place. In that year, John Holland put a gasoline engine in a submersible hull. On the surface, the engine not only powered the boat, but it also turned a dynamo that in turn charged a set of storage batteries. Below the surface, battery-driven electric motors supplied power. On the surface, the craft was capable of 10 knots. Submerged, the top speed was 8 knots.

Both range and reliability were enhanced in 1904 when Maxim Laubeuf replaced Holland's gasoline engine with a diesel. Not only did heavy oil provide greater fuel economy than refined gasoline, but its lubricating qualities reduced engine wear as well. In addition, diesels did not require complicated spark ignition systems. As a result, they were prone to fewer breakdowns—an important consideration when you're underwater and miles away from the nearest shipyard.

Oil as a strategic objective

Besides fueling the new engines of war, oil rapidly became indispensable as a lubricant. It was also an essential ingredient in the chemistry of explosives. As a result, oil supplies, for the first time, became a military objective. Because neither Britain nor Germany had appreciable domestic supplies of oil, both faced the logistical challenges of oil dependency. The skill that they used to anticipate and answer this challenge, as we shall see, had a major bearing on the outcome of the war.

That the Middle East was rich in oil had been known since ancient times. Indeed the biblical tale of Shadrach, Meshach, and Abednego, the victims of King Nebuchadnezzar's fiery furnace (Daniel 3:25), has been read by 20th-century geologists as a reference to the seepage of oil and natural gas in what are now the Iraqi mountains.

At the outbreak of World War I, oil had also been discovered in the United States and Romania. But Mideast oil was generally of superior quality. Besides that, once drilled, it generally flowed freely under its own pressure. Thus there was no need for complicated pumping equipment, and the costs of production were among the lowest in the world.

Competition for supply

By 1910, the vast bulk of British oil was coming from the Persian Gulf, a tense and nearly ungovernable region even then. So to ensure their source of supply, the British took several important steps. First they bought their own oil company. In 1912, the British government spent £2 million to acquire control of the Anglo-Persian Oil Co., which was heavily involved in the exploitation of Persian oil fields.

Next, Britain increased its naval presence in the region. This was done to ward off any attempts by the Turkish and German navies to disrupt supply. With sources thus assured, and the Royal navy protecting the lines of supply, the Allies were able to deploy their remaining forces in a naval blockade of Axis shipping.

Centuries of experience as a maritime power had taught British planners never to underestimate the importance of shipbuilding. Under Churchill's impatient supervision, the conversion of the fleet to oil proceeded rapidly, and substantial numbers of new ships were constructed. At the outbreak of hostilities, the balance of naval material stood at:

	British and Russian fleet	German and Turkish fleet[1]
Dreadnoughts	32	17
Battle Cruisers	11	6
Pre-dreadnoughts	54	45
Destroyers and Torpedo Boats	420	178
Submarines	179	44

This advantage in material, in addition to generally superior British seamanship, eventually proved insurmountable. Slowly but inexorably, the flow of oil so vital to Germany's war effort was reduced to a trickle.

German oil woes

To be sure, the Germans suffered substantially from the Allied blockade. But they were also victims of their own failure to anticipate the demands of a war of attrition. Prior to the war, the American conglomerate Standard Oil supplied 90% of Germany's needs. After the outbreak of hostilities, this supply was cut off, leaving Germany dependent on Galician oil, controlled by Austro-Hungary, and its own meager domestic supplies.

With Persia firmly under British (and Russian) influence, Germany turned toward Romania. Attacking from the south, the Bulgarians, under German command, made rapid progress. But the Allied command in Bucharest ordered the destruction of the oil fields before withdrawing.

By 1917 fuel shortages were evident everywhere in Germany. Trains stopped running, and planes were forced to use substitute fuels, which degraded speed and performance. Germany was the first victim of a successful oil strategy, a lesson that was not lost on Hitler's planners prior to World War II.

---

1. K. Macksey, *Technology and War: The Impact of Science on Weapon Development and Modern Battle*.

Chapter II

Blitzkrieg and Surprise Attack

The History of Oil in World War II

If I do not get the oil of Maikop and Brozny, then I must end the war.

—Adolf Hitler, June 1, 1941

By 1940, the role of oil and war was understood and appreciated by military planners everywhere. However, most accounts of World War II fail to explain the extent that the competition for oil supplies determined the shape and tenor of the conflict.

While only a minor factor in the initial outbreak of hostilities in Europe, oil nonetheless influenced the shape of German battle doctrine and enticed Hitler into a strategically fatal misstep. And in the Pacific, oil was a precipitating factor in the actual outbreak of hostilities.

Oil for the Third Reich

For Germany, the lessons of World War I were twofold. First, the country could never again afford to go to war without ensuring adequate supplies of oil and other vital materials. In Europe, Germany was forced to make secure supplies of oil and other vital materials a major strategic objective. As the war wore on, it was the need for more oil that lay at least in part behind the ill-fated German invasion of the Soviet Union.

The second lesson of World War I was that Germany could never again afford to let itself get bogged down in a war of attrition. In World War II, like World War I, Germany found itself hopelessly outgunned and outmanned by numerically superior adversaries. The need for a doctrine of battle that ensured swift and decisive victory was thus never more imperative.

One German officer who learned well the lessons of Cambrai and World War I was General Heinz Guderian. A veteran of the signal corps, he saw immediately what radio could bring to the problem of coordinating an armored battle. He envisioned one man sitting before a crystal radio and directing an entire squadron of tanks from inside a mobile command post.

Such a formation, he reasoned, could outmaneuver and surprise much larger conventional formations. Out of his vision came a special new kind of armored brigade, ideally suited for a war of concentrated fire and tactical maneuver—the famed panzer divisions.

Guderian also developed a new tactical theory for armored warfare. Instead of using tanks to attack fortified positions (as had been done at Cambrai), he proposed to make his panzers spearheads of infiltration. Using the concentrated violence of massed firepower, he envisioned a force that could break through a defensive perimeter and then maneuver with great speed to attain vital objectives at the enemy's rear. Once the objectives were taken, however, the tanks would withdraw, leaving infantry to secure the new position with anti-tank weapons (which, incidentally, had been vastly improved in the years since World War I).

Genesis of the blitzkrieg

This line of thought meshed perfectly with the war-fighting philosophy of the German high command. As a battle tactic, the swift shock of massive armored attack offered two important military advantages. First, it gave an adversary very little time to react. In addition, it offered the promise of quick capture of foreign stocks of oil and other raw materials, which could then be used to fuel a more sustained effort.

The panzers' first expedition, however, was something less than an awe-inspiring success. In March 1938, Hitler incorporated Austria into the Third Reich. Although the German high command expected no opposition to the Austrian annexation, Hitler wanted a show of force anyway. A better politician than general, Hitler had a keen appreciation of the propaganda value of pictures of cheering crowds greeting German tanks as they rolled into the Austrian capital.

Guderian himself was dispatched to Vienna at the head of the 2nd Panzer Division and the SS-Leibstandarte *Adolf Hitler*. The episode that followed eerily foreshadowed events that would eventually bring down the Nazi war effort: At the border, both units ran out of gas.[1]

Panzer snafu

Fortunately, it was only a case of a bureaucratic screw-up. An army fuel depot was nearby, but no one there had been informed of Guderian's advance. Moreover, the stocks had already been earmarked for other purposes (the defense of the so-called Siegfried Line).

It was late at night when Guderian arrived, and the officer in charge of the depot refused to contravene his orders—which said nothing about releasing fuel to an impatient panzer leader at the head of a column of tanks. Because of the lateness of the hour, the depot commander could not be found, so an exasperated Guderian finally roused the mayor of nearby Passau—who was prevailed upon to provide civilian trucks to ferry fuel from other sources. He also telephoned across the border to ask the Austrian service stations on the road to Vienna to stay open—so that the German columns could buy gas along the way!

(Actually, this was not the only foul-up of the Austrian expedition. While Guderian was foraging for fuel at the border, another division arrived without any maps of the country it was supposed to invade. Guderian finally had to give the general in charge a copy of a Baedeker guidebook so that he could find his way to Vienna.)

Oil squad specialists

Annexation of Austria and later development of the Prinzdorf field contributed another 18,000 barrels per day to German oil production. But it was not nearly enough to fuel the campaign of conquest envisioned by the Nazis. Because captured supplies and conquered oil fields would be necessary to fuel the German war machine in any sustained conflict, the German high command assembled a special squad of oil-field experts to ensure that captured oil would be exploited as expeditiously as possible.

These hand-picked specialists, drawn from the ranks of domestic oil companies and various government bureaus, would be sent in to put out oil-field fires and to get production going again almost before the smoke of battle had cleared. They saw their first wartime action in Poland.

Polish assault

It was at dawn on Sept. 1, 1939, that the world first saw blitzkrieg in action. Germany committed some 2,700 tanks to the attack. In devastating attacks of concentrated fire, closely coordinated with infantry and aircraft, everything that Guderian foresaw was borne out. The panzers broke through Polish lines in short order and spread panic and confusion deep into enemy territory. In one instance, armored columns penetrated 125 miles in only five days. In three weeks, Poland was completely overrun.

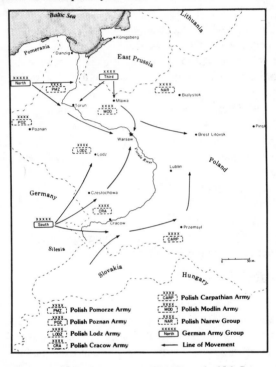

The German Attack on Poland from *Patterns of War Since the 18th Century,* by Larry H. Addington, Indiana University Press, Bloomington, IN, 1984, p. 183.

Even in the midst of victory, problems surfaced that were destined to plague the German army again and again. Pre-invasion estimates of fuel consumption turned out to be vastly underestimated. Guderian's panzer divisions consumed 1,000 gallons of gas per mile on their long drive to Vienna. But when they had to fight their way across open country, fuel consumption almost doubled. On the second day of battle, a unit of the XIX Corps was forced to halt because it ran out of gas.

Oil-field objectives

One of the major strategic objectives of the invasion was the Polish oil fields of Galacia. When forward elements of the German XXII Corps entered Jaslo, members of the oil squad found most of the structures and facilities intact. As German forces pushed farther into Galacia, however, they abruptly found Russian tanks blocking their path.

On Sept. 17, as the German juggernaut was rolling from one victory to the next, the Russians suddenly invaded Poland from the east. Stalin, the Soviet dictator remembered chiefly for his brutal purges of political opponents, was mindful of the strategic importance of oil to Hitler. He ordered Soviet units to capture as much of Poland's oil-production facilities as possible before the Germans arrived.

The Russians won the race. When the smoke of battle cleared, 70% of Poland's productive capacity was in Russian hands—not German. As a result, Hitler was forced to dispatch Foreign Minister Joachim von Ribbentrop to Moscow to negotiate the purchase of the greater part of Polish oil output.

French offensive

Of course, the most conspicuous success of the blitzkrieg came later—on May 10, 1940, when the 94 German divisions that had been amassed along the Western front drove through the Ardennes into France and Belgium. Allied defenses—including France's much-celebrated Maginot Line—folded like matchsticks before the relentless onslaught. For a time, it seemed that no army in the world could stand before an opponent whose tactical coordination bordered on the miraculous and whose stamina was hardly taxed by a 150-mile advance in seven days.

When there was no shortage of fuel, the panzers performed brilliantly. On June 21, the oil squads arrived at the oil fields at Pechelbronn and found that demolition by the retreating French had been sporadic and ineffective. Altogether, more than 7 million barrels of French, Belgian, and Dutch oil fell into German hands—much of it helpfully stockpiled along the Germans' invasion routes. Captured French oil was earmarked for use by the Luftwaffe (the German air force) in what was to become the Battle of Britain.

Failure of will

At Cambrai, the tanks were stopped eventually by the unforeseen

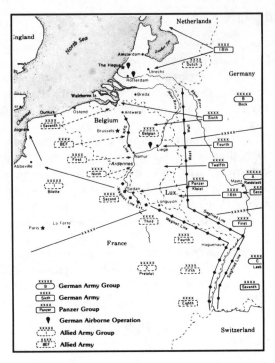

The German Offensive in the West, May 1940, from *Patterns of War Since the 18th Century,* by Larry H. Addington, Indiana University Press, Bloomington, IN, 1984, p. 188.

exigencies of a new kind of warfare. But in 1940, no such obstacles lay in the path of the German advance. In one of the great ironies of history, General von Rudstedt, fearful of losses to his extraordinary tank corps, suddenly became overprotective and ordered the panzers to halt their advance just outside Dunkirk.

Guderian and others thought it was madness not to pursue the attack—and therefore permit the hard-pressed English and French armies to evacuate by sea—but they were overruled. Had they carried the day, the Germans would almost certainly have destroyed the Allies at Dunkirk. The war would have been over.

Strategic shortages

In an effort to avoid the same kind of raw material shortages that hobbled Germany in World War I, Hitler and his generals had put great emphasis on accumulating stockpiles of strategic materials prior

16

to the outbreak of hostilities. Strenuous efforts also were made to develop a domestic synthetic fuels industry.

Once the fighting began, the British Home Fleet took up its war station in the North Sea—as it had in World War I—in an attempt to cut the flow of raw materials into Germany. For a time, the spoils of war more than compensated for the effects of the British blockade. But by the end of 1940, the Germans were beginning to feel the pinch.

Oddly enough, one reason for this was the sheer size of the new German empire. Conquered territories stretched from Poland in the east to the French Atlantic coast in the west, from frigid Norway in the north to the warm waters of the Mediterranean in the south. Even in less chaotic times, this vast area of Europe had never been self-sufficient in oil. In 1938—the last year of peace—the area then under Nazi domination had consumed 575,000 barrels a day. In 1940, the total production under German control amounted to only 234,550 barrels a day—a shortfall of 59%.[2]

Oil-driven tactics

More and more, the need for secure oil supplies began to dictate military policy. For example, Hitler was reluctant to occupy nominally neutral Romania even after it repeatedly attempted to renege on its commitment to export oil to Germany. Remembering the destruction of Romanian oil fields in World War I, Hitler was afraid of inviting a fresh Allied assault if he sent German troops to seize the fields.

(Another irony of the period is that as late as 1940, a good part of the Romanian oil industry was still run by the British. In effect, Englishmen were producing oil that the Germans then used to attack English countrymen and allies.)

By July, the shortages had grown sufficiently acute that Hitler began measuring the Soviet Union for an invasion. There was oil to be had in the Caucasus.

The invasion of Russia

Despite ample warnings from the British—who had broken German codes early in the war—the Russians did nothing to prepare for war. Stalin was preoccupied with bloody political purges at home—which eventually decimated the command ranks of the Red army. So when the Germans moved, the Russians were quite literally caught napping.

It has been called by some military historians the greatest land war

17

ever fought. Into the battle, the Germans threw 142 divisions, 3,350 tanks, and 2,250 aircraft. Opposing them in western Russia were 178 divisions, 10,000 tanks, and 7,000 aircraft.[3]

Operation Barbarossa: the German Plan of the Invasion of Russia, June 1941, from *Patterns of War Since the 18th Century,* by Larry H. Addington, Indiana University Press, Bloomington, IN, 1984, p. 198.

Despite its numbers, the Red army was no match for its peerless adversary. When the battle began at 3:30 a.m. on Sunday, June 2, 1941, most of the Russian army was still sleeping off its Saturday night excesses. The first day, 1,489 Russian planes were destroyed on the ground and 322 in the air, with almost no losses to the Germans.

Panzer-led spearheads carried the blitzkrieg deep into Russian territory in three thrusts. Army Group North attacked the Baltic states, while Army Group Central moved against the Ukraine. General Karl-Heinrich von Stulpnagel, at the head of Army Group South, led the charge toward the Polish oil fields the Russians had seized in 1939. In only 25 days, the panzers had advanced 413 miles against their poorly trained and incompetently led opposition.

Scorched earth

When the oil squads finally reached western Galacia, however, they found that the retreating Russian demolition teams were far more efficient than the French had been a year earlier. Elsewhere, however, the Russians' headlong retreat left behind substantial stores of oil. But to their chagrin, the Nazis found that the oil could not be used without further refinement. Soviet T-34 and Voroshilov tanks ran on diesel fuel, but Guderian's panzers needed gasoline.

From the very beginning, the Russian campaign was a race against time. And as the offensive began to bog down, time began to run out. To its credit, the Red army was able to regroup after the frightening losses during the early weeks of the campaign. (And new fighting spirit appeared among the defenders after Stalin executed five Russian generals for cowardice.)

Logistical nightmare

More important, however, was the Germans' failure to anticipate the logistical demands of maintaining an army so far from home. Prior to the Russian invasion, the panzers had never been in the field for more than six weeks at a time. As early as July, certain Luftwaffe squadrons were forced to begin curtailing ground support missions because they lacked aviation fuel. On Oct. 9, the German quartermaster general estimated that army vehicles were 24,000 barrels short of minimum fuel requirements.

In the summer, dust choked the engines of the mechanized divisions. Fall rains turned primitive, unpaved roads into a quagmire, which did as much to slow the German advance as anything the Russian army could muster. To be sure, the Russian winter firmed up the muddy roads, but lack of antifreeze immobilized hundreds of tanks, trucks, and airplanes.

In the killing cold, even lubricating oils froze solid. All along the front, German soldiers discovered that even their rifles and machine guns no longer worked reliably.

In just six months, the campaign that had begun so optimistically had become a logistical and military nightmare. By then the Germans had suffered 750,000 casualties. They had also lost some 75,000 vehicles—most to mechanical breakdowns. By December, Army Group South—the German units nearest the Caucasus—was out of both fuel and ammunition.

It was spring 1942 before the Germans finally managed to mount an assault on the Caucasus. And it was not until August that the scorched remains of oil fields at Maikop were in German hands. But by then, all the worst fears of the Nazi war-planners had been realized. Once again, Germany found itself bogged down in a long war of attrition.

The war in the Pacific

While oil was an important influence on how the war was fought in Europe, it was only marginally related to the causes underlying the initial conflict. In the Pacific, however, it was the pursuit of oil that led directly to the outbreak of war between Japan and the United States.

In the 1930s, the island nation of Japan was as critically dependent on its navy, and as short of oil, as Britain had been in 1912. But unlike Britain, Japan lacked domestic resources for most other raw materials as well.

In an attempt to remedy the situation, Japan embarked on a policy of paternal domination in Southeast Asia. By 1941, the Japanese occupied Manchuria, China, and Thailand. These conquests were sufficient to assure a supply of most strategic materials, including rubber, tin, and bauxite. But a critical shortage of oil remained. By 1930, production in the East Indies amounted to 170,000 barrels a day—as much as was produced by all Europe, excluding the Soviet Union.

In 1939, Japan imported 80% to 90% of its oil from the United States. The rest came from the Dutch East Indies, where oil fields had been developed by Royal Dutch Shell. With the United States and European powers preoccupied with war in Europe, the Dutch East Indies seemed ripe for the picking. And Japan knew that control of the East Indies would easily assure 100% of its oil requirements.

Additions to empire

Still, Japan was not eager for war with the Allies, realizing that that would mean maintaining long supply lines at sea, which would be extremely vulnerable to attack. So instead Japan concentrated on adding to its empire in Southeast Asia, while the United States looked on nervously.

Mindful of Japanese ambitions, President Roosevelt ordered the American Pacific fleet, then on maneuvers near Hawaii, not to return to its home base on the West Coast. Instead, it was to remain permanently on station at Pearl Harbor.

When the Japanese began their march into Indochina, however,

President Roosevelt felt he had to act. He slapped a trade embargo on all shipments of scrap iron and aviation gasoline to Japan.

Later that year, the Japanese signed the Tripartite Treaty, creating an alliance with Germany and Italy. Next the country invaded Vietnam.

Roosevelt countered with more sanctions. In July 1941, he abruptly issued an executive order that froze Japanese assets in the United States and cut off all oil exports to Japan. The embargo would be lifted, he said, when and if the Japanese withdrew from all their occupied territories.

A fateful choice

The Japanese were caught off guard. Their total oil reserves on the day the embargo was announced amounted to only an 18-month peacetime supply (including only a 90- to 120-day supply for the fleet). Virtually cut off from other sources, they were faced with a tough choice. They could acquiesce to American pressure and give up their newly acquired territories. Or they could seize the initiative while they still had fuel for their fleet.

As everyone knows, they chose the bolder of the two courses. On Dec. 7, 1941, six Japanese aircraft carriers under the command of Admiral Nagumo crept undetected within 200 miles of Oahu in the Hawaiian Islands. At first light, the initial squadrons of a 360-plane attack were launched from their decks. The first wave appeared in the skies over Pearl Harbor at 8 a.m. Two hours later, the U.S. Navy lay in ruins.

The Japanese sank five American battleships and badly damaged three others. They also damaged or sank three cruisers and three destroyers. On the nearby airfield, two-thirds of the American fleet of Army and Navy planes was in flames on the ground. American casualties totaled 3,000, two-thirds of which were fatalities. Nagumo's losses came to 29 planes and 50 airmen.

On Jan. 11, 1941, the Japanese landed in the East Indies. Their supplies of oil were secure.

---

1. H. Guderian, *Panzer Leader*, translated by C. Fitzgibbon, Chapter 3.

2. R. Goralski and R.W. Freeburg, *Oil and War*, p. 63.

3. L. Addington, *The Patterns of War Since the Eighteenth Century*, p. 197.

Chapter III

Forging the Oil Weapon

The Suez Crisis of 1956

Under orders from President Eisenhower, U.S. officials refused to discuss oil [exports] or credit until the British agreed to a ceasefire. Under such devastating pressure, the British and French agreed to a ceasefire and began withdrawing their troops.
—Joseph C. Harsch, *Christian Science Monitor*

While the role of oil in World War II would influence an entire generation of military strategists, it took the Suez crisis in 1956 to really establish oil as a political weapon. Shortly after British Prime Minister Anthony Eden—Churchill's successor—publicly declared that Mideast oil was so critical England would fight to protect it, Egyptian President Nasser gave him a chance to make good on his word.

Indeed Nasser's nationalization of the Suez Canal and the subsequent attempts by France and Britain to regain it amply demonstrated the West's willingness to go to war over oil. But the debacle that followed was hardly a convincing show of strength. Among other things, Western mishandling of the crisis in Egypt set the stage for the superpower competition that continues in the region to this day.

An ancient dream

Whence the original idea of a waterway between the Red Sea and the Mediterranean came lies shrouded in the mists of antiquity. As any student of ancient civilizations is aware, the builders of the pyramids were no slouches when it came to civil engineering. More than 2,000 years before Christ, they dug an irrigation system spanning the vast expanse of what is now northern Egypt. Part of it included a canal extending east from Goshen to the Bitter Lakes. From there, another canal provided access to the Red Sea.

French dreams of empire

A waterway across Egypt was also sought by Napoleon, who in 1798 was searching for a way to break the British monopoly on the trade routes to the Orient. Only 100 miles of flat sand stood in the way of another potential route to India, a route 6,000 miles shorter than the alternative journey around the Horn of Africa.

But because of a naval defeat at the battle of the Nile—a sound thrashing delivered by the British Commander Lord Nelson—Napoleon's grandiose scheme came to naught. Soon thereafter, he was forced to return to Paris, his canal unbuilt. Years later, it took another remarkable Frenchman, Ferdinand de Lesseps, to bring the ancient vision to fruition.

De Lesseps was a French diplomat stationed in Egypt, and by all accounts he was a larger-than-life character. He was said to have awed Frenchmen with his grace in the ballroom and Arabs with his agile horsemanship. But cutting a canal through the Egyptian wilderness was a project that taxed even de Lesseps' legendary persistence and powers of persuasion. Nonetheless, after 10 years of labor, and at a cost of 433 million francs, the waterway—100 miles long, 50 to 100 yards wide, and 26 feet deep—was finally finished. On Nov. 17, 1869, the Suez Canal opened for business.

(In truth, the Suez Canal was only one of de Lesseps' accom—plishments. At the age of 64, he married a girl of 20 and begot 12 children. And before he died (at the ripe old age of 89) he was deeply absorbed in a new canal project—this time across Panama!)

World War II exposure

As we have seen, Britain's dependency on Mideast oil began in the years just prior to World War I. By the time World War II broke out, the Middle East supplied not only Britain, but much of the rest of western Europe as well. A large fraction of this oil went through the canal, which made it an important military objective.

The strategic significance of the waterway was certainly not lost on Hitler's war planners. In addition to denying the Allies access to Mideast oil, control of the Suez Canal would put the Nazis squarely astride the major trade routes to East Africa and India.

Mussolini's muddle

In pursuit of this objective, Mussolini was dispatched to Libya,

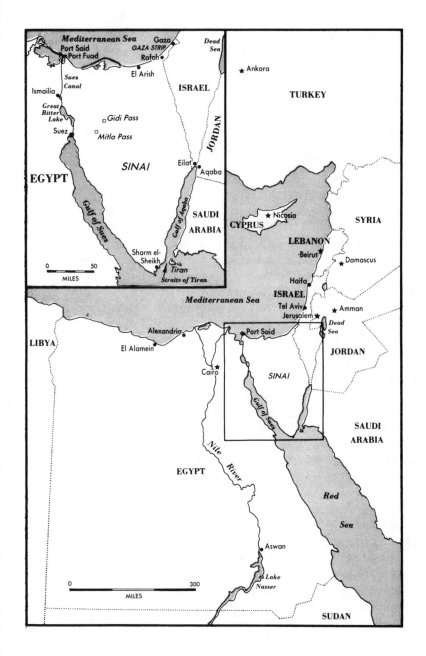

Map of the Suez Canal from *The Lion's Last Roar: Suez 1956,* by Chester L. Cooper, Harper and Row Publishers, New York, 1971, p. 46.

25

Egypt's North African neighbor to the west. In September 1940, he marched across the border at the head of an Italian army 135,000 strong. Mussolini, however, was never noted for his generalship. A few miles inside Egyptian territory he was routed by 30,000 British troops under the command of General Richard O'Connor.

Shortly thereafter, O'Connor launched a counteroffensive that sent the Italians reeling. Mussolini, as it turned out, was no more skillful in retreat than he had been in attack. By January, he had fled back to Libya, with O'Connor in hot pursuit. And on Feb. 9, 1941, he finally caught up with the Italians at Beda Fomm.

The carnage that day was impressive. At the cost of 500 British dead and 1,400 wounded, O'Connor destroyed 10 Italian divisions and killed or captured 150,000 Italian troops. For all practical purposes, the Italian 10th army had ceased to exist.

Had O'Connor been allowed to push on to Tripoli, the campaign in North Africa could have been won in weeks, and the Suez lifeline would have been secure for the balance of the conflict. But British intelligence had picked up hints that the Germans were planning a new invasion of Europe. And at the time, the defense of Europe seemed much more important than the pursuit of obscure victories in North Africa.

Espionage advantage

The British, in one of the great intelligence coups of all time, had broken the German command codes early in the war. As a result, they were uncommonly well-informed about the latest thinking of the German General Staff. And when they learned of new German plans for a blitzkrieg in Greece, O'Connor and the vast bulk of his troops were recalled to reinforce the defense.

But superior intelligence alone is no guarantee amid the fortunes of war. As it turned out, the Allies were right about German intentions—but wrong about nearly everything else. Hitler was indeed planning an invasion of Greece. He feared that Greece—until then formally neutral in the conflict—would bow to British pressure to join the Allied cause. And British air bases on Greek soil would put the RAF within bombing range of Germany's major source of oil—the Romanian fields at Ploesti.

In spite of having had ample warning, Allied defenders were powerless to halt the German advance. The reinforcements that were taken from the Mideast were spent to no avail. Meanwhile, unbeknownst to the British, Field Marshal Erwin Rommel, the celebrated Desert Fox, had arrived in Libya.

Rommel's war

Bringing with him a fresh panzer division from Germany, Rommel quickly rounded up the remnants of the Italian army and melded them into what was later known as the Deutsche Afrika Korps. In short order, he drove the remaining British out of Libya and sent them scurrying for cover deep in Egyptian territory.

When news of Rommel's exploits reached Europe, O'Connor came rushing back to North Africa with additional reinforcements. But it was too little, too late. To add military insult to injury, he was taken prisoner during the headlong retreat.

Rommel aimed to finish what Mussolini had begun and take the Suez Canal. But he needed time to prepare a major assault. In the interim, however, he kept the pressure on by launching raids behind Allied lines. Bombers and fighter aircraft attacked the canal and seeded the waterways with anti-shipping mines. Had the Germans been fortunate enough to sink a passing ship at a critical point, the canal might have been effectively blocked for weeks. Only strenuous measures by the British managed to keep the waterway open.

But while Rommel was preparing, the British were not idle. Field Marshal Bernard Montgomery was brought in to take command of the defense, and reinforcements poured in. Montgomery moved his troops to El Alamein—about 80 miles east of Alexandria—and prepared to make his stand for the defense of Egypt.

Defensive genius

He had chosen his ground well. For three days, direct assaults by the Germans failed to dislodge the British defenders. At length, Rommel tried a flanking maneuver that culminated in the battle of Halfa Ridge, where Montgomery's troops fought the Desert Fox to a standstill.

By now it was clear to Rommel that the Suez campaign was in dire straits. Not only was he substantially outmanned and outgunned by the British, but the British naval blockade of Libya's Mediterranean coast made it difficult for the Germans to get reinforcements and supplies into North Africa. Germany depended on its wartime ally Italy for naval power in the eastern Mediterranean. The Italians had a modern fleet, but they were even more short of oil than the Germans. As a result, Rommel was always being promised supplies that never arrived. Soon he was running low on both gasoline and ammunition. In contrast, the British were managing to keep a steady stream of fresh troops and supplies arriving at the front.

Furthermore, Rommel's already battle-weary troops were being weakened by long exposure to the harsh desert climate. Fearing a British counterattack on his dangerously exposed position, he cabled the German high command in Berlin for permission to withdraw back into Libya. Hitler, however, refused his request.

When Montgomery saw that the Germans failed to make a speedy withdrawal to more defensible terrain, he attacked. For 13 days he threw everything he had at the hapless Germans. By early November, when Rommel finally struggled back to Libya, the once-formidable Afrika Korps had been smashed to pieces. Egypt, the Suez Canal, and the vital oil lifeline were all secure.

Postwar vulnerability

When peace finally came to Europe, the British and the French set themselves to rebuilding their war-torn countries. Slowly, normal trade relations were re-established, and civilian traffic through the canal resumed. But by the 1950s, Western Europe had become more dependent than ever on Suez shipping. Britain received 80% to 85% of its oil through the canal. France imported 90% of its oil from the Middle East, half of which came through the canal.

But while Europeans were once again pursuing the good life, the Egyptians began to chafe under British rule. A principal source of irritation stemmed from the continued presence of foreign troops on Egyptian soil. As much as a decade after World War II was over, Britain had not withdrawn its forces. Seventy-thousand British troops remained on station along the Canal Zone. Although now a member of the United Nations and a leading nation of the Arab League, Egypt still suffered the indignity of occupation by a foreign army.

Condescension and resentment

Actually there had never been any love lost between the British and the Egyptians anyway. For their part, the British found it hard not to treat the Egyptians condescendingly. The British remembered them mostly as hawkers, pimps, and thieves of unrivaled ingenuity. In two world wars, they had proved themselves nothing but liabilities. Worse, they seemed peculiarly ungrateful for the British blood shed to save them from the Germans.

From the Egyptian point of view, the British were taskmasters to an enslaved population. Although Egypt was formally ruled by a nominal monarch, the ineffectual King Farouk, British influence was pervasive. Indeed, the popular perception that the British were behind everything—from the country's abject poverty to its catastrophic defeat at the hands of the Israelis in the 1948 War of Independence—made it easy to blame all the nation's ills on foreign manipulation.

The British recognized the signs of growing unrest. But after the painful and reluctant release of India to independence, they were in no mood to surrender yet another overseas possession. And they were certainly not inclined to turn over something as vital as the Suez Canal to the notoriously untrustworthy Egyptians.

Blood in the streets

By the summer of 1951, the tension had reached a flash point. Egyptian civilians employed by the Suez Canal Co. walked off their jobs. Food supplies to the British garrison at the canal's base were interrupted. But most disturbing of all was a mounting campaign of guerrilla attacks against British installations. Among those chiefly responsible for the attacks were the Muslim Brotherhood (a radical Islamic group) and the Society of Free Officers (SFO), a dissident faction within the Egyptian Army.

In exasperation, the British finally decided to strike back by attacking what seemed a local center of insurgency—the police head-quarters in Ismaili. The news of the British assault spread like wild-fire, and the reaction was instantaneous. Xenophobic mobs took to the streets looting and burning foreign property.

For the entire day, Cairo was in flames, and a number of unlucky foreign nationals lost their lives at the hands of the crowd. Finally the Egyptian regular army was called in to restore order. But orders to subdue fellow citizens who were only venting their frustration on the hated foreigners were not easy to obey.

A year later, members of the SFO were ready to act. On July 23, 1952, the SFO seized control of the army. At the head of the move-ment was a popular veteran of the war with Israel, Major General Neguib. Second in command was SFO's chief ideologue and major driving force, a man named Gamel Abdul Nasser.

Four days later, the army surrounded the Ras-el-Tin palace in Alexandria. And that same evening, King Farouk—the last surviving member of the 150-year-old Mohammed Ali Dynasty—was sent into exile.

Nasser immediately installed Neguib as president and himself as prime minister. But it soon turned out to be a tempestuous marriage. Neguib was popular with the Muslim Brotherhood, while Nasser was not. And when a member of the radical Islamic group took a shot at Nasser as he addressed a crowd of supporters from a balcony in

Alexandria, he seized the opportunity to remove the president from office. Two years after the initial coup, Nasser stood alone at the pinnacle of Egyptian power.

Patriotic agenda

Nasser was not content with merely articulating Egyptian aspirations. As soon as he was able to consolidate his power, he set himself an agenda designed to remedy long-standing grievances among his people and to bolster national self-respect.

First on his list was the problem of the hated British presence. In May 1953, he opened negotiations with London that dragged on for more than a year. Finally, in October 1954, Nasser was able to sign an agreement that committed the British to phased withdrawal over 20 months. At the end of that time, only a cadre of civilian technicians would remain to operate the canal.

Second, Nasser set about trying to repair the damage done by the Israelis to his country's armed forces in 1948. That, however, required modern arms and equipment that Egypt could not produce. So Nasser went shopping.

When Eisenhower demurred and Churchill equivocated, Nasser asked the Soviets. The Russians could scarcely believe their good fortune. Ever since 1945 they had been angling for ways to undermine Western influence in the region. Now, this upstart Egyptian seemed about to drop Europe's vital oil lifeline right into their lap.

In September 1955, Nasser triumphantly announced that Czechoslovakia would supply the Egyptian army. Although the specifics were not announced at the time, the deal included:[1]

- 300 of the latest Soviet model medium and heavy tanks.
- 200 MIG-15 fighter aircrafts.
- 50 Ilyushin heavy bombers.
- 100 pieces of armored artillery.
- 2 naval destroyers.
- 4 minesweepers.
- Large quantities of rifles, small arms, radar, and spare parts.

The third and final item on Nasser's agenda was the High Aswan Dam. Nasser staked not only his personal prestige on this development project, but as it turned out, his entire political future as well. The original Aswan Dam, built across the Nile by British engineers in 1898, had served its purpose well. But Nasser wanted a new one, four miles upstream from the original and vastly larger.

As originally conceived, the new dam would increase Egypt's arable farmland by 17%—an important matter for a desert country struggling to feed its teeming millions. It would also make Egypt self-sufficient in electric power.

The ink was hardly dry on the Czech arms deal when the Russians, trying to make the most of a good thing, offered to build the dam as well. But Nasser had few illusions about Soviet intentions. After all, his military was already dependent on Moscow. To permit Russian influence over the economy as well would be tantamount to re-accepting the yoke of foreign domination—something he had so recently and painfully thrown off. So Nasser turned instead toward the West—where he got a lukewarm reception.

Without much enthusiasm, the British and American governments agreed to open negotiations with Egypt and the World Bank concerning financing for the project. But as the negotiations unfolded, Nasser, true to form, began to bridle at restrictions on the Egyptian economy that Western bankers seemed certain to propose.

Trouble in Washington

The real crisis, however, was in the United States. The Israeli lobby was up in arms over the possibility that the American government might be party to an agreement to aid a hated enemy. In addition, Secretary of State John Foster Dulles was personally furious at Nasser for his diplomatic recognition of Communist China. Furthermore, with the Korean War recently concluded, Congress was in no mood to increase foreign-aid appropriations.

But worst of all, it was a presidential election year. And to Eisenhower's political advisors, it seemed a poor time to go out on a limb for a none-too-friendly country that had just signed an arms deal with the Soviet bloc. So when Eisenhower got cold feet, Churchill's successor, Anthony Eden, backed out as well, and the deal fell through.

An act of political desperation

It was a crushing blow to Nasser's prestige. And in the West, at least, there were few to mourn his predicament. As the Western press and his Arab detractors gleefully speculated on his political demise, it became clear that Nasser had only one option. With his political survival at stake, he decided to hit back, and hit hard.

On July 26, 1956, he addressed an exultant crowd from the same balcony in Alexandria where he had escaped death at the hands of the Muslim Brotherhood two years earlier. As the crowd roared its approval, he announced that the Suez Canal would be nationalized and that its annual revenues of 35 million pounds sterling would be devoted to building the new Aswan Dam. Even as he spoke, Egyptian commandos were quietly taking over offices and installations all along the Canal Zone.

The sheer audacity of Nasser's bold move stunned the Western world. But to the men who occupied the corridors of power in both London and Paris, it was an outrage that simply could not be tolerated. Fury at Nasser and concern for oil supplies created a degree of political consensus not seen between Europe's leading powers since the days of World War II. From the outset, it was clear that both Britain and France were spoiling for a fight.

Conflicting aims

The major difficulty was deciding which objective should come first. Was it "knocking Nasser off his perch," as British Prime Minister Anthony Eden put it, or securing the safety of the canal with its precious cargo? As the crisis unfolded, it became clear that Britain and France could not do both.

Securing the Suez Canal would mean that the British and French invaders would have to strike first at offices and installations along the Canal Zone—before startled Egyptian technicians could sabotage the waterway. But the canal itself was 100 miles long, and even airborne troops would need a certain amount of time to deploy along its entire perimeter.

That would give the Egyptian army plenty of time to organize a counterattack. Worse, a landing of foreign troops would bring forth an outpouring of patriotic fervor that would likely make Nasser stronger and more politically secure than ever.

On the other hand, if the principal policy aim was to depose the Egyptian president, then the British and French would have to destroy his power base—the Egyptian army—and occupy the capital. This would require landing an expeditionary force on Egypt's northern coast and an overland push south to Cairo.

The problem with this strategy, however, was that it too would take time to execute. Even if the tide of battle went all the Allies' way, under no conceivable circumstances could they hope to destroy the entire Egyptian army in one fell swoop. And whatever elements survived were certain to launch retaliatory strikes at the vulnerable installations along the canal.

Russian wild card

One problem with either strategy was assessing the military impact of Egypt's brand-new shipment of Eastern bloc arms. Nothing much was known about the quality of Egyptian pilots and tank crews. But there was always the chance that the equipment might be manned by some of the many of East European advisors known to be in the country. That raised the unsettling possibility of a direct confrontation with the Soviet Union.

An even greater problem was the matter of public opinion. While Nasser was loved by no one in the West, it was by no means certain that another foreign adventure would be welcomed by voters whose memories of World War II were all too fresh.

Failure to come to terms with this fundamental incompatibility of aims virtually ensured from the start that neither objective would be achieved. Ignoring clear-sighted advice to the contrary, the Allies tried to do both. They would drop troops in the Canal Zone and invade the country as well. They would tell the public that the operation was necessary to ensure the safety of international shipping in the Canal Zone.

Israeli connection

In retrospect, it seems incredible that experienced politicians actually thought such an implausible story could be sustained. But the most preposterous part was yet to come. The French conceived the half-baked notion of involving the Israelis.

The Israelis had a score to settle. Not only had Egypt banned Israeli ships and Israeli-bound cargos from the canal, but it had been an enthusiastic sponsor of the bloody raids by the PLO guerrillas that so plagued Israeli settlements. When the French approached Israeli Chief of Staff Moshe Dayan about the matter of starting a war with Egypt, he was intrigued at once.

This was the plan. On Oct. 29, Israel would launch a reprisal attack on Egyptian positions in the Sinai with the intention of advancing as far as the canal. The next day, after formally appealing to both sides for a ceasefire, Britain and France would ask Egypt to permit Anglo-French troops to temporarily occupy the Canal Zone. This was necessary, they would claim, to ensure the safety of this waterway.

It was a request Nasser was certain to deny. But his refusal would give Britain and France an excuse to launch their planned invasion under the guise of protecting free trade and separating the belligerents.

The attack unfolded pretty much as planned. The Israelis attacked as scheduled, but they followed their own military agenda, which did not take them anywhere near the canal. As anticipated, Nasser rejected the Anglo-French request to land troops in the Canal Zone. With the Israelis so far away, he probably thought the British and French were seizing an opportunity to bluff their way back into

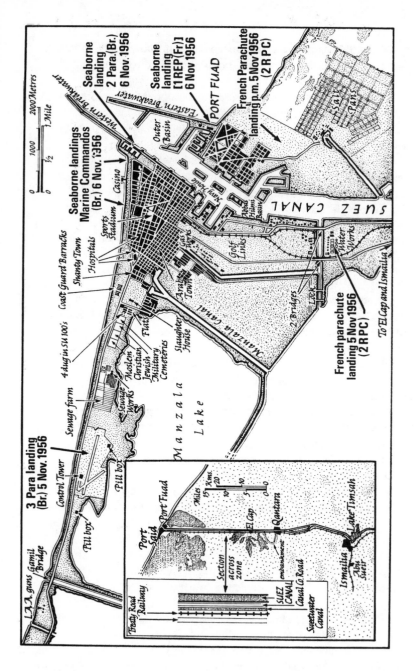

Map of the Anglo-French Invasion Zones from *Suez: The Double War*, by Roy Fullick and Geoffrey Powell, Hamish Hamilton, London, 1979, p. 218.

34

Egypt. Anglo-French forces landed more or less as planned along the Egyptian coast.

Soviet bluster

Interestingly enough, Egypt's new benefactors, the Russians, did nothing. They had their hands full with a crisis of their own. The captive peoples of their East European empire were growing restless. And on Nov. 1, 1956, the third day of the Suez operation, Russian tanks rolled to Budapest to crush a Hungarian political effort toward liberalization. In truth, they were probably delighted that so much of the world's attention was focused elsewhere.

That did not, however, stop them from trying to make the most of their newly self-appointed role as guardian of Mideast peace. Soviet Foreign Minister Bulganin sent thinly veiled warnings to Washington, London, Paris, and Tel Aviv. To Eisenhower, he proposed a joint American-Soviet military operation to "curb aggression" in the Middle East.

In messages to London and Paris, Bulganin warned that "we are fully determined to crush the aggressors and to restore peace in the Middle East through the use of force." More persuasive to the British than Bulganin's bluster was an intelligence intercept outlining orders to the Russian airforce to mobilize for an attack against Britain.[2] In a message to the Israelis, he threatened the very existence of the Jewish state.

While the operation went reasonably well, at least in its early stages, the cover story convinced no one, least of all the Americans. In the years since World War II, the French had grown used to fractious run-ins with Washington. But the British had at least hoped for benevolent neutrality.

Ike's ire

Eisenhower, however, was livid. It seemed to him that the British and French were deliberately endangering world peace to execute a personal vendetta against Nasser. And with the American presidential election less than a week away, the timing could not have been worse. After months of campaigning before the electorate as one of the world's elder statesmen, here he was in danger of being undone by a new war—and one started by allies!

The international outcry was intense, and within days the British began to waver. Some members of the British government took the Russian threats seriously, and British Prime Minister Anthony Eden came under heavy fire in Parliament. Eventually he was forced to convene the Cabinet to consider a unilateral withdrawal.

Edge of financial collapse

The day the Cabinet met, the situation seemed grim indeed. Nasser had effectively closed the canal by scuttling Egyptian ships in the channel. A run on the pound was under way in foreign markets, and the country's foreign exchange reserves were being drained at the alarming rate of 15% a day. Worst of all, British industry was down to less than a month's supply of oil.

As early as 1938, U.S. oil production accounted for more than 60% of the world's total. As a result, the United States was able to use oil as a political weapon in much the same way as OPEC nations did some 20 years later. When Eisenhower cut off oil shipments from the Western Hemisphere to Europe and demanded an immediate cessation of hostilities in Egypt, the British had no choice but to throw in the towel. After briefly wondering if they should not finish the job themselves, the French also acceded to demands for a cease-fire and subsequent withdrawal.

It was an inauspicious moment for the West. Not only was the canal lost, but the Israeli attack had enabled Nasser to cement his supporters with the age-old rallying cry of Zionist aggression. In the aftermath of U.N.-supervised withdrawals, he remained stronger than ever. Only the Israelis managed to achieve their military objectives.

Legacy of defeat

The effects of the Suez crisis were profound. In the oil-rich Mideast, Western influence plunged to a new all-time low. The public humiliation suffered by both Britain and France played a prominent role in the decision by both nations to develop their own nuclear weapons. In England, the Suez crisis brought down the government. France, furious over what it saw as pusillanimous behavior on the part of the British and bullying tactics on the part of the United States, withdrew from NATO and remains outside the alliance to this day.

Nasser, in his marriage of oil to Mideast nationalism, created a powerful weapon that would be used again and again by other ambitious leaders of oil-producing nations. And the Soviet Union, eager to seize the initiative in the wake of Western humiliation, established itself as a power to be reckoned with in the region for years to come.

---

1. C. Cooper, *The Lion's Last Roar: Suez 1956*.

2. P. Wright and P. Greengrass, *Spycatcher*, 1987, p. 107.

Chapter IV

Persian Gulf 1980

America on the Nuclear Brink

I tell you flatly...the country must have at its disposal the necessary resources of both oil and gas...(which) will always be the object of our constant concern.
—Mikhail Gorbachev, speech in Tyumen, western Siberia

At the conclusion of the Suez Crisis of 1956, the power of oil as a political weapon could no longer be seriously disputed. And if anyone required a further demonstration, the Soviets were quick to provide one. In the late 1950s, they imposed an oil embargo to bring down a Finnish government that had somehow neglected to include the local Communist party.

Even so, Western nations were slow to grasp the political disadvantages of oil dependence, and of dependence on Mideast oil in particular. As a result, they found themselves utterly unprepared for events to come—the rise of OPEC and the 1973 oil embargo, to name just two—which could have been anticipated.

By the end of the decade, OPEC was approaching the zenith of its power and had pushed the price of crude above $30 a barrel. The West had grown more dependent on energy imports than ever. In 1979, the United States depended on foreign imports for nearly half its oil supplies. Eighty-seven percent of annual consumption in Europe came from foreign sources. And Japan imported 100% of its annual needs.

To make matters worse, virtually all Mideast oil came by tanker from the Persian Gulf. A cursory glance at a map of Southwest Asia quickly reveals that the Persian Gulf is almost a landlocked lake. Only by passage through the narrow Straits of Hormuz at its extreme southern end can tankers reach the Indian Ocean and thereafter the open seas. The northern shore of this vital chokepoint is Iranian territory. The southern shore belongs to the tiny emirate of Oman.

Importer and Percentage of Oil Imports in 1979 [1]

Exporter	United States	Europe	Japan
South America	8	2	-
North Africa	8	10	--
West Africa	6	5	--
Indonesia	3	--	13
Mideast	15	60	77
Spot or other	8	10	10
Total Percent of Oil Consumption Imported	**48**	**87**	**100**

Indeed, Western oil vulnerability had grown so serious that President Jimmy Carter numbered the Persian Gulf among the vital interests of U.S. foreign policy. In his last State of the Union Address, he declared:

Let our position be absolutely clear: An attempt by any

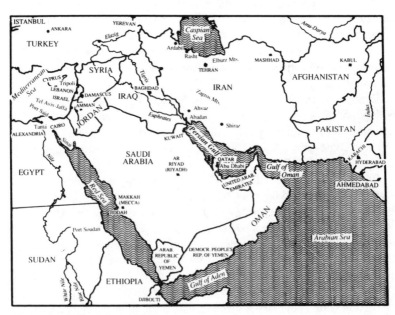

The Persian Gulf and the Middle East.

outside force to gain control of the Persian Gulf region will be regarded as an assault on the vital interests of the United States of America, and such an assault will be repelled by any means necessary, including military force.

Persian ally for the Persian Gulf

Unfortunately, brave words could no longer mask the empty arsenal that lay at the heart of U.S. ability to execute its declared oil strategy. For years American policy in the Persian Gulf had rested on the stalwart goodwill of the pro-Western Shah of Iran. As the autocratic master of an oil-rich country situated on the northern shore of the Persian Gulf and commanding the north bank of the vital Straits of Hormuz, he made a formidable ally.

Although fiercely committed to an ambitious plan to modernize backward Iranian society in a single generation, the Shah never forgot his debt to the West. During the 1973 oil embargo, he stood almost alone continuing shipments to the West. But he was also a tyrant noted for the brutal suppression of his domestic political adversaries. And it was this fact that made it difficult in early 1979, as his grip on power was slipping away, for the Carter administration to come to his aid.

Perhaps it is unrealistic to suppose that with vigorous American support pro-Western leadership in Iran might have been indefinitely sustained. On the other hand, those who urged American acquiescence in deposing the Shah on moral grounds can scarcely claim a moral victory in his successor. And without a doubt, the Shah's departure was an unmitigated catastrophe for American policy in the Persian Gulf.

Faithless ally

American acquiescence in the fall of the Shah also sent a chilling message to other moderate states in the region. If that was the way the United States treated its allies, it would be a cold day in hell before even such nominally pro-Western states, such as Kuwait and Saudi Arabia, ever went out on a limb for Western interests.

In the absence of a pro-Western Iran to police the Persian Gulf, U.S. power to influence events in the region suddenly became practically non existent. In the event of a military emergency, American troops would have to be flown in from the United States—a distance of more than 7,000 miles. Worse, the lack of sufficient airlift capacity meant the troops would have to go without tanks or heavy arms. As Defense Secretary Harold Brown had noted the previous year in

39

congressional testimony, the United States had just enough airlift for a suicidal show of force in the Persian Gulf.

This loss of American power in a strategically vital region of the world did not go unnoticed. On Christmas Eve 1979, the first Soviet military transports began landing in Kabul.

The Afghan invasion[2]

Three days later, columns of T-54 and T-64 tanks, supported by the heavy artillery of the Soviet 40th army, began crossing the Oxus River into Afghan territory. At the same time, a special KGB hit team supported by airborne commandos attacked the fortified Duralaman Palace, the official residence of the Afghan president, Mohammad Hufizullah Amin.

The Soviets had clearly planned this operation with great care. Most of the strategic objectives in and around Kabul were taken in short order—many without firing a shot. The original plan for neutralizing the Afghan president had been no less meticulously thought out. During an elaborately planned banquet that evening, Amin and his bodyguards were supposed to be drugged by their Russian cooks.

Amin ate heartily. But the plan faltered when a number of the guards were inadvertently omitted from the guest list. When the Russians inside the palace tried to pay a postprandial call on the Afghan president, they were surprised to find a contingent of clear-headed palace police blocking their path.

Revolution on a schedule

Now, staging a coup or fomenting a revolution is an enterprise of considerable complexity. Timing is often critical, and the history of revolution is littered with examples of uprisings that got off-schedule and, as a result, fell apart. So the Russians were understandably upset when a platoon of unexpectedly clear-eyed bodyguards threatened to make a shambles of their carefully crafted timetable.

In exasperation, an armored column was called in to assault the palace. But the Soviets were further chagrined to discover they faced an opponent who refused to surrender, even in the face of overwhelming odds. It was a sobering experience, and one destined to be repeated again and again in subsequent years as the Soviets would try without success to conquer the defiant Afghan freedom fighters.

The battle for the palace lasted four hours. By this time, Amin, even in his half-drugged state, must have finally realized what was going on. But all attempts to call for help failed. Communications between the palace and the outside world were completely cut off.

40

Soviet demolition teams had done their work well.

Crimes against the people

When the last defenders were finally dispatched, Soviet troops wearing Afghan army uniforms burst in and shot Amin as he stood by the palace bar, sipping a drink. According to one report, his bartender, one of a number of KGB agents who had infiltrated the Amin household, threw up his hands and pleaded in Russian for his life, thereby escaping instant annihilation. In an effort to ensure there were no witnesses, the Soviets machine-gunned everyone in the presidential family, including seven children. The next day Radio Kabul announced that Amin had been tried, found guilty, and executed by a Revolutionary Tribunal for committing "crimes against the people."

Moscow had chosen its moment well. In the United States, the administration was preoccupied with the brutal taking of American hostages in Iran. Much of the rest of the world was caught up in merrymaking to celebrate the new year. In Afghanistan, heavy snow blanketed the ground, making it difficult for opposition to the Soviets to organize. As a military operation, it was strictly invasion by the numbers—a vignette of Soviet-style blitzkrieg in action, a swift, decisive fait accompli about which the world could protest, but in the end, do nothing.

Fruits of conquest

For the Kremlin, a puppet pro-Soviet regime in Afghanistan conferred a number of strategic advantages. First, it eliminated a hotbed of opposition to the Soviet regime. For more than 100 years, Afghanistan had been a check on czarist ambitions to the north (and, to a lesser degree, on British ambitions in India to the south). When, for example, civil war broke out in Russia in 1917, the Afghans vigorously supported their fellow Asians in Turkestan and Uzbekistan—both of which had long been under czarist domination.

When the Bolsheviks finally consolidated their power and sent the Red army out to reconquer the old czarist empire in Central Asia, they found as many as 20,000 Afghan-supported partisans standing in their way. Needless to say, this was an experience the Soviets never forgot. In the 1970s and 1980s, Afghan opposition took the now-familiar form of Islamic fundamentalism. A puppet regime in Kabul offered Moscow some degree of insurance against the tide of Islamic fervor sweeping into Soviet Central Asia from the south.

Second, the puppet regime afforded a strategic position for some later effort to break through to the Indian Ocean. Possession of a warm-water port—free from ice year-round—has been a principal aim of Russian expansionism since the time of the czars.

But above all, Afghanistan's strategic significance must be measured in terms of the 20th century's most recent index of power—oil. Hardly had the dust of travel been shaken from the khaki uniforms of the airborne commandos when a second army of geologists and oil-drilling technicians appeared, intent on exploiting the captive country's considerable natural resources. Although for years a net exporter of oil, by 1980 the rate of increase in Soviet oil production had dropped to zero. And it was believed that the Russians needed their newfound resources to replace their depleted Caspian Sea deposits.

Even more important than the acquisition of new domestic supplies was the new Soviet power to exert pressure on the most sensitive and fragile link in the Western world's petroleum lifeline—the Persian Gulf.

In the aftermath of the Soviet announcement of military withdrawal from Afghanistan, it has become fashionable in the West to declare a victory over traditional Soviet expansionism. Certainly the Reagan administration lost no time taking credit for rolling back the first Soviet invasion of a neutral power since the post-World War II consolidation of Eastern Europe.

Soviet Vietnam

A more likely interpretation of events is that the Soviets finally came to a conclusion in Afghanistan similar to the one the Americans reached in Vietnam. At home, the war not only consumed resources that would otherwise be much in demand elsewhere in the Soviet economy, but it also distracted attention from the reforms Party Chief Gorbachev was trying to push through the sclerotic Soviet system.

The result was a Soviet decision in favor of a political rather than a military solution. Whether this conclusion represents a victory for the West remains to be seen. It appears that the Soviet withdrawal could be as bloody and destabilizing to the region as the eight-and-a-half years of Soviet occupation. Certainly, it is in the Russian interest for the withdrawal to be as bloody as possible.

If the Soviets cannot have a communist Afghanistan, the next best thing would be a chaotic Afghanistan. That way they can hope to make separate arrangements with various local factions to retain as much influence as possible. To this end, the Soviets have signed more than 400 local deals involving access to oil, gas, and mineral deposits.

Just because the Soviets are withdrawing their troops does not mean they have abandoned the familiar goals of traditional Russian expansionism. Rather it is much more likely that economic trouble at home has merely forced a temporary suspension of expensive foreign adventures. A recovery or consolidation at home could easily ignite another invasion in this volatile and explosive part of the world.[3]

Two centuries of intrigue

As long as the Soviets maintain some sort of foothold in Afghanistan, they will be in position for a future campaign against neighboring Iran. If Afghanistan is marginal to Soviet interests during a period of national introspection, Iran clearly is not.

Actually, Iran has been high on the list of Russian ambitions for several centuries. During the past 200 years, they have attacked Iran nearly a dozen times.

Soviet World War II Occupation and 1946 Main Line of Advance, courtesy of *Armed Forces Journal International*, February 1987, p. 30.

In fact, the territory that now comprises Soviet Azerbaijan was the fruit of conquest in one such campaign. During World War I, czarist troops invaded and occupied what remained of Iranian Azerbaijan. Eventually, it too would have probably been absorbed into the Soviet empire. But in 1917 the Boleshevik Revolution threw the country into chaos, and the Russian troops were called home.

But once the Communists had firmly established themselves in power, interest in Iran revived. Soon Soviet agents were again at work in Iran's northern provinces. While the doctrinaire atheism of communist orthodoxy was anathema to most Iranians, both the Kurds and Azerbaijanis longed for independent homelands, and thus were no friends of the central government in Tehran. In Soviet eyes, such aspirations made them ripe for subversion.

For the Soviets, World War II began on June 22, 1941. On that day, German panzer divisions rolled across the Soviet border and instantly transformed what Soviet propaganda had been calling the Second Imperialist War into what would soon be christened the Great Patriotic War. Earlier that same year, German agents had managed to incite a rebellion by the followers of Rashid Ali in British-controlled Iraq. Already reeling under the onslaught of their erstwhile allies, the Russians began to worry about yet another German attack—this time from the Mideast. In due course, the Stavka, the Soviet General Staff, began to draw up contingency plans for an invasion of Iran.

By summer, the Russians were ready to move. The following account of the start of that campaign comes from Schulze-Holthus, the German intelligence chief in the northern Iranian city of Tabriz.[4]

I had relied on consistent reports from my agents that no troop concentrations had been observed on the North Persian frontier. But the Russians had outdone me in cunning. They had concentrated motorized units farther north, which were only thrown late at night on the frontier. On Monday, Aug. 25, we were awakened brutally out of our sleep at 5 a.m. by the sound of heavy anti-aircraft fire. In the meantime came the hollow thuds of the first bombs.

Invasion by the numbers[5]

The invasion began, just as the war planners had envisaged, with a two-pronged attack into Azerbaijan from along both sides of the Caspian Sea coast. Farther east, Soviet troops advanced in two additional waves: a thrust southward from Quchan toward Shabzevar, and another eastward from Sarakhs toward Meshed.

Iranian resistance was sporadic and uncoordinated, and Soviet forces were able to advance as far as 40 miles in the first day alone. Russian fighters were unchallenged in the sky above the battle, and Soviet bombers emptied their loads on just about every town of any size in northern Iran.

Although ostensibly concerned with securing their southern flank against a German counterattack, once they were established in northern Iran, the Soviets began taking steps aimed at extending their control all the way toward the warm waters of the Persian Gulf. They

Soviet Military Intervention in Iran March 1946, courtesy of *Armed Forces Journal International,* February 1987, p. 32.

provided arms and money in support of the nationalist ambitions of Azerbaijan separatist Jafar Pisherari. Near the western border with Iraq, they encouraged the Kurds to set up an independent state. And on Feb. 1, 1944, the Supreme Soviet accorded official recognition to both.

No rush to leave

When World War II finally came to an end, the Russians somehow weren't in much hurry to leave Iran. In November 1945, they began large-scale distribution of arms to local insurgents, who they hoped to incite in open revolt against the central government in Tehran. Before long, sporadic fighting broke out in the north. And on at least one occasion, troops dispatched by the central government in Tehran to put down unrest were stopped by Soviet uniformed forces at Qazvin, just a short distance outside the Iranian capital.

It was the Shah's intelligence services that discovered the plot against the capital itself. As soon as he learned that Soviet-backed forces were preparing to march on the city, he called for reinforcements. Within hours, staunchly anti-communist troops from distant provinces began to arrive in the capital. Guns and ammunition were smuggled into anti-communist tribes inside the Soviet zone of occupation. Other troops were sent out to hold the mountain passes that guarded the approaches to the city. Inside Tehran, the garrison was reinforced and placed on full battle alert.

Loyalist victories

Such vigorous measures so promptly taken apparently caught the rebels by surprise, and the plan to attack the capital never materialized. In fact, only two battles were actually fought: one at Shahi in the north, and another near Garmsar to the southeast of the capital. In both cases, the Soviet-backed insurgents were put to rout. With their local allies on the run, it soon became clear that if they wanted Iran, the Soviets would have to take it themselves.

With the conclusion of World War II, the Russians were obligated by treaty to begin withdrawing their troops from Iran by the spring of 1946. By March 1946, American and British troops had already departed, leaving them unopposed. On the morning of March 3, the men inside the Kremlin decided to seize their opportunity.

Within hours, Soviet armored divisions began moving en masse southward across the border into Azerbaijan. Several days later, the legendary Soviet tank commander, Marshal Ivan Bagramian, arrived from Moscow to take command of the Russian army of occupation. To provide as much political legitimacy as possible for the operation, Azerbaijan separatist Pisherari was instructed to issue a public statement thanking the Red army for ousting the "tyrannical regime in Tehran."

Edge of victory

The details of exactly what happened next are not clear. What is clear is that the Soviets were apparently on the verge of achieving a centuries-old aim of Russian foreign policy—namely, a warm-water port free from the ice that bottled up the Russian fleet every winter in its home waters. Even without benefit of hindsight, the Kremlin must have also realized that seizure of Iranian oil fields would have given Soviets a strategic advantage of near inestimable value.

On the verge of achieving all this, somehow the Soviets were persuaded to back down. Perhaps the vigorous defensive efforts of the Shah persuaded Soviet leaders that the campaign would be long and difficult. It should be noted, however, that the prospect of a difficult campaign did not keep them from invading Afghanistan some 35 years later. More likely, the Soviet leaders were dissuaded by a blunt private message from President Truman threatening an American nuclear strike if they did not stand down.

Legendary bluntness

Truman, of course, was well-known for his plainspokenness. But in public, he was careful to leave the Soviets a face-saving avenue of retreat. The State Department duly issued the following public protest to the Soviet Foreign Ministry:

The government of the United States has the honor to inform the government of the Soviet Union that it is receiving reports to the effect that there are considerable movements of Soviet combat forces and materials of war from the direction of the Soviet frontier toward Tabriz and outward from Tabriz in the direction of Tehran, Mahabad, and various points in Northwestern Iran.

The government of the United States desires to learn whether the Soviet government, instead of withdrawing Soviet troops from Iran as urged in the Embassy's note of March 6, is bringing additional forces into Iran. In case Soviet forces in Iran are being increased, this government would welcome information at once regarding the purposes therefore.

As public pronouncements go, this is hardly anything that would have backed the Soviets into a corner. In private, however, the men inside the Kremlin must have concluded that it was a fool's gamble to test the resolve of an American president who had twice demonstrated the awesome power of the bomb in the skies above Japan. Hence, there is little reason to doubt President Truman's version of events when he says in his memoirs, "We had to send an ultimatum to the head of the Soviet Union to get out of Persia." It was not, as we shall see, the last time the United States would go to the nuclear brink to stave off a Soviet invasion of Iran.

In late 1980—barely nine months after Soviet tanks rolled into Kabul—American military analysts were forced to concede that Soviet forces could overrun Iranian oil fields and seize the northern bank of the vital Straits of Hormuz in only seven to 10 days. Worse, the United States could do absolutely nothing to stop them—short of outright nuclear attack! Only this time, the United States no longer had a monopoly on the bomb. Sooner than anybody thought, the worst fears of American military strategists came suddenly to the very edge of frightful realization.

America on the brink[6]

Although Western intelligence had picked up signs of unusual

47

activity around the Moscow-based 105th Soviet Airborne Division prior to Christmas Eve 1979, news of the Afghan invasion came almost as a complete surprise to most Western capitals. The United States, in particular, had reportedly suffered a satellite failure over Southwest Asia at a critical moment.

As a result, considerable effort was devoted to bringing fresh intelligence assets to bear on the region during the early days of the Soviet occupation. By late summer, these new sources were reporting very disturbing news indeed. For all practical purposes, it looked as if the Soviets were gearing up for another invasion—this time, of Iran.

This is a story that until now has never been told. Well guarded among the official secrets of the Carter administration, it is a story that former administration officials have been notably reluctant to discuss. A fuller accounting of those tension-filled days of August 1980 will have to wait upon the eventual declassification of documents in years hence. What is known is based on the minutes of a meeting held between then-Secretary of Defense Harold Brown and the Joint Chiefs of Staff. The minutes were obtained by *Armed Forces Journal International* and written about in the September 1986 issue.

Distant early warning

Sometime in July 1980 American intelligence began picking up ominous indications of a major Soviet military operation in Southwest Asia. The 28 Soviet divisions in the Turkestan, Trans Caucasus, and North Caucasus military districts, normally held in a relatively low state of readiness, were suddenly upgraded to a status equivalent to that of elite Soviet forces facing NATO defenses in Europe. Both their radio frequencies and their communications codes were abruptly switched to types believed by Western intelligence to be reserved for imminent hostilities.

A number of units moved from their garrison to the field and took up what looked suspiciously like an order of battle poised for a lightning strike to the south. Some key units suddenly began observing electronic silence, thus making their movements and intentions even more difficult to fathom.

Tactical fighter-bomber wings in the region were reinforced, while stockpiles of ammunition and aviation fuel were increased to levels never before observed by Western intelligence. An airborne division in Eastern Europe was placed on high alert. Finally, units of *Spetsnaz* (elite forces trained for deep penetration raids behind lines) were moved to positions from which they could easily reinforce or spearhead an attack into Iranian territory.

Consternation in the halls of power

Alarmed, high-level policy-makers in Washington quickly convened a series of meetings to consider American options in the event the worst-case scenario came to pass and the Soviets struck south toward the Persian Gulf. But the agonizing truth of the matter was this: Short of a nuclear attack, the United States had almost no options.

The 28 Soviet divisions on alert included about 3,400 tanks, 370 combat aircraft, 350 helicopters, nearly 4,000 artillery pieces, and upward of 8,000 armored personnel carriers and infantry fighting vehicles. Opposing all this, the United States had absolutely nothing!

Concerned about the power vacuum left by the fall of the Shah, Carter had in fact already proposed the creation of a rapidly deployable Indian Ocean task force for just such an emergency as this. But in any match up of this force against the Soviet army amassing along the Iranian border, U.S. forces would be outnumbered 6 to 1 during the first week of mobilization. After two weeks, the ratio would be 10 to 1 in favor of the Soviets, and after 30 days, 14 to 1.

But worst of all, in the summer of 1980 the much-vaunted U.S. Rapid Deployment Force (RDF) was still in the midst of a difficult bureaucratic birth. Although a commander had been appointed and a headquarters had been established, as a useful military strike force the RDF existed only on paper!

As the grim truth dawned, American planners were forced to look for help in the geography of likely Soviet invasion routes. Troops moving through western Afghanistan—one of the few countries in the world without a railway system—would have to traverse difficult terrain with roads that were either primitive or nonexistent.

Tortuous invasion route

Nor would moving an army through eastern Iran be any easier. By air it was only 250 miles to the Iranian capital and only 600 miles to the shores of the Persian Gulf—35 minutes flying time in the newest Soviet jets. But on land, the tortuous miles through the Elburz and Zagros mountains would number upward of 1,000. Furthermore, among the 15,000-foot peaks were literally hundreds of potential choke points—bridges, canyons, and narrow mountain defiles that could accommodate barely a single tank at a time.

The best defensive position for U.S. forces would be in the mountains to the north, before Soviet forces could debouch into the plains surrounding Tehran. So someone suggested dropping in U.S. special forces teams by parachute to attempt to block and hold a number of the most promising potential choke points.

The problem was that these measures were unlikely to stop a determined invader. For one thing, Soviet airborne forces could leap frog blown-up bridges and blocked mountain passes. Second, choke points, even if blocked by artful demolition, wouldn't stay blocked forever. Unless they were defended, they could always be cleared by the Soviet engineer corps.

Unfortunately, U.S. special forces are lightly armed and therefore ill-equipped to take and hold ground against a determined adversary. And inadequate American airlift capacity meant that any air-dropped reinforcements would also have to take the field without heavy weapons. Without tanks and artillery, they would find themselves hard-pressed to hold even the most promising defensive positions.

Thinking the unthinkable

That left only one alternative—tactical nuclear strikes against the Soviet army as it attempted passage through the mountains. It was a topic no one was eager to consider. But it was all that was left. It is clear from the information obtained by *Armed Forces Journal International* that the matter was discussed at the highest levels of American military command. Together, President Carter and Secretary of Defense Brown made up the National Command Authority, the bureaucratic unit of the American government with the power to approve a nuclear strike.

Somehow a nuclear war was averted. For the second time in 35 years, Soviet forces, which had been brought to the fevered pitch of combat readiness, began to stand down. How they may have been persuaded to do so must await a fuller retelling of events. But we do know that Undersecretary of State Warren Christopher was dispatched by President Carter to Europe. At least in part, his mission was to consult with heads of state in Britain, France, and West Germany on how best to coordinate warnings to the Soviets to stay out of Iran. To date, Christopher has declined to be interviewed on the subject.

In the years since 1980, U.S. military capability in the region has been vastly improved. The U.S. Central Command, the successor to Carter's RDF, now includes five Army and Marine divisions, seven Air Force tactical fighter wings, and three Navy aircraft-carrier battle groups. Strategic airlift capacity has been increased to about 45 million tons a day. Equipment, ammunition, and fuel to supply a division-size Marine amphibious force has been pre-positioned at the

Soviet Routes to Tehran courtesy of *Armed Forces Journal International,* January 1987, p. 28.

Soviet Main Line of Advance to Tehran courtesy of *Armed Forces Journal International,* January 1987, p. 30.

U.S. Indian Ocean base at Diego Garcia.

Research windfall

Thirty-five years after the end of World War II, a historian doing independent research on captured German war files made a remarkable discovery. Sorting through a pile of obscure documents, he stumbled across a copy of the Soviet General Staff's 1941 plans for an invasion of Iran. Apparently it had fallen into German hands in the early days of the Eastern campaign, when the Red army was forced into disorderly retreat before the onslaught of Hitler's storm troopers.

Inasmuch as the invasion routes are the same today as they were

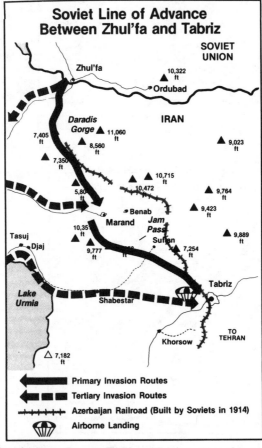

Soviet Line of Advance Between Zhul'fa and Tabriz courtesy of *Armed Forces Journal International*, January 1987, p. 30.

40 years ago, such a document must be presumed to cast considerable light on what the Russians might do in any future attempt to bring Iran into the Soviet empire. Apparently some folks in the upper levels of the U.S. government thought so, too. In 1981, the Department of Defense commissioned the Stanford Research Institute to update the plan to reflect the present balance of power in the region.

In spite of all the improvements made since 1980, there are still some who question whether even today the United States has sufficient conventional forces to hold Persian oil fields against a serious Soviet assault. Among them is the U.S. Central Command commander in chief, Marine Corps General George B. Crist. According to an account of an August 1986 press conference reported in the *Baltimore Sun*, Crist conceded that although he could put up "a hell of a fight," the Soviets, if sufficiently determined, could still push him out of the Persian Gulf.

Former Carter administration Press Secretary Jody Powell put it well indeed. Remarking on improvements in the readiness of U.S. RDFs, he observed that considerable skepticism remains whether even now "we could stop a major Soviet offensive in that area without the use of nukes."[7]

---

1. B. F. Schemmer, "Was the U.S. Ready to Resort to Nuclear Weapons for the Persian Gulf in 1980?" *Armed Forces Journal International*, 1986, p. 98.

2. This account of the last days of independent Afghanistan draws upon the excellent work of Edward R. Girardet in *Afghanistan: the Soviet War*.

3. Author's interview conducted Aug. 18, 1988, with noted Afghan authority Nasir Shansab, author of *Soviet Expansion in the Third World: Afghanistan, A Case Study*.

4. Quoted by Marshall L. Miller, "How the Soviets Invaded Iran," *Armed Forces Journal International*, 1987, p. 30.

5. This account draws on the work of Marshall L. Miller, which appeared in his feature on Soviet military developments in *Armed Forces Journal International*, January 1987-February 1987.

6. Schemmer, *op. cit.*

7. Letter to *Armed Forces Journal International*, September 1986, p. 104.

Chapter V

Oil and the War Against Civilians
The Terrorist Threat

*We are at war and our battle has only just begun. Our first
victory will be one tract of land somewhere in the world that is under
complete rule of Islam....Islam is moving across the earth....Nobody
can stop it spreading in Europe and America.*
—Abd al-Qadir, *Jihad—a Ground Plan*

One of the most chilling contemporary examples of the age-old
connection between economics and war can be seen in the increasingly brutal attacks on unarmed civilian populations. Of course, from
the point of view of military history, the use of terror as a tactic is
scarcely anything new.

In Greek mythology, the twin horses that pulled the chariot of the
god of war were named Dread (Demios) and Terror (Phobos). In his
fourth-century B.C. epic *The Peloponnesian War*, Thucydides reports
the use of "unheard of atrocities" as an instrument of rebellion.[1]

In 1256, the grandson of Genghis Khan, Hulagu, sacked
Baghdad, killed all its inhabitants, and then built a tower using their
skulls as bricks.

Two hundred years later, the father of modern *realpolitik*,
Machiavelli, elaborated on fear as an instrument of state: "...since
men love as they please but fear when the prince pleases, a wise
prince should rely on that which he controls, not on what he cannot
control."[2]

Modern-day terror

Terrorism in the 1980s, however, is a lot different from the way it
was in the time of Thucydides or Machiavelli. First, oil and war in the
Middle East has produced a whole new generation of fanatics bent on

55

destruction. The institutionalization of international terrorism probably started in 1967 when the Soviets began to establish training camps for guerrillas bent on avenging the Arab military debacle in the Six Day War against Israel. In the 1970s and 80s, the Iranians, Syrians, and Libyans replaced the Soviets as godfathers of the international terrorist movement.

In the past, terrorism tended to be indigenous to a specific revolution or particular military campaign. Today, it is international in scope. The same facilities that support fighters from the PLO, also serve the Irish Republican Army, the Red Brigades, and the Baader Meinhoff terrorists.

In the past, the aim of the individual terrorist usually was the assassination of generals and emperors. Today, the march of technology has raised the frightening specter of a band of dedicated fanatics somehow getting their hands on a nuclear weapon.

In this chapter, we will examine the roots of terrorism in the 1980s. We will assess the fitful efforts of the U.S. government to combat the rising tide of international hostage-taking. And finally, we will explore what you can do as an individual—to avoid becoming a hostage, or to survive if you are unlucky enough to become one.

Growing harvest

Terrorism is getting worse despite our best efforts. In 1980, terrorism claimed more victims than in any single year since the Central Intelligence Agency (CIA) began keeping statistics. According to the U.S. State Department, in the decade ending in 1985 more than 6,200 terrorist incidents were recorded worldwide, leaving roughly 4,700 people dead and more than 9,000 wounded.[3]

In 1985, the number of incidents of international terrorist acts were up 30% above the previous year and 55% above the average of the previous five years. By 1988, the CIA was counting more than 900 incidents a year.[4]

One reason that terrorism is so popular is that it has been increasingly adopted as an element of foreign policy by nations on the fringe of civilization. Most experts mark the beginning of this development with the end of the Six Day War in 1967.

After their crushing defeat at the hands of the Israelis, there was little alternative, from the Arab point of view, to some sort of guerrilla campaign. In an effort to expand their influence in this oil rich part of the world, the Soviets began to offer training and equipment to Palestinian guerrillas.

During the 1967-1969 period, several commando training camps were established in Czechoslovakia, staffed with Soviet, East German, and Czech instructors. In time, the camps began to accept not just Palestinians but members of other terrorist groups—including Baader Meinhoff and Red Army Brigades. In return, these groups offered aid and comfort to the PLO outside the Middle East.[5]

There is little evidence that the Soviets actually directed Palestinian operations. But they clearly were responsible for establishing the PLO's capability to train its own.

By 1969—within two years after their smashing military triumph—the Israelis were reporting more than 1,200 incidents of terrorism and sabotage along their borders.

Daddy Warbucks of terrorism

The Soviets played a similar role in North Africa, by arming Libyan Qaddafi, who has aptly been called the Daddy Warbucks of terrorism. Qaddafi has offered aid to almost every international terrorist group—sometimes in the form of training camps, financing and weapons supply, other times offering Libyan embassy facilities abroad as support bases for operations against targets in host countries.

According to the State Department, Libya has provided support to subversive groups in more than 20 countries. Rulers of Libya's African neighbors—including Gambia, Ghana, Niger, Mali, and Sierra Leone and the Sudan—all accuse Qaddafi of trying to overthrow them.

One of the colonel's favorite strategies has been to offer impoverished Muslim tribesmen from neighboring countries jobs in Libya's oil fields—and then force them into his Islamic Legion. His most promising recruits are typically given several months of basic training, and then infiltrated back into their countries of origin to run campaigns of subversion and espionage at the colonel's behest.

Unlike the Soviets, who infrequently directed operations abroad themselves, Qaddafi has for years conducted terrorist operations against his own people. In the opening months of 1980, he warned all Libyan expatriates to return home or face the threat of a homegrown hit squad. Since then, U.S. records note 14 attacks in seven countries by the colonel's assassination teams. Eleven Libyan exiles were killed, one wounded.[6]

When a gun, used on one such attack against a Colorado State University student, was traced to a soldier of fortune with links to

Libyan hit squads, the State Department ordered all Libyan diplomatic personnel out of the country on May 6, 1981.

Russian revenge

Of course the Soviets were not above using terrorists for their own purposes—especially in connection with East European affairs. When the Polish crisis acquired an unanticipated ally with the election of the first Polish Pope, the Soviets knew they had trouble on their hands.

Throughout 1979 and 1980, John Paul II had been working quietly behind the scenes for the peaceful creation of Solidarity, the trade union movement headed by Lech Walesa. But on Monday, Aug. 4, 1980, he received news that seemed to confirm his worst fears. Long-time friend and confident Cardinal Franz König, then archbishop of Vienna, picked up reliable intelligence to the effect that the Russians were on the verge of ordering Polish authorities to conduct a nationwide purge of Solidarity's leadership. Anticipating that this might provoke rebellion in the countryside, the Russians already had put tank crews on alert. Suddenly, all the smoldering tension of the past 18 months seemed about to erupt in a blood-chilling paroxysm of violence.

Knowing that he had to act, John Paul II sat down to write one of the most extraordinary letters ever penned by a pope. It was a single, handwritten page in Russian, on his personal stationary, bearing the papal coat-of-arms. It was addressed to the General Secretary of the Soviet Communist Party, Leonid Brezhnev.

In it, he told Brezhnev that he believed a Russian invasion of Poland was imminent. And if that happened, he warned, he would relinquish the throne of St. Peter and return to man the barricades with his fellow countrymen. With probably unintended irony, John Paul II closed the letter with "Yours in Christ." [7]

Sometime during the second week in August the letter was hand-delivered to the Kremlin by the curmudgeonly Bishop Paul Marcinkus, selected because of his command of the Russian language and the pope's conviction that he would not be intimidated by sitting face-to-face with the most powerful man in the Russian empire. (Two years later, Marcinkus was to achieve notoriety of his own in connection with the Vatican's financial scandal, in which he was deeply involved.)

After the letter was delivered, there were two months of tense and highly secret negotiations among Rome, Moscow, and Warsaw that eventually paved the way for the historic November 1980 agreement between Solidarity and the Polish government.

At this point, Brezhnev, echoing King Henry II of England, probably muttered: "Will no one rid me of this troublesome priest?" The head of the KGB, Yuri Andropov, was listening. And a year later, the 12th-century murder of Archbishop Thomas Becket by the minions of Henry II had its 20th-century parallel played out in St. Peter's Square on May 13, 1981. A few minutes past 5:15 p.m., Mehmet Ali Agca shot the pope three times.

After the shooting in 1981, Italian investigators assembled a wealth of evidence that the Bulgarian secret service had acted at the Soviets' request. It turns out, Agca received his small arms training at a camp in Libya.[8]

Islamic jihad

The dominant religions of the West—Christianity and Judaism—have long been known for their century-old traditions of non-violence (despite the Crusades and the military exploits of the modern nation of Israel). As a result, the frankly martial character of Islam often comes as something of a shock to the Western mind. The Prophet Mohammed himself led troops into battle. In fact, his successful attack on a commercial caravan at Badr in A.D. 624 is celebrated in the Koran as an expression of divine will.[9]

The term jihad, usually translated as "holy war," literally means a great striving in the name of Allah. Of course, this encompasses military struggle. But the great striving also includes political and economic pressures, subversion and propaganda, the penetration and conversion of non-Muslim societies, and terror.

Ayatollah on jihad

During his years in Paris the Ayatollah Khomeini wrote:

> *Holy war means the conquest of all non-Muslim territories. Such a war may well be declared after the formation of an Islamic government. It will then be the duty of every able-bodied adult male to volunteer for this war of conquest, the final aim of which is to put Koranic law in power from one end of the earth to the other.*[10]

By tradition and prescription, jihad is war without scruple, a war that makes easy targets of unarmed civilians.

Indeed Muslim tradition says that those who are martyred in a holy cause are guaranteed free entry into heaven, regardless of the sins they may have committed in earthly life. This kamikaze-like quality makes Islamic terrorists formidable foes. As Western hostage negotiators have learned through bitter experience, it's not easy to bargain with someone determined to die for his cause.

The use of terror tactics in general—and assassination in particular—goes very deep in Islamic tradition. The grandfather of the Muslim kamikaze was Hassan al Sabbah. Born in 1007 and, according to legend, a classmate of Omar Khayyam, he established himself in a mountain stronghold 50 miles from the Caspian Sea in what is now Northern Iran. As his fame grew he came to be known to his followers as the "Old Man of the Mountain."

Lacking the resources to raise and maintain a standing army, he created a secret society dedicated to pursuing a campaign of terror against his opposition—the orthodox Sunni Muslims who ruled from Baghdad—then, as now, a locus of Iranian hatreds and ambitions.

The instrument of his power was a band of fearless political killers that he himself trained. Displaying a flair for indoctrination rarely equaled in subsequent centuries, he elevated ritualized murder to a high art, and established a tradition whereby the techniques of assassination were transmitted from one generation to the next.

Hashish and paradise

His training methods combined the most powerful symbols of Islamic mythology with the most advanced behavioral and biochemical techniques the 11th century had to offer. He recruited his men from among the tough bedouin tribes that inhabited the neighboring Alumet mountains. In small numbers they were drugged with hashish—a concentrated resin from the marijuana plant—and taken to a special hidden garden cleverly appointed with all the trappings of the Muslim heaven.

His aim was twofold: to establish a vision of paradise so desirable that these superstitious folk willingly would die to get there; and to establish his credential as a great prophet.

Marco Polo was one of the few Westerners who managed to meet Hasan al Sabbah face-to-face. In 1273, he wrote:

> *He kept at his court a number of the youths*
> *of the country, from 12 to 20 years of age, such*
> *as had a taste for soldiering, and to these he*
> *used to tell tales about Paradise...then he*

*would introduce them into his garden,
some four or six or 10 at a time, having
first made them drink a certain potion
which cast them into a deep sleep, and
then causing them to be lifted and carried
in. So when they awoke, they found
themselves in the garden...so
charming...they deemed that it was
Paradise.*

*Now this prince, who we call the Old
One, kept his court in grand and noble
style, and made those simple hill folks
about him believe firmly that he was a
great prophet. And when he wanted to
send one of his* ashisisnon *a mission, he
would cause this potion to be given to one
of the youths in the garden, and then had
him carried into his palace. So when the
young man awoke, he found himself in the
castle and no longer in Paradise; whereat
he was not over well pleased...*

*So when the Old Man would have any
prince slain, he would say to such a
youth: 'Go thou and slay so-and-so; and
when thou returnest my angels shall bear
thee into Paradise. And should'st thou
die, nevertheless even so will I send my
angels to carry thee back into Paradise.'*

*So he caused them to believe; and
thus there was no order of his that they
would not affront any peril to execute, for
the great desire they had to get into that
paradise of his. And in this manner the
Old One got his people to murder anyone
whom he desired to get rid of.*[11]

First fedayeen

Sustained by this powerful vision of heaven, and convinced
beyond all doubt of al Sabbah's special place at the hand of Allah,
these men formed a corps known as the fedai—or "men of sacrifice."

Fedai is the root of the 20th-century generic term for Islamic

61

guerrillas—the fedayeen. Because of the special role of hashish, these men were also known as hashishim—according to the Oxford English Dictionary one of the roots of the most familiar term for political killers—assassins.

So eager were the assassins to die, that al Sabbah often paid his fedayeen in advance—so they they could give the money to their families before setting out on a mission from which they would never return. By the time of his death in 1091, al Sabbah's influence stretched from the Persian Gulf to the Mediterranean Sea. And military commanders, kings, and religious figures everywhere all wore chain mail as undergarments to protect against the daggers of the feared assassins.

Hasan al Sabbah was an Ismaili, an offshoot of Shi'ism that is itself an offshoot of Islam. Although Shi'ites have historically been a minority, they are arguably the most visible Muslims today. In large measure, they owe their notoriety to Ayatollah Khomeini and the Islamic fundamentalist revolution.

Origins in blood

Shi'ism was born in a bloody dispute over the true successor to the Prophet Mohammed. In fact, the original term was Shi'at Ali—or follower of Ali. Ali was the fourth Caliph—or Islam's official representative on earth. He also was cousin to The Prophet, and son-in-law by marriage to Mohammed's daughter Fatima.

When Ali was murdered in A.D. 661, the majority Sunni Muslims chose the next Caliph from outside the Ali-Fatima line. But Ali's followers named his son Hasan as their own successor, thereby insuring that they would forever be viewed as heretics by the Muslim orthodoxy. Hasan later resigned the honor bestowed upon him. But that was not enough to save him from assassination.

The first of the suicide attacks for which the Shi'ites are now renowned occurred in the year 680. Hussein, grandson of the Prophet, set out with fewer than 100 troops to defend the family's line of succession to the caliphate. Of course, this was a challenge the sitting caliph was not inclined to take lightly. Accordingly, he sent an army numbering in the thousands to defend the throne. The two forces met at what is now the Iraqi town of Karbala—where Hussein and his entire band of a hundred followers died gloriously.

Today, Islamic mourning houses and religious study centers are called Husseiniyehs. And the annual re-enactment of Hussein's martyrdom at Karbala is one of the most important events on the

Shi'ite religious calendar. In the 1980s, one of the Beirut predecessors to the notorious Iranian terrorist organization Hizbollah was called the Hussein Suicide Squad.

Scorned and treated as heretics by majority Sunni Muslims, the Shi'ites nursed their grievances for 13 centuries. With Napoleon's conquest of Egypt, Westerners for the first time became targets for these centuries of pent-up rage.

Several special factors combined to ignite the wave of Shi'ite fundamentalism that swept the Shah of Iran off the Peacock Throne in 1979. Already mentioned was the Arab humiliation by Israel in the Six Day War. To the Shi'ite clergy, however, the loss of the sacred city of Jerusalem was as disturbing as the battlefield reverses. Muslim losses, despite superior manpower and resources, seemed to be a message from Allah that Islam had somehow lost its way. It was this belief that helped create the fundamentalist movement to return to Islamic roots, and rid the Muslim world of foreign, corrupt, or simply non-Islamic influences.

When the Arab oil embargo startled the world in the 1970s, many fundamentalists saw it as a gift from God. As Daniel Pipes writes in *In the Path of God:*

> *Muslims felt they had finally stopped, and perhaps reversed their long decline. Starved for two centuries for some worldly sign of their special standing before God, for Muslims, the achievements of late 1973 appeared to be a vindication of their faith and a reward for their long-suffering steadfastness....*[12]

Ayatollah's crusade

When the Ayatollah Khomeini came to power, he lost no time in building on the institutional infrastructure for international terrorism that the Soviets had begun years earlier. Nor has his death resulted in any real cutbacks in government support for terrorist activity.

In some sense, the current wave of Shi'ite terrorism dates from a crisp spring day in March 1982, when 380 men wearing large turbans and severe expressions presented their religious and revolutionary credentials at the former Hilton Conference Center in Tehran. Officially, it was a conference on "the ideal Islamic government." But the hosts of this gathering—the Association of Militant Clerics as well as

63

several well-known Revolutionary Guards—belied the innocuous sounding subject matter.

At the conclusion of the meeting, four things were decided: 1) Religion could not be separated from politics; 2) true independence only could be achieved by a return to Islamic roots; 3) there could be no reliance on outside powers; and 4) a large scale offensive should be undertaken to cleanse the Muslim world of the satanic influences from both the East and the West.

It was the start of a crusade that would rock the world.

The nerve center, communications hub, and organizational center for recruiting and deploying cadres of the faithful to spread the revolution was a plain-looking building in downtown Tehran, nick-named Taleghani Center by the CIA. There, personnel from Syrian and Libyan intelligence services worked hand-in-hand with a near endless supply of local fanatics.

This nest of terrorists was personally supervised by Ayatollah Hussein Ali Montazeri, the designated successor to the Ayatollah Khomeini. His annual budget was estimated at $1 billion.

Often, the lights burned late.

Nuclear nightmare

One of the ultimate terrorist nightmares, of course, would be a small nuclear device in the hands of Qaddafi's minions or Khomeini's fanatics, the proverbial "suitcase from Allah."

Such a frightful scenario might unfold in a couple of ways. A small battlefield weapon, such as the American nuclear 155-mm howitzer shell, could be stolen from a storage area in West Germany or the United States.

Published reports exist of one "terrorist group in Europe having tried unsuccessfully to obtain information on NATO nuclear weapon storage facilities, and of another having sought unsuccessfully to enlist the help of a nuclear scientist regarding nuclear weapons they considered stealing..."[13]

Alternatively, a weapon could be co-developed using materials and technology from some sympathetic nation with a nuclear pro-gram. Both Iraq and Pakistan, for example, are Islamic countries with nuclear programs.

More disturbing, nuclear technology is increasingly within the reach of the do-it-yourself terrorist. The Public Broadcast Series *Nova* featured a 20-year-old Massachusetts Institute of Technology student who produced an accurate technical design for a fission bomb in March 1975. A year later, a 21-year-old Princeton physics major designed a bomb with information available solely from public documents.[14]

Nuclear explosives, however, require more than technical know-how. They also require fissionable materials like uranium or plutonium. That supplies of fissionable materials are rare and monitored by a host of international agencies, however, provides only a limited degree of reassurance. In the United States alone, more than 9,000 pounds are missing from the books through 1981.[15] It only takes about 15 pounds of plutonium to make a bomb.

For terrorists unable to build bombs themselves, attacks on nuclear installations make an excellent alternative. As the Soviet nuclear debacle at Chernobyl makes clear, an explosion at a power plant can easily spread radioactive contamination over an enormous area.

In the past 20 years, there have been 155 incidents—among them, bombings, other attacks, and violent demonstrations—at sites of civil nuclear installations in Europe and the United States.[16] With more than 370 power plants operating in more than two dozen countries—and a similar number under construction,[17] there is no dearth of likely targets.

Chemical and biological warfare

A low-tech terrorist threat of almost equal fearsomeness is the possibility of attack with chemical or biological weapons. Like terrorism itself, chemical and biological weapons are not new. The Greeks used sulphur fumes at the siege of Delium in 424 B.C. in what probably was the world's first gas attack. The first recorded use of a biological weapon occurred against a fortress on the Black Sea more than 600 years ago. Plague-infected cadavers hurled over the walls by catapult are generally credited with breaking the three-year siege of Feodosiya in 1346.[18]

Botulinal toxin (botulism) is much more lethal than plutonium, one of the most toxic elements known to man. Assuming a minimum lethal dose, less than an ounce, properly administered, could kill every human being in North America.

The formula for VX, one of the most potent nerve gases in the modern arsenal, has been declassified by both the United States and Britain. It is very cheap to produce. No laws prohibit the manufacture or possession of nerve gas by private citizens.[19] Moreover, the U.S. government has acknowledged that a small amount of its own inventory of VX is unaccounted for.[20]

65

Mail-order poison

T2 toxin, the agent known as yellow rain—used by the Soviets in Afghanistan and by the Vietnamese in Indochina—has from time-to-time been reported available through mail order in the United States.[21]

Since World War I, chemical weapons have been banned by international treaty. And the violations of the treaty that occurred in Afghanistan and Indochina generally were on a very small scale.. Much larger use was made by the Iraqis in the Persian Gulf War, where chemical weapons proved to be one of the most effective means of breaking the human wave attacks mounted by the Iranian Revolutionary Guards. That the Iraqis were able to make such effective military use of these weapons without an international outcry has not gone unnoticed by other antagonists and protagonists in the Middle East.

Toward a counterterrorist strategy

One of the major difficulties in combating terrorism, of course, is that the terrorist is typically a very elusive foe. While the world may be aware of a given group, or even of the identity of its leader or spokesperson, the rank and file and their numbers almost always remain a mystery.

As a result, it should come as no surprise that governments have mostly floundered in their efforts to combat the terrorist menace. Economic sanctions, for example, have been tried repeatedly but found wanting as a counterterrorist strategy.

One problem with sanctions is that they can really only be imposed against states, and not all terrorism is state-sponsored. But in any case, to be truly effective, sanctions require a degree of international cooperation that usually is nearly impossible to obtain. Anyone who believes economic sanctions can change state policy should review the experiences of South Africa.

Barricades and checkpoints

A more effective strategy is to make airports and other popular terrorist targets more secure. For example, tightened airport security and creation of a special corps of air marshals has sharply curtailed airline hijacking inside the United States.

There is a limit, however, to what can be achieved by barricades and checkpoints. The experience of the U.S. government in Washington is typical in this regard. Out of concern about bombings inside the Capitol, new procedures were laid down that require all visitors to pass through a metal detector. Concrete barriers were erected to limit approaches to the building. For the most part, public reaction to these measures was muted.

But when White House officials, worried about the use of car and truck bombs, sought to close Pennsylvania Avenue to the public, the outcry was intense. Clearly, officials can go only so far before members of Western society will fight to maintain some of their most fundamental values—such as freedom of movement and the right not to be inconvenienced.

Failed policy of appeasement

One approach that clearly does not work is giving in to terrorist demands. In 1977, fearing disruption of their Mideast oil supplies, the French actually released one of the most notorious terrorists ever to fall into their hands. His name was Abu Daoud, and he was a commander of the infamous Black September movement. Black September, you may recall, was the group responsible for killing the 11 Israeli Olympic team members during the 1972 Munich Games.

Although the agreement was never admitted publicly, the French Secret Service was believed to have reached a tacit accord with a number of international terrorist organizations. They reportedly agreed to allow terrorists free passage through French territory in exchange for a promise from the terrorists that they would not stage attacks on French citizens or installations. And, in the spring of 1986, the French declined to cooperate in a counterterrorist operation by refusing to allow overflights by American planes on their way to strike terrorist bases in Libya.

In due course, however, the French began to reap the bitter harvest of their policy of appeasement in the fall of 1986 when six bombs exploded in Paris within less than a fortnight. Overall, the 12-day campaign of terror claimed eight lives and injured more than 172 Parisians.

Of course, the French were not the only ones trying to solve the terrorist problem by giving in to terrorist demands. The United States did the same thing in the well-known arms-for-hostages scandal. Of course, that might never have happened had attempts to fight terrorism through counterintelligence and military operations been more effective.

Origin of failure

The inability of U.S. intelligence to develop much of an anti-terrorist capability stems in part from the scandals and budget cutbacks of the post-Vietnam era. U.S. intelligence services lost 25%

of its personnel in the 1970s. At one point, fewer than 50% of CIA analysts even spoke the language of the country they were supposed to cover.

With the end of the Vietnam War, the new intelligence objective became arms control verification—and this pretty much claimed the lion's share of remaining resources. More than anti-terrorist capability was neglected. At one point training and recruitment fell to such low levels that nearly 75% of CIA foreign station chiefs were old enough to be eligible for retirement.

There were other setbacks as well. On at least two occasions, the agency was itself the victim of a devastating terrorist attack. With the seizure of the U.S. Embassy in Tehran, the CIA lost its entire network of intelligence assets in Iran. Another debacle occurred in Lebanon a few years later.

On the morning of April 18, 1983, as Robert Ames, the recently promoted former CIA station chief in Beirut was conducting a meeting with subordinates on the top floor of the U.S. Embassy, an explosive-laden delivery van crashed into the embassy compound. Sixty-three people died in what was at the time the bloodiest terrorist attack ever against an American diplomatic mission.

But if it was a tragedy for the State Department, it was a catastrophe for the CIA. Ames, along with everyone else at the meeting, was crushed to death as the building collapsed beneath them. In one stroke, a single terrorist had wiped out the entire top level of U.S. intelligence in Lebanon.

A further difficulty for U.S. intelligence was that even when identified, international terrorist groups were almost impossible to infiltrate. New recruits are routinely required to demonstrate their loyalty by killing a few civilians. And no American intelligence service could put itself in the position of condoning the slaughter of innocents—no matter how important the cause.

The KGB approach

Sometimes, however, a high-minded refusal to match the ruthlessness of one's adversary puts the United States at a severe tactical disadvantage. When four Russian diplomats were seized by Lebanese terrorists in 1985, the KGB replied in terms well understood by terrorists all over the world. After identifying the hostage-takers, Soviet intelligence operatives seized a number of their relatives and friends. They killed one and mailed parts of his body to the kidnappers along with a note demanding release of all Soviet personnel.[22]

The diplomats were released in short order, and no doubt the terrorists were suitably chagrined. They probably also decided it would be much safer to steer clear of the Russians in the future.

The fight against terrorism also suffered from the kind of bureaucratic paralysis that routinely prevails in Washington. One example of this is bureaucracy's difficulty to even define the problem. One study noted 109 different definitions of terrorism formulated by government officials between 1936 and 1980.[23]

But if bureaucratic bungling is characteristic of the U.S. government, it is a hallmark of the armed forces. And nowhere has that been more visible than in U.S. handling of terrorist attacks against U.S. Marines in Lebanon. Along with French and Italian troops, U.S. Marines were sent to Lebanon on a peace-keeping mission in 1982 as part of a United Nations Multinational Force.

Marine Corps debacle

At 6:20 a.m. on Oct. 23, 1983, a yellow Mercedes Benz stakebed truck roared past Lance Cpl. Eddie DiFranco's guard post at the perimeter of the Marine encampment. As he scrambled to load his weapon—on higher authority, the Marines had been ordered to stand guard with their weapons empty—the driver looked right at him...and smiled.

Seconds later, the building housing 350 sleeping Marines went up in what the FBI later termed the largest non-nuclear explosion since World War II. For the Marines, it was the worst loss of life since the Vietnam War.

Of course, when something like this happens, the government has to blame somebody. A Pentagon commission headed by retired Adm. Robert Long recommended that the Marine commander, Col. Timothy Geraghty, be punished "for failure to take the security measures necessary to preclude the catastrophic loss of life."[24] Of course, no one remembered that Geraghty had been a vocal opponent of orders from above that had specifically violated the Marines' claim to neutrality and made them virtual participants in the Lebanese Civil War.

A month before, the predominantly Christian Lebanese Army suddenly found itself under strong attack by several of the local armed militias in and around Beirut. When the Christian Lebanese appealed to National Security Advisor Robert McFarlane, he sent a cable back to Washington claiming that the Lebanese government would collapse unless the Marines intervened in the factional fighting on behalf of the

69

army. In fact, he painted such a lurid picture that within the Reagan administration his message came to be known as the "sky is falling cable."[25]

Only Col. Geraghty seemed to appreciate that military action on behalf of the Christian-dominated army would violate the Marines' claim to a neutral peace-keeping role. Once the United States was perceived as taking sides in the factional fighting, the Marines would become just another armed militia—and another target.

Officers who were present on Sept. 19 when Geraghty received the order to fire in support of the Lebanese army, report that he argued vehemently against it: "Sir, I can't do that. This will cost us our neutrality. Do you realize if you do that, we'll get slaughtered down here? We could be severely attacked. We're totally vulnerable. We're sitting ducks."[26]

Of course, he was overruled. And he was exactly right. Only 34 days later, the smiling truck driver blasted 241 sleeping American soldiers to kingdom come.

A few minutes after the Marine blast, another truck bomber struck the Beirut headquarters of the French peace-keeping forces. And 10 days later, a third one struck the headquarters of the Israeli Defense Forces in Tyre.

Uncertain retaliation

Immediately after the attack, Israeli warplanes struck back. Two days later, so did the French Air Force. Interestingly enough, the French attack had been originally conceived as a joint U.S.-French counterterrorism strike. On board the U.S. aircraft carrier Kennedy, air crews were awakened several nights in a row and ordered to man their planes.

But each time, the raid was called off at the last minute. In spite of the president's avowal on national television that "those who directed this atrocity must be dealt justice, and they will be," the U.S. government could not make up its mind.[27] Finally, the French flew alone.

At length, the only thing the U.S. chain of command could agree on was that daily reconnaissance flights be sent to try to spot any additional threats against the Marines. On Dec. 3, while on such a mission the crew of a F-14 Tomcat from the Kennedy spotted several corkscrewing exhaust trails coming in their direction—the telltale sign of heat-seeking surface-to-air missiles.

The missiles missed, and the F-14 returned safely. But this time the brass was determined to react. Within 24 hours, the Pentagon had recommended and the president had approved a raid against Syrian anti-aircraft sites in Lebanon. As David Martin and John Walcott remark in their book, *The Best Laid Plans*, "Having failed to shoot back when 241 Americans were blown up, the Reagan administration had no difficulty deciding to retaliate against a few shoulder-fired missiles that had missed."

Even then, Washington could not go ahead without making a hash of everything. After the Joint Chiefs determined the specific targets against which to retaliate—Syrian anti-aircraft sites in Lebanon—the task of planning the raid became the responsibility of Rear Adm. Jerry Tuttle, the commander of the U.S. fleet off the coast of Lebanon. Tuttle was a former carrier pilot, well-known for being an aggressive and hard-driving officer.

Among the ranks he was renowned for his caustic sarcasm— which, from time to time, he also turned upon himself. (He once awarded himself the nickname, SLUF—an acronym for "short, little, ugly fucker.") In short, he was the kind of commander who either inspired utter devotion or undying hatred.

A man of strong and unvarnished opinions, he was not pleased with Washington's choice of targets. Because the Syrian anti-aircraft sites were too small to reliably show up on radar, his pilots would have to go in low and slow enough to spot them visually. This meant they would be exposed to anti-aircraft fire from not just the Syrians, but any local militia man with a shoulder-fired anti-aircraft weapon.

To minimize the risk to his airmen, he planned to attack at high noon. At least that way anti-aircraft gunners would have to look straight into the sun to spot his planes. At 3:30 a.m. on Dec. 4, having worked out the last details of the strike plan, he lay down for a few hours sleep aboard the aircraft carrier *Independence*. While he slept, however, he was countermanded by higher authority.

Somebody in Washington had the bright idea that the raid would have greater political impact if it took place within 24 hours of the original attack. And that meant the planes would have to strike just after dawn. New orders were issued accordingly.

General ignorance

Not only did the four- and five-star know-it-alls on the Joint Chiefs—upon whose sage military advice the safety of the country depends—overrule the well-reasoned judgment of their commander in the field, but they rescheduled the raid at an hour when the targets

71

would be in shadow and American pilots, not anti-aircraft gunners, would have to be looking directly into the early morning sun.

The new orders arrived on board the *Independence* at 5:33 a.m. As soon as Tuttle was awakened with the news, he called back to say there was no way to launch on such short notice. He was ordered to do it anyway. He requested a delay long enough at least to get his air crews properly organized. He was denied.

For better or worse, military men are trained to follow orders— even when issued by imbeciles. Having exhausted the available alternatives, Tuttle scrambled his airmen, told them they had only minutes to review maps and pictures of their targets, and ordered them to their planes.

On the aircraft carrier *Kennedy*, two of the fliers scheduled for the mission, Lts. Bill Davis and Tom Corey, raced for the flight deck. But when they arrived, they were astounded to discover that their A-6 aircraft had not even been armed with any missiles or bombs.

With only minutes to flight time, they screamed at the ordnance men to attach some in a hurry. Unfortunately, the only munitions at hand were 1,000-pound iron bombs, great for attacking large fortifications, but notoriously inaccurate against small targets like the one they were assigned to assault.

Even so, inaccurate bombs were better than none at all. But there was time only to strap on a pair of the thousand-pounders before the plane was ordered to the runway. It was almost like going to battle unarmed.

Worse, it was the rule rather than the exception. Only one of the A-6s took off with a full load of munitions, flown by Lts. Mark Lang and Robert Goodman. Only the fact that theirs was the last plane in the take-off line had allowed sufficient time to make sure it was fully armed.

And a few moments later, it was tumbling out of control, the victim of a surface-to-air missile. As the flaming wreck spun toward the ground at two-thirds the speed of sound, Goodman and Lang somehow managed to fire their ejection seats. Lang's parachute barely had time to open before he hit the ground.

As a result he landed with such impact that his left leg was severed. He bled to death under the gaze of the gunners who had shot him down. Goodman also landed hard, breaking a rib and separating a shoulder in the process. The remaining planes from the *Kennedy* were so lightly armed that all of their munitions could have been carried by a single plane.

Another plane was shot down, but its crew was safely rescued. So, at the cost of one American dead, another captured, and two planes lost, a pair of Syrian gun positions were damaged, and an anti-aircraft radar was put out of commission for about 48 hours.

Brass hat cover-up

Back in Washington, the chain of command was busily covering up what a disaster the raid had been. Not surprisingly, no one was willing to admit responsibility for making a dangerous mission more dangerous because of an irrelevant political consideration. It's a wonder the brass didn't find a way to blame Adm. Tuttle as they did Col. Gerarghty.

Not only did the United States fail to avenge the fatal terrorist attack on the Marines, but it could not even manage even to effectively defend reconnaissance aircraft whose mission it was to help protect the Marines from further attack. According to the peculiar logic of the defense bureaucracy, there was apparently nothing to be done but give up reconnaissance. A short time later, all flights over the most dangerous areas of Lebanon—and therefore the ones most in need of watching—were quietly halted.

Even where international terrorist incidents involving Americans have been brought to a successful conclusion, the U.S. government has frequently been more of an obstacle than a help. Consider, for example, the case of U.S. Brig. Gen. James Dozier, a NATO commander assigned to Verona, Italy.

Unscheduled guests

On Dec. 17, 1981, just as Dozier was sitting down to dinner with his wife, somebody started ringing the doorbell. He went to the door where he found two men in coveralls who explained (in Italian) that they were trying to find the cause of a leak in the apartment below. Once inside, they pulled silenced pistols. In short order, the general was gagged, blindfolded, and dumped in a steamer trunk.

The terrorists then put the trunk in a refrigerator carton, which they carried downstairs and deposited in a panel truck. After a short drive, it was transferred to another vehicle. A couple of hours later, Dozier was taken out of the trunk and chained to a steel cot inside a pup tent that was set up inside an apartment.

His captors announced that he was a prisoner of the Red Brigades. To make sure they could not be overheard, they strapped headphones on him, and treated him to rock music at amplitudes sufficient to cause permanent hearing damage.

When news of the kidnapping reached the U.S. Defense Department, a new bureaucracy swung into action. The commission that had investigated the failure of the Carter administration effort to rescue the American hostages in Iran found that the operation had been done in by the lack of a proper organization to direct the mission. The bureaucracy's reaction, predictably, was to create another bureaucracy. In this manner, the Pentagon's Joint Special Operations Command (JSOC) was born.

The JSOC immediately sent a six-man team of intelligence and communications specialists to the Mediterranean. But once they arrived in the operating area of the European Command (EC), EC commanders claimed them. As a result, America's elite and highly trained counterterrorist force spent its first few weeks on the job arguing about who was in charge.

When they finally went to work, the communications specialists scanned the airwaves in hope of overhearing the kidnappers conversing via walkie-talkie. Presumably, lots of conversations were overheard. But none belonged to the kidnappers.

Psychic insights

No stranger to inter-service rivalry, the Air Force figured out a way to outdo the JSOC in the race to leave no stone unturned. Displaying a flair for imagination rarely found in military organizations, operation Distant Viewing was launched. This consisted of consulting a number of local psychics who claimed they might be able to find the general by means of extrasensory perception.

One said he was being held on a farm in Austria; another said he was confined in the hold of a ship. Again, every lead was duly catalogued and turned over to the Italian police. None led anywhere. Finally, the overburdened Italian investigators had to ask the Americans to stop trying to be of so much help.

Another effort to aid the investigation was the offer of a $500,000 reward for information leading to a rescue. No sooner had the reward been announced than it was discovered that no office, embassy, agency, or branch of service involved in the case had legislative authority to dispense reward money outside the United States. The federal government, which had no trouble overspending its $800 billion budget, somehow could not manage to come up with a half-million dollars of reward money.

Bureaucratic gridlock

It was a good thing the money was never needed. But it is worth noting that the one man who finally was able to break the bureaucratic logjam was a young Marine major who had originally come to the White House as an "easel-carrier," one of the nameless assistants whose duties included handling charts, slides, and other visual aids for his superiors. A few years later, he would become legendary for his ability to circumvent Washington's perpetual bureaucratic paralysis. His name was Oliver North.

That Dozier was ever rescued owed more to the thoroughness of the largest manhunt in Italian history—involving some 5,000 officers—and the shrewdness of the U.S. ambassador to Italy than all the hamstrung efforts of the U.S. government. Aware that many captured leaders of the Red Brigades were still directing operations from behind bars, Ambassador Maxwell Rabb persuaded the Italian Minister of the Interior to put all jailed members in one place and cut their lines of communications to lawyers and relatives.

Soon, the now leaderless kidnappers began to falter. The first major break in the case occurred on the 39th day of Dozier's captivity. During one of the sweeps in which more than 400 suspected terrorists were detained, police picked up the brother of one of the imprisoned Brigade members. He revealed the name of one of the men who had carried Dozier out of his apartment.

As part of a plea bargain, this man led police to a second-floor apartment in Padua where Dozier was being held. After watching the apartment for several days, the Italian counterterrorist brigade stormed the building, using the sounds from a nearby bulldozer to mask the noise of the assault. Dozier was rescued unharmed—except for his hearing loss. Five terrorists were captured along with a cache of weapons and ammunition. And not a shot was fired.

Preferred target

Increasingly, Americans are becoming the preferred victims of international terrorists. The director of the CIA recently reported that U.S. persons, property, and institutions are victims in one out of every two terrorists incidents.[28]

It is not hard to see why. First, as we have observed, the U.S. government rarely is able to react with decisiveness or dispatch. And that helps minimize the terrorist's personal risk. Second, Americans make ideal hostages. Because of the U.S. preoccupation with individual human rights, hostages become an instant media event. And as a result, the centralized communication facilities of the nation end up at the service of the hostage-takers.

As of this writing, your odds of becoming the victim of a hostage-taking still are very low. (They're about the same as your chances of being struck by lightning.) One thing, however, is certain. As terrorists around the world continue to zero in on Americans, those chances are going to increase. Hence, it is only prudent to investigate what you as an individual can do to avoid becoming a victim.

One thing you can do is to be aware of unsafe destinations. Terrorism is frequently a crime of opportunity, and most often occurs at the world's least secure airports. In the Middle East, Beirut tops the list. Tripoli and Istanbul, along with the South Asian airports of Dakar and Bombay, also are considered among the worst. The airports of Jeddah, Baghdad, Accra, Algiers, and Karachi are only slightly safer. Tel Aviv, however, is one of the world's most secure airports. Zurich is considered the safest European airport, Athens the most dangerous. Rome, Barcelona, and Palma de Majorca also are considered unsafe, while London gets high marks for security precautions.

In South America, Rio de Janeiro, Mexico City, and Lima rate low on security. In Sub-Saharan Africa, Lagos stands out as unsafe.

In Eastern Europe, Polish and Soviet airports get high ratings for security. Security, however, does not necessarily mean safety in the Soviet Union. Soviet government directives to resist hijackers at all cost have caused injuries to passengers and several crashes. Some of the many Soviet air accidents rumored in the West are suspected to be the result of authorities' attempts to thwart hijackers trying to defect.[29]

Hotlines and phony passports

The State Department maintains a telephone hotline that you can use to stay abreast of security conditions in countries around the world (202)647-5225. An updated listing of these briefings also is available on-line to computer owners through the Compuserve database service.

Usually, the first thing a hijacker will do is collect passports from his band of victims. From these, he can easily identify each person's nationality. One way to avoid being identified as an American in this way to carry a camouflage passport.

These are passports bearing your signature and photograph, but which establish you as a citizen of one of several countries that no longer exist. They will not help you cross any of the world's border checkpoints. But they may help you conceal your national identity.

They are legal—as long as you don't try to use them in any official connection or transaction. One that I recently saw was purportedly issued by British Honduras and appeared totally authentic—that is, to anyone who failed to realize that British Honduras ceased to exist as a country in 1981. (It is now Belize.) But the Ayatollah's minions have seldom been noted for their grasp of Latin American history.

(For under $200, an outfit called International Document Service, *3106 Tamiami Trail, North Naples, FL 33940*, will supply a camouflage passport and two additional pieces of supporting identification.)

Surviving as a hostage[30]

If you are unlucky enough to become a hostage victim, there are a number of things you should—and should not—do to maximize your chances of emerging unharmed.

The most dangerous period of a kidnapping or a hostage-taking is the initial capture. At this moment your first impulse may be to freeze or to run or to fight. The safest thing to do is to freeze. At all costs, avoid sudden movements. They can easily get you killed.

If there is shooting put your head down. Better still, lie on the floor. That way you'll be a smaller target. If you wear glasses or other aids, protect them. Slip them into a pocket. Don't put them down.

If shooting breaks out on an airplane in flight, there is some likelihood that a bullet will penetrate the aircraft's outer skin. A handful of bullet holes, however, will not be enough to depressurize the aircraft. A greater danger is the possibility that a stray bullet might hit a fuel tank somewhere in the plane's hull.

(To minimize this risk, the ammunition used by U.S. air marshals are specially designed for use in confined spaces. While lethal within a range of 50 feet, at greater distances these bullets rapidly lose power and are unlikely to penetrate aircraft bulkheads.)

Listen carefully to what your abductors say, and follow their instructions precisely. If you have to endure a beating, try your best to roll with the punches as much as possible. Fortunately, you can probably count on your body's own coping mechanisms—adrenalin and shock—to increase your tolerance to pain. Most former victims report that they felt very little pain when abused during a capture.

In the event of a rescue attempt, you should not under any circumstances attempt to disarm any of your captors. Nor should you try to seize a gun during the confusion. Your rescuers will be trained to shoot anyone holding a weapon—and there will not be time to explain that you are not one of the "bad guys."

The period of confinement in a hostage-taking may be as short as several hours or as long as several years. Many of the insights on how best to survive an extended period of captivity come from the experience of William Niehous, a vice president of Owns-Illinois' foreign subsidiary in Venezuela, who was kidnapped and held captive for 1,219 days.[31]

Five points of survival

Niehous outlines a five-point plan for surviving an extended confinement. Taken together, these five points comprise the acronym FACES.

F stands for faith that you will be able to endure the emotional roller coaster of captivity. There is a range of psychological reactions that you are likely to experience immediately after capture. The most common emotions are incapacity, fear, denial, and withdrawal.

Initially, you may be so afraid that you think you won't be able to cope. Knowing that anybody in the same boat would go through the same thing may help you control your fear. Many former hostages have expressed surprise at their own capacity to endure what appeared unendurable.

Be aware that overwhelming fear sometimes manifests itself in neurotic reactions. Claustrophobia is a typical example. In an airplane especially, you may panic at being confined by seatbelts, or even the plane itself. Escaping into irrational behavior may be an effective form of denial, but it is an unconstructive one. A better strategy would be to seek relief in the minutiae of your experience rather than in total unawareness.

Try to distract yourself by memorizing every detail of your captors and what they do. Write a diary in your head and include everything you observe—including colors, smells, and textures. Omit no details—no matter how trivial they seem. Not only will the effort help you control your emotions, but the information may be useful later.

A is for aspirations or goals. William Niehous reports that he sustained his spirits by setting himself objectives. "I would live until a specific date, whether it was my son's graduation, or my wife's birthday, or Christmas. As the date came and went, with my release not imminent, I did become despondent; however, I then set another goal for life sometime in the future. I kept telling myself that those holding me surely would release me by the date of my next goal."[32]

One way to combat the sometimes overwhelming sense of powerlessness is to organize the space allotted to you. Even if all you have is a cramped economy-class airline seat, designate special places to keep different objects. Make it one of your goals to keep your area orderly. External order will help your internal order.

C is for communication. If you have a medical problem that requires special medication or attention, inform your captors at the first non-threatening opportunity. They may accommodate you. Generally, it is in their interest that you stay healthy. A sick hostage is a burden and a liability.

If you are given a chance to read newspapers, try to stay abreast of events in the outside world. If you are allowed to send letters to relatives or loved ones, putting your thoughts on paper can have a beneficial effect—even if they are never delivered.

If you are allowed to communicate with other hostages, take care not to spread any suspicions you might have concerning any of them. Discord can only further devastate the morale of the entire hostage group. If held together with other hostages, do not hoard food without group consent. Secrets are hard to keep in captivity. And if you are found out, it will only may make you a target for hostility.

E is for exercise. Contrive to establish some form of exercise that can be done in your confined circumstances and do them regularly. Maybe all you can do is wiggle your toes and fingers. But even that much will aid circulation—especially if you are being held in cramped conditions.

Moreover, it is important to do what you can to keep your body as agile as possible. If a chance to escape presents itself, you don't want to be so debilitated that you cannot seize it.

Stockholm Syndrome

S is for the Stockholm Syndrome—the well-documented emotional attachment that frequently develops between the captive and captor. (The term comes from a barricade-hostage incident that took place during a 1973 bank robbery in the Swedish capital.)

Falling in love with the hostage-taker is a common manifestation of the Stockholm Syndrome. Sometimes this attachment is strong enough to cause a hostage to become so eager to please his captives that he acts against his own best interests and that of his fellow victims. For example, hostages have been known to help terrorists escape.

The degree to which a hostage experiences the Stockholm Syndrome varies by individual. Some remain largely unaffected, while others are nearly blinded by it. According to one study of hostage incidents, more than 80% of the kidnap victims experienced some degree of fear and anger toward the police—especially if the police overtly threatened the hostage-takers.[33]

Be aware, however, that this attachment works both ways—and you can therefore use it to your advantage. For this reason, you should seize every opportunity to establish a personal relationship with your captors.

If you have a chance, for example, try to get them talking. Be as friendly as they allow you to be, but not so friendly that you lose their respect. The more that you can get them to think of you as a fellow human being—and not as a depersonalized political objective—the greater your chances of emerging unhurt.

One further note: Ever since Kozo Okamato, the surviving terrorist of the Lydda Airport massacre, admitted "a strange ecstasy" in meting out death to innocents,[34] a number of authorities have warned that women terrorists may be more inclined to engage in acts of senseless violence than their male counterparts.[35]

Indeed, a host of studies confirm that terrorist acts by females have thus far been characterized more by gratuitous violence than those of their male counterparts—whose use of force usually appears more calculated and directed toward some well-defined political goal. Whether this will continue to be the case is, predictably, a matter of considerable dispute.

Hopes for the future

In view of the statistics that show terrorism is growing steadily worse, and the befuddlement that has plagued U.S. efforts to combat it, what hopes should we have for the future? In the great game of military competition, high technology traditionally has been one of America's strong suits. And while technology can scarcely persuade fanatics to take up more leisurely pursuits, it can be pressed into service to make the task of the unrepentant more difficult.

Black powder markers

One promising possibility lies in steps that could be taken to reduce the anonymity of explosives. Back in the early 1970s, a 3M Co. research chemist developed a means of tracing explosives by seeding them with tiny chips of multilayered melamine plastic. These tiny chips, no bigger than one-thousandth of a millimeter across, could contain as many as 10 separate layers, each with a different color laminate.

Dubbed microtaggants, these chips could be mixed in with explosives early in the manufacturing process without affecting their chemistry or performance. More importantly, they would always survive among the explosive debris, providing a positive link to a particular production batch. Government regulations require considerable record-keeping on the buying and selling of explosives. These microtaggants would for the first time make it possible to link a particular explosion to a particular recorded purchase of explosives.

A dramatic real-life test occurred on May 10, 1979, when a truck exploded in the parking lot of Bethlehem Steel near Baltimore, killing the driver and severely wounding his passenger. After sweeping the area, technicians from the Bureau of Alcohol, Tobacco, and Firearms (ATF) discovered the telltale taggants among the debris.[36]

A call to 3M revealed that the color code matched a batch of Tovex 220, a water gelatin explosive widely used in road construction and quarrying. Records showed that this particular batch had been sold to the Jenkins Explosives Co. in Martinsburg, WV. A visit there led federal agents to James McFillin, the man who had purchased the explosives. He also was the murderer.

Legislative failure

That same year, two bills were introduced in Congress (H.R. 2441 and S. 333) to mandate the use of microtaggants in all explosives manufactured in the United States. Widespread tagging in the United States, especially if coupled with some kind of international treaty, could create a significant obstacle for international terrorists. It would mean that law enforcement agencies would no longer have to speculate about who might be behind a particular terrorist bombing. The evidence would be at the scene of every explosion. (Switzerland passed legislation mandating the tagging of all explosives in 1980.)

Even if not universally adopted, such a treaty would provide useful clues. For one thing, if the bomb debris was untagged, it would be strong evidence that the explosives came from some country not supporting the treaty. Furthermore, the pursuit of untagged explosives might force terrorists to resort to alternative materials—none of which are likely to be as safe or as easy to handle as what they now use.

But the technology of microtaggants has yet to be adopted—incredibly, neither of the bills introduced in 1979 was ever passed. 3M got tired of waiting and finally shut down its microtaggant production line in 1983. Both bills were casualties of a spirited campaign against them by the gun lobby.

The di-electric scanner

Another promising technology that met a similar fate was developed by William Gregory of the physics department at Georgetown University. Called di-electric analysis, it works on the principle that different materials exhibit distinctive behavior in two important respects—their abilities to store electric charge and to conduct electric current.

Gregory built a simple device that measures these two characteristics—and found that virtually any material he tested exhibited a characteristic fingerprint. By compiling a library of these fingerprints, Gregory maintains that a set of portraits could be developed covering just about any innocent items found in a suitcase—socks, shaving cream, blow dryers, etc. Security personnel could hand-inspect anything the machine didn't recognize.

As it turns out, di-electric analysis is especially sensitive to the chemistry of explosives. This gives it an important advantage over the X-ray machines and metal detectors now in service. Neither of these can pick up the presence of an explosive, especially if it is packed in some innocent-looking container—such as a tube of toothpaste. Furthermore, the di-electric scanner should be able to easily spot the metal detector's newest nemesis—the ceramic and plastic handgun.

Gregory got a chance to prove his device when the U.S. Information Agency (USIA) was plagued by a rash of letter bombs. With considerable public fanfare, a scanner was installed in the mailroom of USIA's Washington headquarters in February 1977. Apparently the mere announcement was enough to deter aspiring bombers. The year that the scanner was in operation, no additional explosive packages were received.

Letter-perfect performance

During that time, however, the scanner was tested by USIA security on a daily basis, and it performed flawlessly. The ATF was so impressed that it arranged another series of exhaustive tests. The results showed a 99% rate of accuracy.

Although Georgetown University has licensed the technology to interested manufacturers, it remains unmarketed and undeveloped. No di-electric scanners are in service at any of the world's major airports.

As helpful as adoption of these technologies might be, at best they merely complicate the terrorist mission. Any effort to truly strike back at international terrorists inevitably amounts to another military mission of the kind that have gone awry so often in the past.

The grim conclusion that the United States probably will never be able to match the surgical precision and efficiency of the Israeli Defense Forces in the battle against terrorists. As we have seen, it almost looks as if the surest way to screw something up is put the American military establishment in charge.

High-priced weapon systems, for example, continue to fail when they are most needed. In 1980, three of eight Sea Stallion helicopters malfunctioned on the way to their Desert One landing zone, forcing U.S. counterterrorist forces to abort the planned rescue of American hostages at the U.S. Embassy in Tehran. Six years later, seven out of nine U.S.-built F-111 fighter-bombers failed to drop their bombs on Qaddafi's headquarters. And that was after the largest peacetime expansion of the Pentagon's budget in modern times.

Some might argue that while military miscarriages inevitably make the headlines, successful counterterrorist operations may never be publicized for fear of revealing too much about U.S. intelligence assets and techniques. This may indeed be the case. But if the whole truth were known, surely more debacles than we yet know of would also come to light.

Downed by gunfire

Consider, for example, the case of an Itavia DC-9 bound from Bologna to Sicily on the evening of June 27, 1980. Somewhere over the Mediterranean, the jet exploded and crashed into the sea, killing all 81 aboard.

At the time, this was thought to be just another in a wave of terrorist bombings. But now, almost six years later, the true story finally can be pieced together.

Not much was ever found of the plane. Thirty-nine bodies were eventually fished out of the sea, along with a few seat cushions, but it was the cushions that provided the first clue.

Tests performed on the debris in England revealed traces of a chemical known as T4, a military explosive commonly used in air-to-air missiles. Furthermore, small particles of the explosive were found deep inside the fabric of the cushions, which suggested that they had been traveling at extremely high speeds—speeds much higher than would have been caused by a bomb inside the plane.

Twenty-two days after the explosion, shepherds in a remote area about 300 miles from the scene of the crash made a startling discovery. There, on the side of a mountain, lay the wreckage of a Soviet-built MIG-23 jet fighter. The body of the pilot was still in the cockpit. Both the pilot and his craft bore the markings of the Libyan air force.

When word leaked out, authorities immediately sealed off the area. And, although the date of the crash was never officially established, the state of decomposition of the pilot's body suggested that it certainly could have occurred on the same day that the DC-9 exploded.

83

The Italian government has denied any link between the two events. But NATO documents confirm that a major military air exercise was conducted over the Mediterranean in June 1980. They also indicate that a squadron of four Libyan MIG-23s overflew the exercise area almost every day.

A radar study by the National Traffic Safety Board in the United States found that an unidentified object flying at high speed crossed the DC-9's flight path shortly before the explosion. Events of the final seconds of the flight, however, are obscured by a mysterious eight-minute gap in military radar reports at the time of the crash.

Although the Italian Defense Ministry has denied that any NATO planes were in the air at the time of the crash, it is difficult to avoid the conclusion that an aerial dogfight must have broken out between NATO pilots and the Libyan flyers. One MIG-23 was shot down by NATO fighters. It is also clear that the unarmed DC-9 must have suffered a similar fate. What we don't know is which side fired the missile that brought it down.

---

1. Thucydides, *The Peloponnesian War*, trans. Rex Warner, p. 209.

2. Niccolo Machiavelli, *The Prince*, trans. George Ball, p. 98.

3. Press release issued by U.S. State Department, September 1986.

4. Speech by CIA Director William Webster before the American Bar Association meeting in Toronto, Aug. 9, 1988.

5. Special National Intelligence Estimate, prepared by CIA analyst J. Azrael, 1981.

6. *ibid.*

7. This account draws on the excellent work done by G. Thomas and M. Morgan-Witts, *Pontiff*, p. 406.

8. *ibid.*

9. The Koran, 1:119.

10. Quoted by J. Laffin, *War Annual 1*, p. 61.

11. Quoted by B. Lewis, *The Assassins: A Radical Sect in Islam*, p. 7-8.

12. D. Pipes, *In the Path of God*, p. 295.

13. *Report of the International Task Force on Prevention of Nuclear Terrorism*, Nuclear Control Institute, Washington, DC, June 25, 1986.

14. *Princeton Alumni Weekly*, Oct. 25, 1976.

15. Rear Admiral Thomas Davies, "Terrorism's Nuclear Potential: What Might The Means and Targets Be?," Conference on International Terrorism: The Nuclear Dimension, Nuclear Control Institute, Washington, DC, June 1985, p. 3.

16. "International Task Force on Prevention of Nuclear Terrorism," cited by L.R. Beres, *Terrorism and Global Security*, p. 40 f.

17. *ibid.*

18. Stockholm International Peace Research Institute, *Weapons of Mass Destruction*, p. 41.

19. R.C. Clark, *Technological Terrorism*, p.110.

20. N.C. Livingston, *The War Against Terrorism*, p. 110.

21. *Washington Post,* Sept. 23, 1981.

22. Gerald F. Seib, "Soviets' Big Stick gets Better Results than that of U.S. Gulf Actions Show," *Wall Street Journal*, Aug. 10, 1987.

23. D.C. Martin and J. Walcott, *Best Laid Plans: The Inside Sotry of America's War Against Terrorism,* p. 53.

24. Report of the DoD Commission on Beirut International Airport Terrorist Act, Oct. 23, 1983.

25. D.C. Martin and J. Walcott, *op. cit.,* p. 118.

26. R. Wright, *Sacred Rage: The Wrath of Militant Islam,* p. 78.

27. P. Taubman, *New York Times Magazine*, April 14 , 1985.

28. CIA Director W. Webster, Speech before American Bar Association meeting, Toronto, Aug. 9, 1988.

29. F. Modderno, *Traveler's Health and Safety Handbook.*

30. *ibid.*

31. "How to Survive as a Hostage," Diplomats and Terrorists: What Works, What Doesn't—A Symposium, Institute for the Study of Diplomacy, Georgetown University, 1982.

32. *ibid.*, p. 34.

33. F. Modderno, *op. cit.,* p. 9.

34. *ibid.*, p. 6.

35. D.E. Georges-Abeyie, "Women as Terrorists," in L.Z. Freedman and Y. Alexander, *Perspectives on Terrorism*, p. 78.

36. S. Kindel, "Catching Terrorists," *Science Digest*, September 1986, p. 37-82.

Chapter VI

Oil and War Today

The Geopolitical Roller Coaster

The Soviets are likely to play a patient and persistent game in the Persian Gulf....They will pressure existing regimes, exploit regional tensions, and carry out subversion in an attempt to expand their influence gradually while weakening that of the United States....The Soviet interest in the Gulf is not oil per se, but the manipulation of Western dependence on oil.
   —David Deese and Joseph Nye, *Energy and Security*

From the development of the first oil-fired engines of war to the invasion of Afghanistan and the rise of the Organization of Petroleum Exporting Countries (OPEC), the story of oil and war has chiefly been concerned with the military significance of a scarce resource getting scarcer. Oil grew scarcer because of more demands on existing supply, as ever more applications for oil-related technology were developed. And it grew scarcer because of curtailments of supply, either in the form of higher prices or production cutbacks.

All that changed, however, in 1986 when the first cracks began to appear in OPEC's seemingly inpenetrable facade. One cause of OPEC's distress, of course, was the power of market forces. Another cause grew out of certain political developments surrounding the Iran-Iraq War. As we look to the decade ahead, the ebb and flow of power in the Persian Gulf looms as one of the most profound influences on the future of oil and war. So do the developing shortages in Eastern Europe and the Soviet Union.

OPEC reached the zenith of its power in the early 1980s, when the price of oil rose above $30 a barrel. In due course, however, the

87

group fell victim to its own successes. By ratcheting up the price of energy more than tenfold, OPEC members set in motion forces that would inevitably result in the creation of alternatives to OPEC oil.

One of these forces was the substitution of other fuels for oil. The high price of oil suddenly made a wide range of alternative fuels competitive. Gasohol appeared in service stations across the United States. Research accelerated on the conversion of coal—an abundant resource—to oil and natural gas. Cities across the United States built methane-fired power plants fueled by another abundant resource—garbage. Even nuclear energy, which for years had been plagued by safety considerations, got a new lease on life. Investments in more exotic technologies, such as geothermal and solar, proliferated.

Of course, not all of them were successful. The Carter administration, thoroughly taken in by lobbyists who had mastered the latest set of energy buzz words, decided to adopt an enormously expensive synthetic fuels program. At the time, it seemed a politically expedient thing to do. After all, long lines at the nation's filling stations ensured that the energy crisis was at the top of everyone's concerns. But like so many government programs, it failed in everything it was advertised to accomplish. Not only did it never produce a single unit of economically useful energy, but in the end, it even failed to advance the political popularity of its sponsor.

Exploratory excess

A second force set in motion by OPEC-induced price increases was a boom in energy exploration. In non-OPEC countries, the discovery of new supplies suddenly assumed a new urgency. The demand for oil rigs and drilling equipment skyrocketed. Energy exploration companies became the new stars on Wall Street, and investors who were shrewd enough to see the crisis coming made a killing. Major new oil fields were discovered and developed—in Mexico, Alaska, the North Sea, and elsewhere. Britain and Norway set new oil production records in 1983, 1984, and 1985. Developing countries such as India and Brazil, which had previously imported large amounts of petroleum, suddenly achieved self-sufficiency.

Conserving success

The third force was conservation. In the early weeks of what came to be known as the energy crisis, respected economists of every stripe assured us that the demand for oil was "inelastic." After all, they reasoned, folks have to drive to work. Oil, they said, was the most essential raw material required by the U.S. economy. Of course we could cut back, but only by shutting down U.S. industry and turning out the lights.

The dominant—and utterly wrong-headed—thinking of the day is nicely illustrated by a slim volume entitled *The Limits to Growth,* which appeared in the 1970s. In it, author Donella H. Meadows and others sagely argued that what they called the reckless depletion of non-renewable resources would inevitably usher in a new dark age. On Nov. 19, 1973, the cover of *Newsweek* featured the fearful legend: "Are We Running Out of Everything?"

Apocalypse delayed

Well, a funny thing happened on the way to the apocalypse. People starting riding the bus to work. Consumers started demanding smaller, more fuel-efficient cars. There was a boom in home insulation and solar-powered water heaters. After decades of decline, the market for wood stoves abruptly reawakened. American industry did not shut down but found ways to increase energy efficiency. In due course and without much fanfare, what was said to be impossible came to pass. The United States imported 2.328 billion barrels of oil in 1979. By 1986, that number had declined to 1.213 billion barrels—a decline of nearly 48%.[1]

With supply increasing and demand declining, it wasn't long before OPEC began to feel the heat. In an attempt to keep prices from plummeting, members of the cartel adopted offsetting measures. They cut output. In the short run, they indeed were able to keep prices from falling—but only at the cost of surrendering market shares to the new non-OPEC producers. In 1980, OPEC producers supplied 60% of all oil purchased on world markets. By 1986, their share of the market had declined to 30%.

Honor among monopolists

But there was another problem. Loss of market share meant fewer OPEC barrels sold. And that meant fewer dollars in revenue. Even though this strategy kept the price up—at least in the short run—it required a sacrifice of oil earnings to execute. OPEC, which included the world's lowest-cost oil producers, ended up subsidizing high-cost producers in the United States, Mexico, and the North Sea.

To no one's surprise, tensions began to surface within the cartel. Countries that got along fine as long as revenues were increasing became more and more at odds when revenues started falling. To understand more clearly what happened in 1986—and what could happen in the future—it will be useful to learn something of the internal dynamics of the cartel.

OPEC and NATO

OPEC, as Edward L. Morese has argued,[2] is a lot like NATO, the familiar post-World War II alliance between the United States and European powers for the defense of Western Europe. Both are comprised of one dominant member and a host of smaller, less influential members.

In the case of NATO, the dominant member is the United States. Generally speaking, the U.S. objective with regard to NATO is to maximize American freedom of action vis-a-vis the Soviet Union. But at the same time, the United States has to make sure that the Allies do not undermine these bilateral arrangements. On the other hand, the objectives of the Allies themselves are quite different. They aim to maximize their own freedom of action—that is, to pursue independent foreign policies, unconstrained by the United States. Much of the disagreement within NATO—from the withdrawal of the French from the alliance in the 1960s to the initial reluctance of the Allies to send minesweepers to the Persian Gulf in 1987—is the direct result of these conflicting objectives.

It is a very similar situation within OPEC. Here the dominant member is the kingdom of Saudi Arabia, which has within its borders 24% of the world's proven oil reserves. In the long run, the Saudis want to preserve the central role of oil in the world economy—and thereby the kingdom's influence over world affairs—for as long as possible. For this reason, they are inclined to be champions of stability in the oil market. They also want freedom to conclude whatever arrangements seem appropriate to that long-term goal.

But the other countries within OPEC, especially those with lower proven reserves and larger, more demanding populations, tend to take a short-term view. For them, maximizing oil revenues today is far more important than any distant concern about the role of oil in the 21st-century economy. As a result, they—like the NATO allies—tend to be fiercely protective of their own freedom of action.

Grand compromise

The grand, decade-long compromise struck between these conflicting aims was for Saudi Arabia, OPEC's biggest producer, to absorb the lion's share of the production cutbacks required to maintain the high price of oil. Time and time again, the Saudis argued for moderation in pricing at OPEC ministerial meetings. And time and time again—especially in the mid-1980s—other OPEC members tried to maximize revenues by cheating on their production allotments.

Eventually, the Saudis reached the end of their patience. By the mid-1980s, more than half of their production capacity had been shut in. Annual revenues, which had been as high as $120 billion in 1981, plunged. Having embarked on an ambitious construction program during the fat years, they were loath to cut back when revenues dropped. Instead, the government drew upon its external reserves to finance its budget shortfall. In a few years, however, these external reserves would be exhausted, and then the Saudis would either have to cut back or become one of the world's unlikeliest borrowers. (In fact, the Saudis did become borrowers—but not until three years later.)

Concessions to reality

Sheik Ahmed Zaki Yamani, Saudi Arabia's venerable oil minister, understood this arithmetic perfectly. By 1985, non-OPEC production was setting new records for the third year in a row. At the ministerial meeting in December, OPEC members were again in disarray over who should bear the burden of yet further production cuts. Widespread cheating on production quotas that were supposed to be in effect already had called into question OPEC's ability to police its own accords.

At the urging of Yamani, OPEC finally agreed to face reality, and the fiction of setting production quotas was formally abandoned. Henceforth, each member of the cartel would be free to sell as much as the market would bear. Soon OPEC producers were in the midst of a free-for-all scramble to reclaim lost market shares.

Saudi Arabia led the way. And when the Saudis jumped in with both feet, the splash was heard around the world. On Jan. 20, 1986, the price of oil, under pressure from increased Saudi production, crashed below $20 a barrel. A few months later, it plunged below $10.

In the short run, the new Saudi policy aimed to restore lost revenues by increasing sales. But in less than a year, the Saudi ship of state was floundering like a stricken tanker in the perilous waters of the Persian Gulf, another victim of the long-running war between Iran and Iraq.

The Iran-Iraq War

What turned out to be one of the most intractable of all oil-related conflicts began in the fall of 1980, when the Iraqis decided that the time was ripe to seize some long-disputed real estate along the Iranian border.

Like most conflicts in this region of the world, the Iran-Iraq War has its roots in centuries of bloody conflict between the Arab and Persian empires. In the 16th and 17th centuries, for example, Persia (which included what is now the state of Iran) occupied Iraq three times.

In later centuries, border wars were fought over control of a vital waterway—the mouths of the Tigris and Euphrates rivers, now called the Shatt-al-Arab. The first Treaty of Erzerum, concluded in 1823, was an early attempt to negotiate a settlement. Scarcely 20 years later, however, tensions between Iraq, then a vassal state of the Ottoman Empire, and Persia were again approaching a flashpoint. In 1847, the second Treaty of Erzerum attempted to settle the question of disputed territories by awarding Abadan Khorramshahr and the East Bank of the Shatt-al-Arab to the Persians.

Seeds of strife

After World War I, the collapse of the Ottoman Empire changed the balance of power in the region again. Iraq declared its independence—which, of course, Persia refused to recognize. At the same time, another Central Asian tribal group—the Kurds—seized the moment to free itself from foreign rule. Claiming lands on both sides of the disputed border, the Kurds began a guerrilla campaign against both Baghdad and Tehran that continues to the present day.

When Iraqi nationalists—who came to power in 1958—were succeeded by Saddam Hussein's radical Ba'ath Party 10 years later, the recovery of Arab lands from Iranian control suddenly became a national priority. The Iranians replied by sponsoring a Kurdish campaign against Baghdad, which by 1976 had become a full-scale rebellion. (Incidentally, the Kurds also received the backing of the United States.)

During this period, the Iraqi city of Najaf became something of a hotbed of Islamic fundamentalism. Muhsin Hakim, the chief Shi'ite theologian of the period, was a resident of Najaf, as were his three sons who later became major figures in Iranian politics. Najaf also was home to one of the intellectual godfathers of the Shi'ite revolution, Sayyid Muhammad Banquir Sadr. Near him in exile lived another religious figure-turned-revolutionary leader, who was especially troublesome to the ruling Shah of Iran, the Ayatollah Ruhollah Khomeini.

While the Iraqis wanted an end to Iranian sponsorship of the Kurdish rebellion, the Shah of Iran wanted to rid himself of this troublesome priest. In due course, a bargain was struck on those terms. The Iranians closed their border to the Kurds, and in return, Saddam Hussein sent the Ayatollah packing—this time to Paris.

Like all previous agreements between Iran and Iraq, this one also was short-lived. The Kurds are still a thorn in Iraq's side. And sending Khomeini further into exile did little to help the Shah in his troubles with Iran's restive Shi'ites. It did, however, incur Khomeini's lasting hatred of Saddam Hussein.

The land war north of the Persian Gulf.

Iranian revolution

After the fall of the Shah on Jan. 16, 1980, Iran quickly dissolved into chaos. Competing factions, driven by homicidal hatred, settled old scores and made new enemies with bloody abandon. Khomeini's triumphant return from Paris seemed only to increase the daily public

93

executions that already had marked the Iranian revolution as one of the most murderous on record.

Because the Ayatollah feared the possibility of a military coup staged by loyalist remnants of the Shah's American-equipped army, military officers were executed with particular enthusiasm. With its streets in chaos, its army decimated by purges of more than 23,000 men—and cut off from American resupply by Khomeini's fanatical animosity toward the United States—Iran certainly looked like a target of opportunity. The Iraqis seized the moment and took possession of some long-disputed real estate along the border.

On Sunday, Sept. 21, 1980, forward elements of the Iraqi army crossed the border into Iran from the west. Using methods pioneered in World War II, the Iraqis opened with heavy artillery bombardment of enemy positions. Next came a blitzkrieg-style tank assault supported by ground-attack aircraft. Behind the tanks came the Iraqi infantry to take up defensive positions in the newly acquired territory.

Strategic blunder

The initial Iraqi assessment of Iranian defense capabilities was correct. Opposition was haphazard and uncoordinated, as the Iranians were forced to fall back toward the interior. Within a few short weeks, the Iranian cities of Qasr-e-Shirin, Mehran, Bostan, and Abadan had all fallen into Iraqi hands. In the midst of their brilliant tactical success, the Iraqis made the first of a series of strategic blunders that would ultimately cost them victory in the war. Instead of pursuing and demolishing what remained of the Iranian army, they staked out territory, started defensive fortifications, and offered to talk peace.

As a country with a population less than a third of the size of its adversary, Iraq's hope of victory had to lie in destroying the enemy's means of resistance—that is, its armed forces. By settling for territorial gains instead, they gave the Iranians time to regroup. Political and religious quarrels with Iran were patched up in the face of an external adversary. Revolutionary Guards were ordered to the front as the Iranians began to bring the greater resources of a vastly larger country to bear.

In the spring of 1981, the reorganized Iranian army launched twin counteroffensives against Abadan and Bostan. In both cases, the Iraqis were pushed back. In early 1982, three more Iranian offensives managed to regain yet more ground. During these offensives, Iran first began to use human-wave attacks reminiscent of those used during World War I and the Korean War.

Visions of Muslim paradise

While Iran was never able to match the firepower of Iraq's Soviet-supplied tanks and artillery, the eagerness of fresh conscripts and Revolutionary Guards to die for Islam gave Iranian attacks a fanatical ferocity unmatched on the modern battlefield. Muslim tradition promises anyone who dies defending Islam on the field of battle a place in heaven regardless of his sins. It was this belief that gave so many Iranian military missions their distinctively suicidal character.

One of the most frequently recounted stories of the war, for example, concerns a 15-year-old Iranian fighter who was wounded and taken prisoner by the Iraqis. As he lay bleeding and sobbing, an Iraqi medic sought to reassure him by telling him that his wounds were not serious. At this the boy cried even harder.

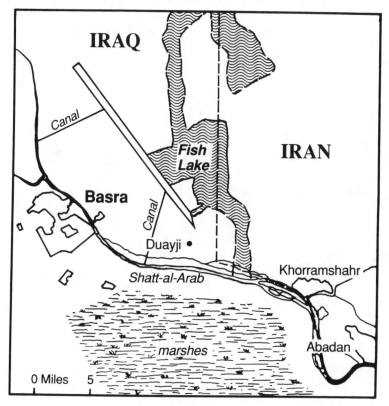

Southern war zone.

"That is not why I cry," he sobbed. "I cry because I didn't die. God does not want me!"

Similar sentiments echo in the metaphor contained in a letter written by another Iranian fighter, Mohsen Naeemi. "My wedding is at the front and my bride is martyrdom. The sermon will be uttered by the roar of guns. I shall attire myself in my blood for this ceremony. My bride, martyrdom, shall give birth to my son, freedom. I leave this son in your safekeeping. Keep him well."[3]

Martyrdom is made to seem even more attractive by a vision of Muslim heaven that sounds rather like a male sex fantasy. Among the rewards promised to the martyrs of Islam are strong liquor—which, of course, is strictly forbidden in earthly life—and enjoyment of the houris, or maidens of paradise. Not only do these heavenly beauties attend to every desire of the faithful "upon jeweled couches," but they have the miraculous capacity to recover their virginity before each episode of love-making.[4]

Reeling under the Iranian assaults and fearing worse to come, the Iraqis used the lull that followed the last Iranian offensive to withdraw to a better defensive inside their own borders. In so doing, they gave up virtually all that remained of the territory they had captured in the early weeks of the war.

Urban defense works

Particular attention was paid to defending the approaches to Baghdad, the Iraqi capital, and Basra, the second largest city. To the east of the capital, the Iraqis constructed a defensive line of heavily fortified tank positions. Behind these heavy concrete and sandbag installations, Iraqi tanks were set up as defensive artillery. But the fortifications were built in such a way as to permit the tanks to withdraw in the event Iraqi lines were breached and mobile defense became necessary.

Interestingly enough, these defense works were not designed to allow the tanks to move forward in a smashing counterattack once an Iranian assault faltered. This meant that as early as 1982, the Iraqis had virtually conceded the battlefield initiative to their enemies. It also showed the increasingly single-minded preoccupation with defense that is characteristic of a siege mentality.

Similar defensive positions were deployed around Basra. To provide yet another obstacle to the Iranians, the Iraqis flooded the north of the Shatt-al-Arab. This area appears on some recent maps as "Fish Lake."

When the Iranians resumed the attack in the fall of 1982 and five more times during the course of 1983, the Iraqis shot them to pieces. On the few occasions when Iraqi lines were actually breached, poorly trained Iranian conscripts, long on enthusiasm but short on military discipline, proved incapable of exploiting the opening.

In 1984, the Iranians launched the first of their "final offensives." They hurled upward of 300,000 men against Basra. Using artillery, close air support, and mustard gas, the Iraqis killed them by the thousands. The Iranians tried again in 1985 but with the same result.

Price of folly

Throughout it all, the Iraqis failed to launch a single serious counterattack. They would use their air power in support of front line positions but not to attack stragglers from a broken Iranian attack. Neither would they risk any aircraft in attacks on troop concentrations in the enemy rear.

This turned out to be a serious strategic miscalculation, because by 1986 the Iraqis no longer enjoyed unchallenged superiority in the air. This was not because of any sudden improvement in the Iranian air force. The new threat to Iraqi aircraft was on the ground.

By then the Iranians were beginning to receive new supplies of American arms as part of the then-secret arms-for-hostages negotiations carried on by the Reagan administration. American shipments included some anti-aircraft weapons. But perhaps more important was Iranian acquisition of sophisticated shoulder-fired anti-aircraft missiles from Sweden.

Sweden boasts several world-class weapons manufacturers whose principal market is supposed to be the Swedish army. Sweden, however, is too small a country for an independent arms industry to be able to survive without exports. Arms exports, however, pose a moral dilemma for a nation committed to both armed neutrality and disarmament at the same time. In an attempt to limit arms trade to countries nice enough not to use them, Swedish law strictly forbids exports to any nation at war. That certainly would seem to have included the Iranians in 1986.

At the time, however, Swedish Prime Minister Olof Palme was the United Nations-designated emissary charged with trying to mediate a cease-fire between the Persian Gulf belligerents. When he visited Tehran, he found the Iranians far more interested in trying to arrange the purchase of Swedish arms than they were in any peace talks.

Arms for influence

To no one's surprise, these efforts came to naught. But Palme was a clever man. A few secret shipments of Swedish arms to Iran would bolster his influence in Tehran in any subsequent round of talks. An experienced diplomat, Palme knew how to use that influence to enhance his reputation as international peacemaker. And that was just the sort of thing that would go over well in the upcoming Swedish election.

A short time later, several hundred RBS-70 missiles manufactured by the Bofors Co. were delivered to a Singapore intermediary, from which they were transferred to Iran. When they started arriving at the front, the Iranians reported that they were able to shoot down 45 Iraqi aircraft in a single month.[5]

(Palme didn't survive long enough to enjoy the benefits of this intricate scheme. As the election drew near, he reportedly reneged on another shipment after the Iranians had paid for it. According to the peculiar ethical code fashionable in Tehran, this was a moral outrage. It was avenged several months later on a dark street outside a Stockholm theater, where Palme went down in a hail of bullets. Among the groups thought to have had a hand in the killing was the Kurdish Workers' Party, a terrorist group backed by Iran.)[6]

Bolstered by their new high-tech weapons, the Iranians began another offensive. This time, instead of trying to take Basra by direct assault from the east, they tried a more imaginative approach—a flanking maneuver to the south. The Iranians crossed the Shatt-al-Arab in early February, and, after a bloody five-week campaign, occupied the Faw Peninsula.

In a desperate attempt to relieve the pressure on their southern flank, the Iraqis finally launched a diversionary attack in the north and recaptured Mehran. It was the first Iranian territory captured since 1982. By July, however, Mehran was back in Iranian hands. Nonetheless, Iran was forced to divert material from the southern front, and the campaign on the outskirts of Basra bogged down.

Stalemate on the ground

On Christmas Eve 1986, the Iranians began yet another series of assaults on Basra. This time they managed to come briefly within artillery range of their objective. Attacks continued throughout 1987 with little significant exchange of territory. In an August 1987 interview with the Western press, Dr. Kamal Kharvazi, a member of the Iranian Supreme Defense Council, acknowledged that the military leadership in Tehran had conceded the futility of further mass attacks on Iraqi positions. Henceforth, he claimed, Iran would settle down to a war of attrition and seek to foment political instability inside Iraq. In any case, stalemate on the ground had already begun to give way to action on the high seas, as each side began to attack the others' oil-exporting facilities.

Both Iran and Iraq are members of OPEC, and both depend on oil revenues to finance the war. But in Iran, where oil accounts for almost 95% of budget revenues, dependence was particularly acute. Under the Shah, Iran had enjoyed a healthy agricultural sector and was a net exporter of food. But under the Ayatollah, agriculture succumbed to the twin assaults of the chaotic fundamentalist revolution and the demands of the war effort. Consequently, Iran was forced to import most of its food—which had to be paid for out of oil revenues.

So when the Saudis and their allies within OPEC, the Kuwaitis, started to drive down the price of oil, the Iranians felt the squeeze first. Realizing that they might soon have to choose between continuing the war and paying for food, they first launched a vitriolic propaganda attack on Saudi Arabia. This public campaign was accompanied by a behind-the-scenes gambit in power politics conceived and executed by the Iranian oil minister, Gholamreza Aquzadeh.

During a secret visit to the Saudi capital of Riyadh, Iran's oil minister is believed to have threatened attacks on Saudi shipping—and worse—if King Fahd did not get rid of the chief architect of lower prices, Ahmed Zaki Yamani. In October 1986, King Fahd gave in to Iranian pressure, and Yamani was dismissed.

Six months later, oil was again more than $20 a barrel. But it is hard to say exactly how much this price recovery owed to the change of heart in Riyadh. That is because another factor was at work. In oil markets all over the world, fears of disrupted supplies also drove prices higher, as the Tanker War erupted in the Persian Gulf.

Both Iran and Iraq were dependent on giant oceangoing oil tankers to transport their oil to export markets. In both cases, these slow-moving vessels had to load their volatile cargo in the narrow waters of the Persian Gulf. From there, they had to pass through a choke point, known as the Straits of Hormuz, to reach the open waters of the Arabian Sea and the Indian Ocean. Iran, because of its relative lack of overland pipeline facilities, was much more dependent on Gulf tanker traffic than Iraq. Accordingly, the Iraqis generally took the lead in escalations of the Tanker War.

Few of the attacks that took place, however, involved vessels directly registered to one of the belligerents. The vast majority were attacks on tankers owned and operated by other countries. Of these other countries, Kuwait felt itself particularly vulnerable.

Geography had been both kind and cruel to Kuwait. On the one hand, a population of less than 2 million sat on top of 92.7 billion barrels of proven reserves—enough to last 250 years at present production rates. On the other hand, the New Jersey-sized emirate was uncomfortably sandwiched between two powerful neighbors— Saudi Arabia to the south and Iraq to the north—and therefore was not able to avoid taking Iraq's side in the 7-year-old war with Iran. Iraq's French-built Mirage fighters regularly flew over Kuwaiti territory on their way to missions in the Persian Gulf. And once a month in the dead of night, Iraq's principal arms supplier, the Soviet Union, unloaded material at Kuwait's Shuaiba Harbor for overland transport to the north.

Reflagging request

Concerned about Iranian attacks on its shipping, Kuwait asked the United States to let its tankers sail under the stars and stripes. But their request arrived just as the Iran-Contra investigation was getting under way in Washington. And the last thing the Reagan administration wanted to do was stir up more Middle East controversy.

When the Kuwaitis realized that the Reagan administration was stalling for domestic political reasons, they shrewdly let Washington know that the Soviets already had agreed to a similar request. That got an immediate response. Rather than let the Soviets increase their presence and influence in the area, the Reagan administration not only agreed to the reflagging of Kuwaiti vessels, it also sent the U.S. Navy in to escort neutral shipping in and out of the Gulf.

Seeing this, the Iranians stepped up their propaganda attacks on Kuwait, Iraq, Saudi Arabia, and the United States. They also began to sow mines like the malignant seeds of some sinister crop along the shipping lanes on both sides of the Straits of Hormuz.

For almost a year and a half, the war of the tankers appeared to gain in intensity as the land war between Iran and Iraq seemed to stalemate. For the United States, the two most important events were the accidental Iraqi attack on the *U.S.S. Stark*—in which more than two dozen sailors lost their lives—and the accidental U.S. downing of the Iranian airliner in July 1988—which killed everyone aboard.

But then, just as U.S. diplomatic installations around the world were bracing for a wave of retaliatory terrorist attacks, the Iranians startled the world by agreeing to accept a United Nations-sponsored proposal to negotiate a truce.

Sunrise or false dawn?

To some, Iran's new enthusiasm for peace seemed to signal the end of the pugnacious phase of the Islamic fundamentalist revolution—a revolution that once seemed bent on the overthrow of Saudi Arabia, Kuwait, and the other oil-rich sheikdoms of the Persian Gulf. More likely, the Iranian acceptance of cease-fire talks—like the Soviet withdrawal from Afghanistan—signalled less a change of heart than a change of tactics.

For a long time, it seemed that the Iranian fundamentalist revolution led something of a charmed life. Long after most revolutions would have evolved into some kind of return to normalcy, the mullahs were still going on one radical binge after another.

For eight years, they seemed able to ignore with impunity the absurd political and economic contradictions of their own policies. But in the end, even a secure place in Allah's heaven could no longer delay the inevitable. In all likelihood, the real reason Iran began to consider a ceasefire was that the country was in such a shambles that failure to achieve at least a temporary cessation of hostilities would have put the revolution itself at risk.

Harbingers of decay

In the cities and countryside behind the front lines, the signs of distress had been multiplying for some time. As foreign-exchange reserves dwindled, the mullahs imposed increasingly harsh currency controls. But that only created a roaring black market—in which inflation ran as high as 50%. Among the countless items in short supply were automobile tires, a pair of which reportedly cost about a year's salary for a middle-level public employee.

Economic growth slowed to a trickle and then went into reverse as private investment stopped dead in its tracks. Iran's gross national product dropped 50% between 1985 and 1986 alone. War damage to plants and equipment was so extensive that one study estimated it would take Iran as long as 20 years to recover the level of economic development it enjoyed in 1965.[7]

For nearly a decade, the mullahs debated the theological basis of private property and employer and employee rights without reaching any definitive conclusions. Not surprisingly, few were willing to risk their capital in an enterprise without some assurance that who owns

101

what would not be instantly revised on the word of some choleric cleric.

Even more disturbing was the fact that the country that was once an agricultural exporter was now forced to spend $2 billion of its meager foreign-exchange earnings annually on imported grain. Iran's population was also growing between 3% and 4% a year—one of the highest growth rates in the world.[8] As a result, it became increasingly clear that the choice before the Ayatollah was not so much between guns and butter, but between war and famine.

Of course, the worse these problems grew, the more the leadership needed the war to maintain itself. A patriotic call for self-sacrifice in defense of the motherland frequently covers a multitude of other shortcomings. (Of course, the Ayatollah was not the first dictator to discover this.)

Hence, it was only when the increasingly routine debacles of everyday Iranian life finally made their appearance on the battlefield that the moment of truth arrived. It began on April 17, 1988, when the Iraqis suddenly broke the battlefield stalemate and recaptured the Faw Peninsula—an area at the extreme north end of the Persian Gulf that had been occupied by the Iranians for more than two years. (It was from these positions that the Iranians had launched their much-heralded series of "final offensives" against Basra.)

Encouraged by their success, the Iraqis launched a series of assaults against the town of Shulamcheh to the north on May 27. Again, the Iranians fell back under the withering artillery fire, which included attacks with chemical munitions. On June 27, the Iraqis captured the oil-rich region around the island of Majnoon, held by Iran since 1984. In late July, as speculation concerning a cease-fire intensified, Iraqi forces broke through faltering lines of defense and plunged deep into Iranian territory for the first time since 1982.

Several factors combined to account for these battlefield setbacks. First among them was that the ruling clerics managed the military with all the skills they had so conspicuously displayed in management of the economy.

To begin with, the regular army had never really recovered from the purges of the early years of the Islamic revolution. Three quarters of those executed were officers. As a result, trained military commanders were in very short supply. Worse, the few that remained were still regarded with suspicion by the mullahs—so their advice often went unheeded.

Limits of fanaticism

With the professional military under a cloud, the war against Iraq was increasingly fought by the fanatical Revolutionary Guards (and other equally fanatical local militias), which were noted chiefly for their human wave attacks. Although largely untrained, their eagerness to achieve martyrdom on the battlefield served them well—as long as they were on the attack.

But when it came to mounting a creative tactical defense against mechanized Iraqi units with vastly superior firepower, their lack of military training became a major liability. At just the moment when the regular army could have been of the most help, the corps was largely hamstrung by meddling mullahs with little or no military expertise.

Moreover, the army and the Revolutionary Guards were locked in a bitter competition for increasingly scarce supplies of ammunition and spare parts. During Iraq's much-heralded "war of the cities," for example, the Iranian air force could marshal only a couple dozen air-worthy fighters.

In due course, Iraqi pilots brought home to the average Iranian what he had long suspected—both the war and the country were on the verge of falling apart. In the Iranian capital, citizens tasted the terror of aerial bombardment for the first time. Elsewhere, the entire industrial infrastructure of the country lay open to Iraqi attack.

Soon fresh calls to arms by the mullahs were falling increasingly on deaf ears. Non-regular army forces—including the Revolutionary Guards— reportedly fell more than 30% below their manpower levels of two years prior.

Eight years of bloody fighting had cost Iran upward of $200 billion (as estimated by the Tokyo-based Institute of Middle Eastern Economies) and more than a half-million dead. With nothing to show on the battlefield, the very legitimacy of the Islamic revolution was called into question.

Unity of command

These are the factors that led to the consolidation of military command (of both the regular army and the Revolutionary Guards) in the hands of Hojatulislam Ali Akbar Hashemi Rafsanjani, the speaker of the Iranian Parliament and one of the leading figures in post-Khomeini Iran.

Rafsanjani's first major decision was to accept cease-fire negotiations. Seen in this light, it appeared to reflect more a tactical retreat

103

than a reflection of any outbreak of genuine pacifism among the mullahs. If a permanent peace could be negotiated on favorable terms, so much the better. But if it could not, even a temporary halt to fighting provided a much-needed respite during which to shore up the sagging Islamic revolution.

I believe it is a mistake to label Rafsanjani a moderate, simply because he appears to have engineered the Ayatollah's blessing for the cease-fire. In the past, he personally has encouraged Lebanese terrorist groups to step up attacks against the United States and other Western countries. And after Khomeini's death, he hastened to Moscow for a state visit even before the official 40-day mourning period was over.

Hawks and doves

Drawing fine lines of distinction between moderates and conservatives or radicals has long been a staple of Western political science. For example, you often see statements issued by the U.S. State Department refer to hawks and doves among the leadership in the Kremlin. During the Iran-Contra hearings, witnesses testified that a major reason for entering the ill-fated arms-for-hostages negotiations was to cultivate "moderate" elements in Iran.

The plain truth of the matter is that this kind of analysis doesn't amount to much in the murderous free-for-all of Iranian internal politics. (Already, there have been numerous attempts on Rafsanjani's life.) Trying to separate the moderates from the fanatics among the mullahs is a little like trying to sort members of the Mafia according to their stands on abortion and women's rights. Differences of opinion undoubtedly exist, but they simply don't matter very much.[9]

Barring an outright collapse, there is no reason to expect Rafsanjani to shut down Taleghani Center (see Chapter 5) or to halt efforts to encourage Islamic movements around the world. Now that the war with Iraq has been concluded, attempts at subversion of the other Gulf states may be the only available means of exporting the Islamic fundamentalist revolution. Indeed it was the Ayatollah Khomeini himself who declared that Gulf rulers who did not give in to Iran would be "put to the sword and dispatched to hell, where they shall roast forever."[10]

It is hard to overestimate the geopolitical importance of the Persian Gulf. Gulf states account for 57% of the world's proven reserves of oil. Japan is dependent on the Gulf for 50% of its supplies, Europe for 26%, and the United States, 5%. And all the Gulf states have significant Shi'ite populations within their borders that may be more or less susceptible to the Ayatollah's call to arms.

Shi'ites as a fraction of total population[11]

Bahrain	70%
Kuwait	24%
United Arab Emirates	18%
Qatar	16%
Saudi Arabia	8%
Oman	4%

The Saudis were among the first victims of attacks by Shi'ite terrorists. In December 1979, a band of 500 armed insurgents attempted to take over the Great Mosque at Mecca. In the battle that followed, more than 300 were killed along with their leader, Muhammad al-Quraishi. Had he succeeded, the political damage could well have brought down the Saudi royal family.

Since then, Shi'ite extremists have staged terrorist attacks in other Gulf states, notably Kuwait and Bahrain. Of these, Kuwait is a particularly soft target. A few well-placed charges at the emirate's six power and desalinization plants could bring the entire country to a virtual standstill.

During the 1987 Haj, the annual Muslim pilgrimage to the holy city of Mecca (which lies inside Saudi borders), Iranian pilgrims staged violent demonstrations that resulted in the deaths of 402 people. At that time, Rafsanjani was calling for the "uprooting of the Saudi royal family."

Regardless of what is or is not settled between Iran and Iraq, it is clear that Shi'ite fundamentalism will be a threat to Persian Gulf oil supplies for some time to come. Another threat, as always, comes from the Soviet Union.

Superpower rivalry

In the bipolar world of superpower politics, global competition for power and influence is a zero-sum gain. Accordingly, any disadvantage stemming from Western dependence on Mideast oil is, by definition, an opportunity for the West's principal adversary, the Soviet Union. Even though the Soviets under Gorbachev appear increasingly preoccupied with economic problems at home, there is no reason to suppose they have abandoned their traditional efforts to court influence abroad—especially in this vital and volatile area of the world. For some time, the Russians tried to play both sides of the Gulf War.

Efforts to cultivate Iran have so far included resumption of Soviet purchases of natural gas and several joint economic projects. Among them are construction of a rail link and a pipeline that would allow the Iranians to export oil to or through the Soviet Union.

Of course, any increase in Soviet influence in Tehran must be viewed with a certain amount of alarm in the West. At this point, however, it is probably premature to worry about Iran being enticed into the Soviet orbit. The dogmatic atheism of communist ideology is certain to be anathema to the mullahs, despite Rafsanjani's warm reception in Moscow. Moreover, they can scarcely afford to let themselves be taken in by the main supplier of arms to Iraq.

Steady shipments of military equipment and supplies have been the major source of Soviet influence in Baghdad. Furthermore, this means that any Iraqi success against its larger and more powerful neighbor has to be seen as a victory for Soviet arms.

Russian oil dependency

Beyond making trouble for the West, the Soviets may have an interest in Persian Gulf oil for their own consumption. Since the end of World War II, the Russians have remained generally self-sufficient in oil. In 1984, however, Soviet oil production fell after increasing every year since 1945. In the Soviet Union, as in the United States, most of the easy-to-find oil already has been exploited. To keep their reserves from declining in future years, the Soviets will increasingly have to devote precious resources to exploration of the intractable Siberian wilderness.

Soviet self-sufficiency is not yet threatened, but Russian exports to Eastern Europe already are under pressure. Bulgaria, Czechoslovakia, East Germany, Hungary, and Poland are dependent on the Soviets for more than 90% of their oil supplies.[12] If the Soviets were forced to cut back, they would loosen some of the glue that holds their East European empire together. And nothing encourages military adventures so much as a restive empire—*glasnost* and *perestroika* notwithstanding.

Another nation to feel the pinch of tightening supplies is Japan. In 1941, as we have seen, Japan went to war to secure access to adequate petroleum supplies. In the 1980s, Japan is still as dependent on imported oil as it was 40 years ago. This dependency recently has helped fuel the debate over whether Japan—officially a pacifist nation since the end of World War II—should start to rebuild its once-mighty military power. But this is a topic for the next section, "Pearl Harbor II."

Investment implications

Much has been said thus far about the present status as well as the future of oil and war. Now it is finally time to begin assessing the implications for your financial future.

There are two major conclusions that can be drawn from this most recent chapter in the 70-year-old history of oil and war. The first concerns the new volatility of oil prices. While oil is unlikely to scale the heights of the late 1970s and early 1980s (at least, in inflation-adjusted terms), there likely will be many somewhat lesser swings of increasingly short duration.

OPEC will continue to be torn by political conflicts. Sometimes they will be patched up. Other times not. Either development, however, is sufficient to move oil away from its equilibrium price. Of course, the ebb and flow of armed conflict in the Middle East always raises the possibility of a disruption in supplies.

Another legacy of the rise and fall of OPEC is a world far more sophisticated in its ability to accommodate rising and falling energy prices. As a result, markets react and adjust with much greater speed than they did 10 years ago. This suggests that whatever short-term variations occur are likely to be of increasingly short duration.

While unstable oil prices create considerable uncertainty, they also create investment opportunities. If you have an inclination to speculate, you will find some ideas on how to turn this volatility to your trading advantage in Chapter 13.

A troubled peace

The second conclusion is that the risk of oil-related conflict has not diminished despite Soviet military withdrawal from Afghanistan and the truce between Iran and Iraq. The end of the war has enabled Iraqi president Saddam Hussein to turn his attention once more to Iraq's traditional adversary, Israel.

Even more disturbing is the fact that the Iraqis have pioneered the first large-scale use of chemical weapons since World War I. Attacks on Iranian positions have included the use of mustard gas and newer and much more potent nerve agents.

(According to Belgian sources, some of the nerve gas used by Iraq against its rebellious Kurdish minority have included samples from Soviet stockpiles. Fragments from a shell casing that bore Russian

107

markings have been recovered from the region near the Turkish border. More disturbing, it contained traces of a poison never before seen by Western intelligence.)

Open violation of all existing international treaties against the use of chemical weapons may have well ushered in a new and frightening dimension in the arms race. Unlike nuclear weapons, chemical weapons require neither rare materials nor great technical sophistication. The CIA estimates that there are now 20 countries building chemical stockpiles. In addition to Iraq, Syria is among them. [13]

Chemical weapons are cheap and almost impossible to control. Many conventional substances are very efficient killers, and almost any laboratory capable of making either pesticides or fertilizers could easily be converted to making other toxic agents. Methyl isocyanate, for example, which killed more than 2,000 after leaking from a Union Carbide facility in Bhopal, India, is widely used in the brewing of pesticides. It would also make a highly effective munition.

In addition to the increasing popularity of chemical weapons, another disturbing military trend is the proliferation of ballistic missile technology in the Middle East. In the spring of 1988, the Iraqis finished development work on their al-Hussayn missile that has a range of about 600 kilometers. Presently under development is the al-Abbas missle, which Western analysts expect to be able to hit targets as far away as 900 kilometers.

One of the persistent rumors one hears from sources in southern Lebanon is that the Iraqis are about to supply the Christian militia with missles capable of hitting the Syrian capital of Damascas. Of course, either the al-Hussayn or the al-Abbas has more than sufficient range to strike targets in Israel.

The Israelis also could be hit by the Saudis CSS-2 missile, recently purchased from China. The CSS-2 can carry a nuclear payload. But any of these missiles can carry chemical munitions.

Following is a short list of the variety of ballistic missiles that presently bristle in the weapons inventory of Mideast nations: [14]

Egypt	Range
Frog-7	70 km
Saqr-80	80 km
Scud-B	300 km
Badr-2000	800 km

Iran

Oghab	40 km
Shahin-2	115 km
Nazeat	115 km
Scud-B	300 km

Iraq

Astros	68 km
Frog-7	70 km
Scud-B	300 km
al-Hussayn	600 km
al-Abbas	900 km

Israel

Lance	110 km
Jerihco-1	450 km
Jericho-2	1,450 km

Kuwait

Frog-7	70 km

Saudi Arabia

Astros-2	68 km
CSS-2	2,200 km

Syria

Frog-7	70 km
SS-21	120 km
Scud-B	300 km

North Yemen

SS-21	120 km

South Yemen

Frog-7	70 km
SS-21	120 km
Scud-B	300 km

Because ballistic missiles fly too fast to be shot down by air defenses, their proliferation will encourage potential adversaries to consider a pre-emptive attack at the first hint of conflict. The effect of this use-them-or-lose-them mentality is to put the Mideast tinder box on more of a hair trigger than it would otherwise be.

And if all this weren't bad enough, there remains the question of U.S. vulnerability in the next oil-related conflict. While we have been enjoying plentiful supplies of gasoline, American dependence on imported oil is increasing again. We now import something in excess of 42% of our oil—about the same fraction as we did before the oil shocks of the 1970s. If present trends continue, we will be more than 50% dependent on foreign sources by 1990.

From a humanitarian point of view, it certainly is laudable that the pace of killing may be slowing in the Persian Gulf. But it is equally important to realize that peace—however desirable—is not without its own risks. In the Middle East especially, the combination of centuries-old animosities, chemical weaponry, ballistic missiles, and growing U.S. dependence on foreign oil can be safely counted upon to produce another explosion—if not sooner, then later.

In an era of nuclear weapons, of course, there always is a chance that such an explosion could escalate into an apocalyptic nightmare sufficient to render any investment strategy totally irrelevant. More likely, however, is a new conventional war on either land or sea.

Precious metals

This possibility alone is sufficient to create a speculative opportunity in precious metals. Whenever war threatens, those with assets to protect scramble to move them to safety. For many of them, this means converting assets to gold. Gold prices, you may recall, hit their all-time high as Russian troops fired the opening rounds of the Afghan invasion.

Precious-metals investments offer two benefits. They are a haven of safety in war-torn times. And they allow you to profit directly from increases in world tension. For this reason every investment portfolio should contain a small amount of gold. In especially troubled times, it is prudent to increase the fraction of your investments in precious metals. For some specific recommendations on what to buy, see Chapter 13.

Transnational citizenship

Perhaps the best defensive measure of all, however, is to loosen your identification with the country of your birth and become a citizen of the world. At some time or other, most every nation has blundered into foolish or ill-conceived military adventures. One of the best ways to protect your savings from the ravages of war is to spread them around the world.

One way to do this is to have savings accounts in several countries. Swiss banks, for example, offer legendary safety and stability. A visit to a British bank, in addition to superb financial services, offers all the sights and sounds of London. The following is a short list of non-U.S. banks accustomed to dealing with Americans. Some of them may even permit you to open an account by mail.

Foreign Commerce Bank, *Bellariastrasse 82, CH-8038 Zurich, Switzerland;*

110

Barclays Bank, *Hanover Square Branch, Box A8/9, London W1A4CW, UK;*

Lloyds Bank Ltd., *Threadneedle Branch, 39 Threadneedle St., London EC2R 8AU, UK;* and

Isle of Man Bank, *2 Athol St., Douglas, Isle of Man, British Isles.*

(Note: U.S. tax law requires you to report the existence of foreign bank or brokerage accounts totaling $10,000 or more on your annual tax return.)

You may want to put a little money in either stocks or real estate around the world. See Chapter 13 for specific recommendations for foreign stocks.

If you are new to banking or real estate outside the United States, I recommend one of the following books:

Christopher Webster, *The Austrian Advantage: Confidential Banking in the World's Low-Profile Financial Havens*, Investment Insights, Harrison, New York, 1987.

Marian Cooper Molinaro and Patti Watts, *European Real Estate Treasures...A Dreamer's Guide*, Agora Inc., Baltimore, 1987.

Adrian Day, *Investing without Borders*, Alexandria House, Alexandria, VA, 1982.

Robert Czeschin, *The Complete Report of Banking Safety and Privacy*, Agora Books, 1989.

For most of its long history, the story of oil and war has been a chronicle of a scarce resource getting scarcer. For a time, the 1986 collapse of OPEC appeared to usher in a new era of abundance, as oil prices plunged to their lowest levels in decades. More recently, new shifts in the precarious balance of Mideast power have raised fresh fears of impending scarcity. Even in the 1980s, the wisdom of Henry Berenger still applies. Oil is still the catalyst of competition and conflict between nations—the same trip wire of world war—that it was 40 years ago. And so it is likely to remain.

---

1. Figures from U.S. Census Bureau Office of Trade Information Tariff Schedule #4751010.

2. E. L. Morse, "After the Fall: The Politics of Oil," *Foreign Affairs,* 1986.

3. "The Devil's War Against Islamic Iran," published by the Revolutionary Guard Corps, Theran, 1982, cited by Robin Wright, *Sacred Rage*, p. 36.

4. For scriptural references to the houris, see the Koran, Suras 55:72 and 56:22; for a more secular discussion of these divine lovelies, see Crim, Keith, Abingdon, *Dictionary of Living Religions,* p. 239.

5. The story of the Palme connection first appeared on the CBS broadcast of *60 Minutes* on Nov. 29, 1987.

6. In due course, Palme, who was posthumously awareded India's Nehru Prize for his contributions to non-violence, was discovered to have been one of the world's most effective arms salesmen. For example, he sold India the howitzers it subsequently used to shell Pakistan. He also arranged for another Swedish company, Boghammer Marin, to sell the Iranian Coast Guard the speed boats they used to harass U.S. Navy vessels on patrol in the Persian Gulf.

Like the Bofors RBS-70s, the speedboats were transhipped through Singapore. According to the Swedish Bureau of Statistics, Singapore, which has one of the world's tiniest armies, was the leading destination for Swedish arms exports every year from 1977 to 1986.

Nor was Palme the only one to die under mysterious circumstances, as the story of these shipments began to leak out. Carl Fredrik Algernon, a bureaucrat whose job it was to enforce Sweden's export ban on weapons sales to warring nations, somehow stumbled into the path of an onrushing train a half-hour after denying that he knew anything about illegal exports.

Unsurprisingly, all this had created a substantial embarrassment for the Swedish government. Three-and-a-half years after the Palme assassination, government prosecutors finally tried to pin the murder on a Stockholm vagrant with a history of pyschotic episodes. Whether the real killer will ever be found remains very much in doubt.

7. K.R. Timmerman, "The Gulf," *Wall Street Journal*, Feb. 17, 1988, p. 29.

8. "No Singing in the Wilderness," *The Economist*, Feb. 6, 1988, p. 44.

9. Consider, for example, the May 1987 kidnapping of British diplomat Edward Chaplin. While Western leaders tried to figure out which faction from what section of the political spectrum might want to create an international incident that could well lead to the severing of diplomatic relations, the real reason for the kidnapping had nothing to do with international politics. It was entirely personal.

It seems that an Iranian national previously arrested by British authorities and charged with larceny was the brother of the head of one of Iran's revolutionary committees. The man simply decided that a retaliatory kidnapping was far better than allowing his family's honor to be besmirched by his brother's conviction for theft. (See *Financial Times*, Sept. 15, 1987.)

10. H. Algar, trans., *Islam and Revolution: Writing and Declarations of Imam Khomeini*, Mizam Press, Berkeley, CA, 1981.

11. *Financial Times*, Aug. 6, 1987.

12. R. Goralski and R. Freeburg, *Oil and War*, p. 330.

13. D. White and P. Marsh, "The Deadly Brew of Nationalism," *Financial Times*, Jan. 7, 1989.

14. "Third World Missiles," *Economist*, May 27, 1989.

Section II

Pearl Harbor II

Chapter VII

The Japanese Postwar Economic Miracle

From Ruins to Riches

American commercial policy translated into foreign policy has created a real threat to the United States: that of economic attack by the Japanese.

—Malcolm McIntosh, *Japan Rearmed*

For the Japanese, World War II came to an end on Aug. 20, 1945, when Emperor Hirohito went on the radio to admit defeat. It was the first time the Japanese people had ever heard his voice. Later, he renounced his centuries-old claim to divinity and joined the ranks of mortal men.

This also marked the start of one of the most dramatic economic recoveries in recorded history. How Japan climbed from the devastation of World War II to the status of economic superpower in the 1980s is a fascinating story. It is a story of superpower politics, of ham-fisted government intervention in the economy, and of the native ingenuity and adaptability of the Japanese people.

Without a doubt, the war was a catastrophe for the Japanese economy. Aerial bombardment by the U.S. Army Air Force—including atomic attacks on Hiroshima and Nagasaki—had utterly destroyed 119 major Japanese cities. About 2.2 million homes were reduced to rubble, and more than 9 million homeless civilians wandered the streets in search of shelter.

Unfortunately, even the figures in the following chart do not tell the whole story. Thousands more homes were lost to wartime confiscation and forced evacuations. If these losses are added in, more than 20% of the civilian housing stock was destroyed.

Number of Residences Damaged
During World War II[1]

	National Totals	Urban Area Totals
Total Damaged	2,362,000	2,264,000
Completely Burned	2,188,000	2,119,000
Partially Burned	49,000	39,000
Completely Demolished	64,000	55,000
Partially Demolished	61,000	51,000

In addition to residential housing, factories, roads, bridges, and port facilities were devastated as well.

Damage to Economic Assets
During World War II[2]

	% Damaged
Energy Utilities	11
Furniture and Household Goods	21
Production Goods	25
Commercial Buildings	25
Transportation Facilities	29
Industrial Machinery	34
Ships	81
Naval Vessels and Planes	100

As the above figures indicate, shipping suffered the most damage. Before the war Japanese shipping capacity stood at 6.3 million tons. Afterward, only 1.53 million tons remained. To make matters worse, most of the surviving ships were unfit for long voyages. They had been hastily constructed during the war, when the military had first claim on the nation's output of raw materials.

Total wartime damage to the economy was estimated to be 99.2 billion yen—based on the prevailing price levels of 1945. At current price levels, that is equal to 32.7 trillion yen—or in today's dollars, about $218 billion.[3]

When the war ended, 6 million demobilized soldiers returned to the civilian economy. At the same time, another 4 million civilian workers lost their jobs, as wartime industries shut down. Total unemployment reached 13.1 million.

War losses in 1944 alone accounted for 35% of Japanese national wealth—a number approximately equal to the nation's entire gross national product in 1946. The cost in human terms was also staggering. By the end of the war, military and civilian casualties numbered almost 3 million.

Loss of empire

Defeat also cost Japan her Asian conquests. The loss of territories in Manchuria, China, and Indochina reduced the size of the Japanese empire by more than 56% from its wartime peak. Consequently, the Japanese mainland was cut off from the vital flow of raw materials that formerly came from its overseas possessions.

Even the topography of the land had been laid to ruin. Entire forests had been stripped of timber. Wartime neglect of reforestation resulted in widespread devastation from massive flooding in 1946. Over-cultivation during the war, when fertilizers were only haphazardly available, contributed to the rapid depletion of agricultural land. Crop failures in 1946 were the worst in decades, and famine further debilitated an already destitute population.

Economic Measures of Production and Consumption[4]

Production	1946 Levels as a % of Prewar Levels
Real GNP	62
Per Capita GNP	55
Coal Production	53
Steel Production	10
Textile Production	7
Per Capita Consumption	
Grams of Rice	70
Fish	65
Soy Sauce	53
Fruit	34
Sake	23
Eggs and Poultry	16
Sugar	6

With access to foreign markets cut off, the sudden increase in the domestic population (raised by returning soldiers) resulted in a demand for raw materials and basic daily necessities that far outstripped meager supplies. Massive shortages soon developed, and living standards dropped to unprecedented lows.

No strangers to adversity

In spite of these considerable hardships, there were early indications that the Japanese people would recover from the crushing burden of military defeat. Five days after the emperor's historical broadcast, blackout and curfew regulations were lifted. Soon Japanese children, who had been sent into the countryside to escape the heavy bombing of cities, were returning to their families. On Oct. 9, 1945, professional baseball resumed in Japan.

Throughout their history, the Japanese often have been well-acquainted with adversity. Living on a tiny chain of volcanic islands, they are skillful at survival and accustomed to picking up the pieces after the eruptions, earthquakes, typhoons, and tidal waves that devastate the islands with disconcerting regularity.

Over the course of their 1,000-year history, they have tasted the bitter medicine of military defeat many times. But always they have learned from their conquerors. When the Portuguese first arrived with firearms in 1543, the Japanese copied their designs. Within a few short years they were making their own, which rivaled those of European manufacture. It was no different in 1945. Displaying the same spirit of adaptability that has served them so well in the past, the Japanese set about learning English with a vengeance. Within weeks, English language texts topped the Japanese best-seller lists.

With the country's infrastructure destroyed, native ingenuity came to the rescue. Open-air markets appeared and flourished in bombed-out buildings that had once contained stores and shops. Portable stalls were set up in vacant lots alongside busy thoroughfares. Soon, items appeared for sale that had not been available during the war. Prices, however, zoomed toward the stratosphere.

Although the government pledged to provide food rations, surrender had impaired its ability to do so. During the war, farmers were easily compelled to provide produce at the low official prices. After the surrender, they found it easy to defy the central government—especially when black market sales brought 50 or 60 times the official price. With the crop failures of 1945 and 1946, prices rose even more. White rice traded at 150 times the official price as panic buying spread throughout the black market.

The scourge of hyper-inflation

Other forces were at work as well. The value of redeemable Bank of Japan notes in circulation increased 40% in the last 15 days of April 1945. By February 1946, this measure of the Japanese money supply stood at exactly twice the level of the previous April—a 100% increase in only eight months.[5]

During the war, the Japanese government had raised the colossal sums necessary to support the armed forces by issuing bonds, for which there was no market. Some of these war bonds were bought by the Bank of Japan, which, in effect, printed the money to pay for them. This produced an immediate increase in the money supply. But other bonds were forced on the civilian population.

Bonds bought by civilians were paid for out of savings. While the war was still being fought, strict economic controls prevented the bonds from being cashed in. Thus, an enormous reservoir of purchasing power built up in the civilian economy. When the war ended, the government began to redeem the bonds. But this huge release of latent purchasing power came at a time when the war-torn civilian economy could scarcely produce any consumer goods.

To make matters worse, in the four months after the surrender, the government paid out millions to business owners as compensation for their contributions to the war effort. The government also offered business loans to finance the shift from military to consumer production, further increasing the amount of money in circulation.

True to one of the strictest canons of monetarist theory (which says that inflation is caused by overexpansion of the money supply), prices smartly followed suit. According to a Bank of Japan survey, black market prices rose 30% between September and December 1945. By February 1946, they had doubled.

As in the case of postwar Germany, the roots of hyper-inflation lay in the familiar story of too much currency chasing too few goods.

Other hardships had to be dealt with as well. With communications in disarray, the average Japanese had little access to reliable information. Rumors of an impending war profits tax or of a forced devaluation encouraged distrust of the nation's banks and created a climate of uncertainty and fear. Hoarding of scarce food and consumer goods was common.

Bungled economic policies

Influenced by American Keynesians, and under the thumb of occupation authorities headed by the Supreme Commander for Allied Forces (SCAF), the government tried several ham-fisted solutions. On Feb. 16, 1946, the government announced the Emergency Economic Crisis Policy, which included: efforts to strengthen the food rationing system by vigorously prosecuting farmers who sold their produce illegally on the black market; a general crackdown on black market transactions involving consumer goods in short supply; a freeze on bank deposits; and the creation of a new currency.

117

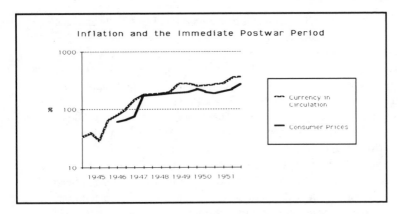

Inflation and the Immediate Postwar Period

Currency in Circulation
Consumer Prices

As any student of free-market economics could have predicted, these measures only made things worse. Even beefed-up enforcement agencies were no match for the ingenuity of farmers and others who depended on black market sales to make ends meet.

Profitable enterprises, by their very nature, simply cannot be legislated out of existence. Making them illegal serves only to force them underground. The truth of this can be seen in the decades of futile efforts on the part of Western governments to stamp out gambling, prostitution, and narcotics trade. So it was with the black market in postwar Japan.

The monetary provisions of the Emergency Economic Crisis Policy had a dramatic, if short-lived, effect. As a result of the freeze on bank accounts, not only did the Japanese lose free access to their savings, but cash in circulation was effectively confiscated as well.

The government announced that the old yen notes would cease to be legal tender as of March 2, 1946. They would, however, still be accepted for deposit in the otherwise frozen bank accounts until March 5. Thereafter, they would be worthless paper. Withdrawals from the frozen accounts were in new yen. They were strictly limited according to the family and income status of the depositor.

The aim, of course, was to shrink the money supply—usually defined as bank deposits plus currency in circulation. Confiscating currency and restricting access to bank accounts reduced the money supply by some 50 billion yen practically overnight. Inflation halted in its tracks—for a time.

These measures did nothing, however, to help expand production of food and other scarce consumer goods. Law-abiding urban dwellers suffered greatly as they tried to survive on the meager withdrawals of their own money that they were permitted under the government's program.

118

In rural areas, however, few people had bank accounts. And farmers who sold on the black market quickly accumulated cash balances in new yen. So the net effect of the monetary provisions of the Emergency Economic Crisis Policy was to increase the return on black marketeering—the very thing earlier provisions of the same policy were trying to stamp out!

By September 1946, inflation was again roaring out of control, and the danger of famine had become so acute that the occupation authorities had emergency relief sent from the United States.

Shifting American attitudes

Increasing volumes of aid coincided with a slow but profound shift in the attitude of the American government toward Japan. The United States, of course, had borne the brunt of the war in the Pacific. And in the early days of the occupation, the American high command was in no particular mood to be generous.

SCAF's original proposals for postwar "democratization of Japan" were couched in the high-minded rhetoric of the United Nations Declaration on Human Rights. But to any neutral observer, it was clear that what SCAF had in mind was the complete disarming of Japan and the total destruction of the political, social, and economic systems that had made it possible for the country to wage war.

The first priority of the occupation authorities was the demobilization of the army and the demilitarization of the government. Former leaders were ordered to stand trial for war crimes. In spite of the increasingly desperate situation of the Japanese people, SCAF seemed in no hurry to repair the economic damage that the war had caused. For example, an early directive to General MacArthur from Washington stated, "You are not to assume any responsibility for the reconstruction or strengthening of the Japanese economy."[6]

Democratization of Japan included:
a) drafting a new constitution that
   i) gave women the vote and the right to hold office.
   ii) abolished all laws and state organs that restricted human rights.
   iii) renounced war and the maintenance of armed forces;
b) giving workers the right to organize labor unions;
c) instituting universal education at state expense;
d) working on agricultural land reform; and
e) working toward economic democratization.
Something of the Allies' true intent could be seen in this eco-

nomic democratization. This included the purging of more than 180,000 people in senior administrative and business posts who were thought to be right-wing, nationalistic, or militaristic. It also involved breaking up the *zaibatsu*,[7] the large financial and industrial holding companies that had dominated Japan's economy for 50 years.

In November 1945, the government froze all of the assets of the 15 largest *zaibatsu*. Other attacks on the *zaibatsu* came in the form of legislation. In April 1947 the Law Relating to the Prohibition of Private Monopoly and to Methods of Preserving Fair Trade, patterned after U.S. antitrust legislation, was enacted.

Eight months later, the Law for the Elimination of Excessive Economic Concentration was passed to provide the legal basis for the dissolution of any company deemed to be monopolistic. This was to be done by severing the holding company from its various parts and purging the prominent members of the founding *zaibatsu* families. Under this law, 325 *zaibatsu* were slated for dismemberment.

Pauley's plan for deindustrialization

If SCAF clothed its true intentions in the noble language of human rights, others were more candid. U.S. Ambassador to Japan Edwin W. Pauley helped produce a report outlining war reparations that the Japanese would be forced to pay. It called for the physical removal of the existing plants and equipment of more than 1,000 factories from Japan.

Pauley's Final Reparations Report was a program for gutting what remained of Japanese industry—for returning Japan to the status of an underdeveloped agricultural country. A Brookings Institute report, prepared about the same time, urged that Japanese living standards not be allowed to rise above what they were in 1930—more than a decade before the war began.

As the 1940s drew to a close, however, events elsewhere in the world began to influence the U.S. attitude toward Japan. American relations with the Soviet Union began to sour. Britain, preoccupied with recovery from World War II, was no longer exerting the influence in Asia that it once had.

But most disturbing of all to President Truman and his advisors was the series of defeats suffered by another American ally, nationalist Chinese leader Chiang Kai-shek, at the hands of Mao Tse-tung's ragtag band of revolutionaries.

Against this backdrop of deepening geopolitical concern, punitive attitudes toward the Japanese began to give way. As the only industrialized country in Asia, Japan was increasingly seen by U.S. policy-makers as the Western world's only opportunity to erect a bulwark against the rising tide of Asian communism.

In due course, American policy began to tilt away from punishment and toward economic recovery. Before long, the Pauley Report was completely forgotten. Of the 325 *zaibatsu* slated for dissolution, only 30 were ever dissolved. Virtually all of Japan's big banks survived intact.

Soon the anti-monopoly laws of 1947 were being substantially rewritten to allow the new *zaibatsu* to dominate their old markets. Many were even allowed to re-establish themselves under their former names and trademarks.

Mitsui and Mitsubishi were among the first to take advantage of this newly relaxed attitude. Little did American policy-makers realize that they were replanting the seeds of giant industrial monopolies that would plague American manufacturers 40 years later.

The Dodge Line

In February 1949, just six months before Communist victory in mainland China, Truman replaced Pauley. The new U.S. ambassador to Japan, former Detroit banker Joseph Dodge, arrived with specific instructions to contain inflation and get Japanese industry moving as rapidly as possible.

In a famous press conference in Tokyo, the new ambassador first presented what later became known as the Dodge Line. The Japanese economy, according to Dodge, was like a man walking on stilts. One of the stilts was U.S. aid. The other was loans from the Japanese government's Reconstruction Finance Bank. Pursuing his metaphor, Dodge said that the economy was in danger of toppling over and falling on its head, that the stilts had to be removed, and that the economy had to learn to stand on its own two feet.

To accomplish this, Dodge called for: the government to pay off its debts; a slash in spending sufficient to produce a budget surplus— in essence a deflationary fiscal policy; an end to loans to business; the relaxation of rationing and price controls; and a devaluation of the yen to promote the growth of Japanese exports on world markets.

This last measure was especially important because it would affect the international competitiveness of every sector of the Japanese economy. Making export growth the engine of Japanese economic independence required a yen low enough to ensure that Japanese products could be attractively priced abroad.

121

Manipulating the yen to promote exports

As always, the Japanese learned from their conquerors. Manipulation of the yen to levels that permit Japanese exporters to undercut their competition has been a hallmark of Japanese economic policy right down to the present day.

The Dodge Line actually made more sense than earlier government efforts to manage the Japanese economy. Because of the strong deflationary measures it contained, spectacular progress was made in the fight against inflation. The Consumer Price Index declined 10% in 1949. On the black market, prices declined as much as 30%.

The Dodge Line also marked the beginning of the end of the black market as a major economic force in postwar Japan. With the end of rationing and price controls, a free market was officially re-established for the first time in nine years. The effect was immediate. For the first time since the end of the war, fresh bananas appeared on grocery shelves. In urban areas, beer halls began to reopen.

But the Dodge Line also had a darker side. Reduced government spending and an end to government loans left many businesses starved for capital. The sudden end of inflation also devastated profit margins. Many businesses were caught with expensive inventory that they could only sell at a loss as the general price level declined.

Bankruptcies swept over the country like a Pacific tidal wave. The daily newspapers were filled with articles on the suicides of presidents of smaller and medium-sized companies. Popular magazines carried stories of the suicides of entire families.

Company president commits suicide

On July 5, 1949, three days before he was due to announce the first of more than 100,000 employee layoffs, the president of Japan National Railways was found dead on one of his company's tracks. All across the country, workers were dismissed on a massive scale. Labor disputes increased in both number and intensity. Reports of riots made the headlines on a daily basis. On top of all these miseries came the harshest winter since the end of the war. For most Japanese, 1949 was the darkest year in postwar history.

Dodge, a puritan at heart, refused to contemplate any reduced dosages of the deflationary medicine he had prescribed. And it is likely the country would have fallen into civil anarchy had geopolitical events not intruded.

In Peking on Oct. 1, 1949, Mao Tse-tung proclaimed the People's

Republic of China. In December, Chiang Kai-shek's forces fled across the Formosa Strait to the island of Taiwan. And on June 25, 1950, war broke out in Korea. On July 8, General Douglas MacArthur led the U.S. Army, formerly on occupation duty in Japan, in the first action in support of the beleaguered South Korean army.

Japan, of course, was the industrialized country nearest the war zone. Within weeks, enormous orders poured in for goods and services to support the troops in Korea. (Much the same thing happened again during the Vietnam War a decade-and-a-half later.) In the early years of the conflict, these orders were mostly for military supplies—sandbags, barbed wire, army blankets, and ammunition. When the war ended, the demand shifted to goods and services needed for reconstruction in South Korea—the repair of trucks and aircraft and the construction of military bases and communications and transportation services.

During the period from 1950 to 1955, foreign currency earnings of Japanese business were as high as $3.6 billion.[8] War-related orders amounted to 60% to 70% of exports, reversing Japan's balance of payments in a single stroke.

Korean War boom

The Korean War boom also set off the explosive growth in Japanese exports that has continued for nearly 40 years. During one 12-month period alone (June 1950 to May 1951), Japanese exports increased 55%. The unsold inventories created by the Dodge Line deflation were sold almost overnight.

The war also set off an explosion in profits. One measure of Japanese business profits doubled twice between 1950 and 1951.[9] For the first time since the end of the war, the profitability of Japanese companies reached levels that permitted significant increases in equity capital accumulation. By October 1950, mining and manufacturing had surpassed prewar levels.

By the end of 1951, the Japanese gross national product exceeded its highest prewar peak. On the Tokyo Stock Exchange, the Nikkei Dow surged 81%. The postwar recovery had been achieved.

Seeds of conflict

By the time the Korean War boom wound down, the Japanese economy—in the words of Joseph Dodge—was back on its own two feet. But the seeds of future Japanese-American tension had already been planted. And nobody at the time foresaw the bitter harvest that would follow some three-and-a-half decades later.

123

In the 1980s, American manufacturers reeling under the assault of Japanese competition regularly air their grievances before the media and the U.S. Congress. One of their loudest complaints concerns the monolithic character of their Japanese competitors.

American companies are restrained from collaboration by the provisions of U.S. antitrust legislation. Indeed, the anti-competitive nature of antitrust law has long been criticized by such noted legal

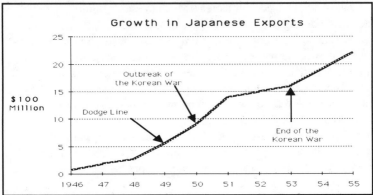

Growth in Japanese Exports

scholars as former Attorney General Edward Levi and former Federal Appeals Court Judge Robert Bork.

The Japanese, on the other hand, are under no such constraints. They routinely collaborate on both basic research and product development for export markets. Had the occupation authorities not lost sight of their original intention to subject the *zaibatsu* to American-style trust-busting, Japanese companies would be subject to the same antitrust legacy as their American counterparts. As a result, they would not enjoy the competitive advantage that they do today.

Inhibiting competitiveness

It is easy to understand the geopolitical concerns of the period. With communist revolution sweeping through Asia, one cannot fault the U.S. government for scraping any legislation that would have hindered rapid economic growth in Japan. The questions that remain to be answered are these: Why did the government think the same kind of legislation that would inhibit growth abroad would not also do so at home? And with American industry in headlong retreat before foreign competition, why are these laws still permitted to remain on the books?

The close coordination and mutual support among Japanese companies and between Japanese government and industry that

124

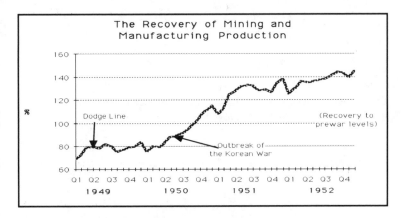

The Recovery of Mining and Manufacturing Production

American companies find so to their disadvantage are the direct results of American intervention in the rebuilding of the Japanese economy. One aspect of this is the Japanese practice of export-led industrial growth.

Much of the shouting in recent years has been an expression of outrage at the Japanese practice of manipulating the value of the yen so that Japanese exporters can undercut their competition while maintaining their profit margins. As long as the yen was held at artificially low levels, Japanese manufacturers enjoyed cost advantages that American and European competitors found nearly impossible to match.

One cannot fault American policy-makers of the 1940s for failing to anticipate the situation more than three decades later. Or for allowing original policy aims to lapse because of the Korean invasion. An analysis of the threats to American interests that accompany Japan's rapid ascension to the status of economic superpower follows in the next chapter. As we Americans look with envy and increasing resentment at the Japanese miracle, we should remember that, in some sense, we brought it on ourselves.

1. Economic Stabilization Board, *Taiheiyo senso ni youru waga kuni no higai sogo hokokusho,* 1949.

2. *ibid.*

3. *ibid.*

4. T. Uchino, *Japan's Postwar Economy: An Insider's View of its History and Future,* p. 29.

5. Uchino, *op. cit.*

6. Uchino, *op. cit.*, p. 23.

7. From the Japanese roots *zai* (wealth) and *batsu* (clique).

8. Uchino, *op. cit.*, p. 57.

9. According to a Mitsubishi Institute study cited by Uchino, the profit rate on available capital rose from 2.2% in eary 1950 to 7.9% in late 1951.

Chapter VIII

Buying Up America
Orientals with Open Checkbooks

Japan, an abject loser in World War II, has achieved its pre-war goal of a Greater East Asia Co-Prosperity Sphere....France, the Netherlands, and the United Kingdom have all gone home and the United States itself is under siege from an expanding Japanese economy.

—Gen. T.R. Milton, *Air Force Magazine*

About 25 miles east of I-75, in the heart of Kentucky, lies the little town of Harrodsburg. On the outskirts of town sits an ominous-looking World War II tank, a memorial put up by local veterans in honor of the 29 Harrodsburg men who died at the hands of the Japanese during the infamous Bataan Death March in 1942. Just a few hundred yards east of the tank stands a brand-new Hitachi Ltd. factory.

In the last chapter, we examined how American influences on the Japanese recovery from the economic ruin of World War II sowed the seeds of future Japanese-American conflict. In this chapter, we will examine the increasing—some would say disturbing—dependence of American economic well-being on Japan.

Capital surplus

One of the pillars of Ambassador Dodge's plan for Japanese economic recovery was export-led industrial growth. American orders for goods and services during the Korean War then touched off an explosion in the growth of Japanese exports that has continued to the present day.

127

Of course, the proceeds from all those sales abroad went back to Japan, where most of them were reinvested in new plants and equipment for the production of yet more exports. Relatively little was spent to purchase foreign goods. During the intervening decades, growth in exports consistently outpaced imports—with the inevitable result that money started to pile up in Japan.

The same thing happened to the Arabs in the late 1970s, when OPEC quadrupled the price of oil. Suddenly, a surplus of capital began to accumulate in countries with rather limited local opportunities for productive investment. Sooner or later that capital had to find a home abroad. At the zenith of OPEC's power, the Arabs had about $385 billion invested abroad. But the Japanese are beginning to make that look like small potatoes.

Japanese foreign direct investment has been increasing at double digit rates for nearly a decade. And more and more of it is coming into the United States. In 1988 alone, Japanese direct investment rose 44% above the levels of the previous year.[1] And more and more Americans are divided in their reactions. In this respect, Harrodsburg is a metaphor for the entire nation. This profoundly ambivalent reaction—welcome on one hand, suspicion and resentment on the other—is one we shall see again and again.

The first wave of Japanese direct investment came when the big Japanese automakers—Nissan, Honda, Mazda, Mitsubishi, and Toyota—built assembly plants in the Midwest. By the end of the 1980s, the Japanese auto industry will have spent about $4.5 billion on U.S. plant and equipment capable of producing about 2 million cars and trucks a year—25% of American production. Already more than 350 Japanese auto parts companies have built U.S. factories in order to supply both Japanese and American manufacturers.[2]

For the Japanese, it was one of the simplest ways to circumvent American import restrictions. U.S.-elected representatives might vote to limit importation of Hondas from Japan, but they are not likely to oppose the sale of Hondas manufactured in their districts—in factories employing hundreds of their constituents.

Indeed, some fret that substantial Japanese direct investment will ultimately lead to undue influence. Cutbacks in government funding for universities, museums, and public broadcast stations, have encouraged fund raisers to turn to Japan. As a result, Japanese companies donated $85 million in 1987, and almost $140 million in 1988.[3] At the Massachusetts Institute of Technology, for example, Japanese companies have endowed 16 chairs at about $1.5 million each and spent about $4 million a year for access to research.[4] About 80% of the funding for Japanese studies now comes from Japan. And, according to Patricia Steinhoff, director of the Center for Japanese Studies at the University of Hawaii, some of these Japanese scholars are very eager to express Japan's official point of view.[5]

The Japanese are also spending $50 million a year on high-powered Washington lobbyists. That is, in addition to millions more spent for consultants' advice, speeches, and background papers.[6] Recent victories for Japan's lobbyists on Capitol Hill have included defeat of the plan to impose harsh sanctions on the Toshiba Corp. after it sold to the Soviet Union equipment designed to make its submarines better able to evade U.S. detection.

As early as mid-1986, 63% of respondents in a *Business Week*-Lou Harris poll said that Japanese investments will result in "too much influence over U.S. governmental policies."[7] Two years later, the Washington consulting firm of Smick-Medley & Associates found 78% of those polled favored restrictions on foreign business and real estate investment.[8]

But while some worried, others welcomed foreign investment with open arms. All across the nation, local jurisdictions hired economic development directors whose job it was to bring in investment and industry. The governor of Tennessee, for example, announced his goal was to "get the Tennessee economy integrated with the Japanese economy."

Real estate investments

After the first wave of factory building subsided, the Japanese turned to real estate. According to U.S. Commerce Dept. figures, Japanese real estate holdings in the United States rose from less than $500 million in 1981 to almost $43 billion seven years later. By the end of 1986, the Japanese had surpassed the British to become the largest foreign owners of commercial real estate in the United States. About 40% of Japan's U.S. real estate holdings are in Hawaii. California accounts for about 31%, and New York for 18%.[9]

Leading the way was Mitsui Real Estate Development, Japan's largest property company, and a direct descendent of the prewar *zaibatsu*. Virtually all of Mitsui's overseas assets are in the United States. Among its more notable purchases are the 42-story ATT Center in Los Angeles, the Madison Avenue Hotel in New York City, and the Halekulani Hotel in Hawaii. Other major players include Kumagai, with Manhattan developments totaling in excess of $1.2

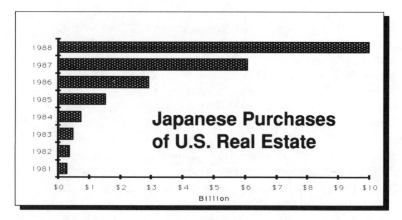

Japanese Purchases of U.S. Real Estate

1988	
1987	
1986	
1985	
1984	
1983	
1982	
1981	

$0 $1 $2 $3 $4 $5 $6 $7 $8 $9 $10

Billion

billion, and Shuwa Investments (whose name means "excellent harmony"), which has been spending $1 billion a year on U.S. real estate.

So far, the Japanese have been most interested in the bluest of the blue-chip properties and have often been willing to pay substantially more than market value for buildings in prime commercial locations. This can add up to a seller's dream. Shuwa's 1986 purchase of Arco Plaza in Los Angeles for $620 million was at the time the largest all-cash real estate transaction in U.S. history. A year later, it bought the Washington, DC, headquarters of *U.S. News & World Report* for about $480 per square foot—at the time, the highest price ever paid for an office building in the U.S. capital.

(The Japanese are also landlords to a number of U.S. government offices. Washington's Judiciary Center is Japanese-owned, as is the headquarters building of the Peace Corps. The federal government pays approximately $11 million in annual rent for these two properties.)

Mike McCormack, head of a major Hawaiian realty firm, tells the story of a homeowner who thought his house was worth $400,000, but sold it to a Japanese buyer for $800,000. That buyer turned right around and sold it to another Japanese buyer for $1.2 million.[10]

If you're interested in selling property to well-heeled Japanese investors, one of the hottest places to advertise is the Japanese-language magazine *Worldwide*. Some advertisers have reportedly gone so far as to hire Japanese interpreters to help them handle inquiries.

Although sellers are delighted to have customers who pay top dollar in cash, not everyone is pleased to see the Japanese coming

130

with open checkbooks. The mayor of Honolulu recently sponsored legislaton to limit foreign real estate purchases after a Japanese buying spree pushed residential prices up 32%. And the *Los Angeles Times* recently noted the complaints of a local developer about the "danger of being owned by foreigners."[11] The irony is that the complainer, a Mr. Goldrich, is himself a Polish-born, naturalized American.

Commercial bank lending

While the Japanese push into U.S. real estate still is in progress, yet another assault is under way as well—this time in the financial sector. The world's five biggest commercial banks (measured in terms of deposits) are all Japanese, and lately they've been making a big splash in the United States.

One way they've made inroads is by landing money in markets shunned by other banks. At a time when an American bank would scarcely consider making additional loans to ailing firms in rust belt industries, National Steel got $350 million from Japan. Nomura Securities has been lending money and underwriting mortgage-backed bonds for troubled American savings and loan associations. Still, other Japanese banks are becoming involved in lending new money to hard-pressed Third World countries.

Almost a score of Japan's largest banks now have branches in the United States. That's an increase of nearly 100% from the number five years ago. Much of their rapid growth has been achieved by a business philosophy that puts market share ahead of profits. Frequently, they offer loans at interest rates from one-half to one percentage point below those offered by the competition—much to the distress of American banks. But few complaints have been heard from satisfied borrowers, who have been able to acquire financing at bargain-basement prices.

Investment banking

It is much the same story in investment banking as it is in commercial banking. Japan's leading brokerage house, Nomura Securities, has a market capitalization of approximately $70 billion—more than 10 times that of the largest U.S. broker, Merrill Lynch & Company. In fact, Nomura alone is worth more than all the securities firms in the United States combined.

Nomura, Daiwa, Nikko, and Yamaichi, make up the big four of the Japanese securities industry. Along Wall Street, it is feared that

131

they hope to do what Toyota, Nissan, Honda, and Mitsubishi did in the automobile industry.

As underwriters, these firms have been doing exactly the same thing as the big Japanese banks—sacrificing profits to undercut the competition. Nomura, for example, was recently selected as lead underwriter of a new General Electric Credit Corp. bond issue, because it underbid U.S. competitors by more than 10 basis points. The same tactics have established the big four as the lowest financial services firms in the European market as well.

To staff their growing U.S. branches, the big four have been forced to hire American talent. And in the crucible of colliding cultures, the disillusionment of the big four's American employees has matched the dismay of their helpless over-matched American competitors.

One American vice president of a Japanese subsidiary relates, "Every night everyone's desk is examined, and...[someone] reports back to Tokyo what you did each day. So we all learned to clean out our desks each night. They also said we couldn't have pictures of our families at work and told us not to go home for dinner with our families. We were meant to be out with clients every night."[12]

Buyers of American bonds

Nowhere is the theme of profound American ambivalence stronger than in the securities markets themselves—where surplus Japanese capital is increasingly finding a home. The Japanese are major investors in U.S. government securities.

In 1985, net Japanese purchases of Treasuries totaled $28.3 billion, nearly a threefold increase over the preceding year. And they have been steadily increasing every year since. By some estimates, the Japanese account for more than 15% of all purchases of treasury bills, bonds, and notes.

On the one hand, this inflow of Japanese capital is absolutely essential. In recent years, federal deficits have more than doubled the national debt. For the first time in many decades, the United States has become a debtor nation—that is, it owes more to foreigners than foreigners owe to Americans. Total U.S. debt is now more than all that of Brazil, Mexico, and Peru combined!

When the government spends more than it takes in, it has two choices for making up the shortfall. It can either print more money, or it can borrow it. Expanding the money supply enough to cover the budget shortfall every year would surely risk recreating an inflationary nightmare worse than what we experienced in the 1970s.

The only other alternative for making up the shortfall is to borrow. (Most U.S. government borrowing amounts to the issuing of bonds. In effect, any owner of a T-bill, bond, or note is a lender to the U.S. Treasury.) Without the inflow of Japanese capital, government borrowing would surely consume the lion's share of the capital available inside the United States—crowding out other borrowers, such as home and automobile buyers or businesses desiring to finance expansion. Interest rates would rise to the ruinous levels of the late 1970s—and perhaps beyond. The economy would slide into recession.

Make no mistake, many of those in the U.S. government are grateful for the inflow of Japanese capital. After all, they want to get re-elected. And there is no surer danger to the current batch of officeholders than another recession—or worse.

No control over monetary policy

At the same time, the United States has effectively lost control of its own monetary policy. If the Japanese stopped buying, interest rates

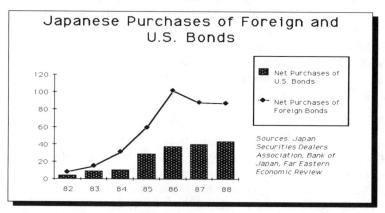

would spiral upward, and the Federal Reserve could do little about it. If the Japanese decided to cash-in their chips, the results would be equally dramatic. Substantial selling could knock the bond market for a loop.

(Japan's Vice-Finance Minister for International Affairs, Toyoo Gyohten, has already warned that the Japanese appetite for U.S. securities should not be taken for granted.)[13] This would result in an additional increase in interest rates beyond already elevated levels. (Remember the financial axiom that holds bonds down, interest rates up, and vice versa.)

As foreign ownership of U.S. securities increases, interest rates—especially in the short run—are increasingly beyond the control of U.S. monetary authorities. The same can be said for exchange rates. If the Japanese ever decide to withdraw their investments from the United States, they would presumably want to convert the proceeds into yen. This selling of dollars for yen could weaken the greenback on the world's foreign exchange markets. Massive selling could knock it over the edge.

Just as major earthquakes often are preceded by a series of minor tremors, so it is with upheavals in financial markets. In April 1986, the Japanese liquidated $1.5 billion worth of bonds in two weeks, and the tremors unsettled investment markets both inside and outside the United States. Fortunately, the Japanese resumed buying a short time later—and no catastrophe ensued. But the experience drove home the fact that U.S. investment markets are increasingly at the mercy of events outside the United States.

The extent to which U.S. investment markets are increasingly at the mercy of outsiders was frightfully confirmed in October 1987 when the Dow Jones Industrial average plunged 500 points in a single session. Several months later, the chairman of the commission appointed to investigate causes of the crash, Nicolos Brady, later to become Secretary of the Treasury, concluded the Japanese selling of U.S. bonds was one of the triggers of the worst debacle in stock market history.[14]

Pension fund buying

If present demographic trends continue, Japan will soon have one of the oldest populations of any major nation. By the year 2000, 16% of the population will be 65 or older—compared with 13% in the United States. An older population, unfortunately, generally is a less healthy one. At present, the costs of health and retirement benefits for one elderly person are divided among six working Japanese. By the year 2000, the burden will be divided among four workers.

One reaction to these trends has been an extraordinary increase in the amount of money flowing into Japanese pension funds. Assets of corporate pension funds, for example, tripled between 1981 and 1986. Many of these funds are charged with the task of investing these assets to be able to cover the staggering load of retirement benefit payments that lies ahead.

Where can all this money possibly go? Pension fund managers

are notoriously conservative investors, and properly so. When you hold the financial well-being of thousands of elderly people in your hands, you cannot afford to speculate. Consequently, the first concerns of any pension fund manager are liquidity and safety.

A suitable market for pension fund investments must be liquid enough so that it can absorb large blocks of buying and selling without difficulty. And as far as possible, it must be a market in a politically stable country—where the risk of revolution or wartime devastation is nearly zero.

Let's examine the liquidity issue first. The world's four largest stock markets are:

Country Market Capitalization ($Billion)[15]

Japan	2,965
United States	2,532
United Kingdom	632
West Germany	236

Note that, after the United States, the next most liquid market is only 20% the size of the Japanese stock market. And the fourth most liquid is only 8% the size of the Japanese market. In terms of liquidity, the major destination for surplus Japanese pension fund capital must be the United States.

In terms of political stability, the United States probably ranks ahead of even Japan. The last revolution here occurred more than 213 years ago. And U.S. territory has not been devastated by the clash of arms since the outbreak of the Civil War in 1861. With the exception of Japan, the United States is, therefore, the natural destination for Japanese pension fund capital.

For the foreseeable future, the flow of Japanese capital in and out of U.S. stocks will continue to be a major influence on whether the market rises or falls. Foreign buying in general—and Japanese buying in particular—was a principal factor in the spectacular bull market of the 1980s. Foreign selling also was a factor in the crash of 1987. So it will be in the future.

This is the heart of the essential American ambivalence toward foreign investment—we need money from abroad to pay for our own government's overspending. Yet to the extent that we enjoy this benefit, we place ourselves increasingly at the mercy of events outside our borders—and outside our control. And, as in the case of the unforeseen results of the American plan for the economic recovery of postwar Japan, it is a state of affairs that we have largely brought upon ourselves.

1. *Investor's Daily,* March 16, 1989, p. 7.

2. A. Viner, *The Emerging Power of Japanese Money,* p. 171.

3. *Business Week,* July 11, 1988, p. 73.

4. *ibid.,* p. 70.

5. *ibid.,* p. 70.

6. *ibid.,* p. 67.

7. *Business Week,* July 14, 1986, p. 54.

8. E. Rubinfien, "Reverse Land Rush: Americans Pitch Property to Japanese, " *Wall Street Journal,* June 15, 1988, p. 1.

9. P. Apodaca, "Japanese Investors Fuel Resurgence," *Investor's Daily,* Dec. 4, 1987.

10. *ibid.*

11. *Los Angeles Times,* Feb. 1, 1987, p. 5.

12. P. S. Forbat, "Japan's Yen for American Assets," *Registered Representative,* July 1987, p. 32.

13. N. Holloway, "Japanese Move Cautious Over U.S. Investment Prospects," *Far Eastern Economic Review,* March 9, 1989, p. 88.

14. "Task Force's Brady Says Japanese Sales of U.S. Bonds Touched Off Oct. 19 Crash," *Wall Street Journal,* April 22, 1988, p. 18.

15. John Dessauer in a speech delivered before the Agora International Swiss Investment Conference, Lugano, Switzerland, May 20, 1987.

136

Chapter IX

The Next Pearl Harbor

Japanese Rearmament in the 1980s

The balance of military power in the 1990s could well depend on the successful application of super intelligent computers in the control of highly effective advance weapons systems. The fact that Japan has computer technology which is at the forefront of knowledge with extreme military applications puts Japan in a very powerful position.
—Malcolm McIntosh, *Japan Rearmed*

In Chapter 7, we saw how none of the American occupation authorities foresaw that economic decisions in 1945 would help set the stage for Japanese/American conflict 40 years later. History is full of the stories of unforeseen consequences. And ignorance of history results in repetition of old mistakes.

In the 1980s, American politicians find it easy to blame the problem of the trade deficit on Japan. Calls for protection of American industry from Japanese competition abound—from "voluntary restraint agreements," to import quotas to the construction of new tariff barriers aimed at goods from the Orient. But few of those clamoring for protection in the 1980s have read the history of the 1930s. And even fewer realize that they could be putting civilian rule at risk in Japan.

Japan has always been a natural resource–poor nation, utterly dependent on access to raw materials and markets abroad. Denied access in the 1930s, the Japanese economy plunged into its deepest depression of the 20th century. During the civil unrest that followed, new military rulers came to power whose motto was: "A rich nation, strongly armed." Their efforts to secure by force what had been denied by protectionism is the story of events that culminated in the Pacific campaign of World War II.

Post-World War I protectionism

In the aftermath of World War I, formidable barriers to international trade were flung up all over the world. Some were wartime measures that were simply retained because governments sought to protect staple industries. Some governments found import duties an attractive source of additional revenues. The rise of Nazism in Germany, for example, was accompanied by severe protectionist measures. France and Italy also imposed a round of new tariffs. Britain enacted the Import Duties Act of 1931. And in the United States, the infamous Smoot-Hawley Act was signed into law by President Hoover.

As Professor Bronfenbrenner has observed:

> *The Depression immediately accelerated protectionist attempts by the West—particularly the USA and the British Empire—to export unemployment and real-wage cuts to their trading partners. Protectionism was rationalized, as it affected Japan, by savage attacks on the Japanese wage level as "exploitive."...The resulting tariffs, quotas and preferences were slanted, possibly for racist reasons, in an anti-Japanese direction. This leads both rapidly and naturally to Japanese trade paranoia.[1]*

The effect of these measures on Japan was devastating. As international trade plunged, the country quickly fell into depression. Bankruptcies soared. Farm prices dropped 30% to 40%. In urban areas, starvation was widespread. In rural areas, daughters were sold into prostitution.

These bitter developments quickly brought home to the Japanese the extent to which they were the captives of outside forces. China, Russia, the United States, and European powers either had critical natural resources within their borders or colonial empires to supply them. Japan, alone it seemed, had nothing.

Enactment of specifically anti-Japanese measures only further increased the nation's sense of being unfairly treated by the rest of the world. The 1924 Exclusion Act, for example, specifically prohibited Japanese people from living in the United States.

As the depression deepened, civil disorder increased and Japanese politics lurched sharply to the right. Between 1930 and 1936, two

138

prime ministers and two finance ministers were assassinated by right-wing militarists. In 1931, young army officers occupied part of Manchuria and declared the puppet state of Manchunokuo. Manchunokuo offered both territory and raw materials to the emerging Japanese imperial empire.

The new Japanese militarists took their inspiration from the 1887 *Ikensho* (Opinions) of the early Meiji General Viscount Tani Takeki:

> *Make our country secure by military preparedness—*
> *encourage and protect our people at home. Then wait for*
> *the time of confusion in Europe which must come*
> *eventually...for such an event will agitate the nations of the*
> *Orient as well...[then] we may become chief of the Orient.*[2]

The rise of militarism in Japan, however, had little in common with European-style fascism. Japan's new military rulers were driven primarily by a sense of national frustration over the extent to which the nation always seemed to be at the mercy of foreign powers. To restore the nation's independence, they set out to secure access to these critical raw materials—at the point of the bayonet if necessary. Announcing a plan for paternal domination of much of Southeast Asia, they sent troops into Thailand, Vietnam, and China.

Alliance with Axis powers

In 1940, Japan signed the Tripartite Axis Pact with Germany and Italy. This alliance helped contribute to the European disarray anticipated by Viscount Takeki. But more importantly, the Axis powers ratified Japanese ambitions in Southeast Asia. Article II of the Tripartite Pact read:

"Germany and Italy recognize and respect the leadership of Japan in the establishment of a new order in Greater East Asia...."

By 1941, Japan had acquired sufficient overseas possessions to afford secure supplies of rubber, tin, bauxite, and most other strategic materials. Only in the case of oil was the country still dependent on a foreign supplier—in this case, the United States.

The story of how President Roosevelt's oil embargo against Japan led to the infamous attack on Pearl Harbor appears in an earlier chapter, so I shall not repeat it here. But the lesson of the 1930s is clear. If protectionist measures had not been directed against Japan, it is doubtful that Japanese militarists would have ever come to power. And without aggressive, acquisitive leadership in Japan, the war in the Pacific would probably never have occurred.

Growth of Japanese military forces

Article IX of the Japanese Constitution—essentially written by American occupation authorities—contains a formal commitment to official pacifism. But over the years, this commitment has been artfully reinterpreted. In the 1950s, for example, Japanese courts suddenly discovered their constitution included a right of self-defense. At the behest of an American government concerned by Communist expansion in Asia, the Japanese then created the Self-Defense Forces (SDF).

In the decades since the 1950s, this constitutional right of self-defense has required more and more from the Japanese military establishment. In 1952, the SDF had 118,000 men under arms. By 1954 that number had risen to 152,000, and by 1983, 272,000. Defense spending has grown by 5% per year for a decade. Today Japan has the eighth-highest defense budget in the world—Article IX notwithstanding. With 800 combat aircraft, the Japanese air force ranks 15th in the world. The country's surface warfleet numbers 54 ships—more than Britain, another island nation, and fifth largest in the North Atlantic Treaty Organization (NATO).[3]

State-of-the-art military technology

Japanese sophistication in electronics and computers has put Japan at the very forefront of new military technology. Japan today leads even the United States in state-of-the-art anti-submarine technology. Sales of advanced equipment by Toshiba to the Soviet Union not only stirred up a hornets' nest of anti-Japanese feeling on Capitol Hill, it also led to a quantum jump in the capability of Soviet submarine warfare. If American fears about unauthorized technology transfer can be assuaged, Japanese electronics and computer firms are certain to be involved in the research and development of the Reagan administration's Strategic Defense Initiative (SDI).

It should be noted, however, that much of this growth in the Japanese military establishment has been encouraged and applauded by the United States, which has been eager for Japan to shoulder a greater share of the defense burden in the Pacific. But in Japanese postwar politics, military spending has always been a controversial matter. There are, however, indications that popular support for rearmament is on the rise.

In 1971, the well-known playwright Yukio Mishima committed *seppuku* (hara-kiri) at an SDF rally to protest the lack of traditional values—among them, old-fashioned patriotism. In 1982, history texts were rewritten in such a way as to minimize Japanese atrocities during World War II. Right-wing politicians today openly call for outright repudiation of Article IX. In addition, they also have sought to rekindle popular awareness of the grandeur of Japan's imperial past. Attempts have been made to re-establish the old imperial dating system, in which the calendar is numbered according to the year of the current emperor's reign.

Shrine of military strength

One of the most important symbols of Japan's imperial past is Yasukuni, the Shinto shrine said to hold the souls of everyone who died fighting for Japan (including those hanged as war criminals after the end of World War II). Yasuhiro Nakasone visited the shrine as a private citizen in 1984, and again as prime minister in 1985. This immediately caused consternation among the rulers of neighboring Asian nations. They saw Nakasone's gesture as a ratification of Japan's wartime militarism and an indication of support for right-wing elements of the ruling Liberal Democratic Party.

Forty years have passed since the end of the World War II. As a result, less than half of the Japanese today have any memory of the horrors of war or the bitterness of defeat. Younger generations no longer carry a burden of wartime guilt. Increasingly, they see little reason to apologize for Japanese economic success—or to automatically defer to U.S. leadership on foreign policy matters. Nor are they shy about suggesting that Japan adopt a more forceful foreign policy and act more aggressively in its own self-interest.

Japanese nuclear weapons

In the early 1970s, Yasuhiro Nakasone, then director general of the Defense Agency, produced a report entitled *Concerning Our Nation's Independent Defense and its Potential Power* that recommended that Japan acquire tactical nuclear weapons. The Japanese nuclear dilemma is very much like that of Western Europe.

On the one hand, the country is ostensibly protected by the American nuclear umbrella. But the Japanese—like the French a decade before—have begun to have doubts whether a U.S. president would launch a nuclear attack on behalf of an ally if the United States was not itself directly threatened. There is also the issue of national pride. Shouldn't the world's second-largest economic power be able to look to its own defense?

141

In 1978, the government announced that the constitution would allow Japan to deploy nuclear weapons if it wished. With 33 operating nuclear power plants and great technological sophistication, there can be no doubt that the Japanese could rapidly produce an arsenal of nuclear warheads. Perhaps they already have.

The seeds of official pacifism, planted by American occupation authorities 40 years ago, have taken surprisingly deep root. Still, it is hard to believe that a reservoir of feeling for a truly independent nation does not still exist below the surface in present-day Japan. If the Japanese ever glimpsed some possibility of suddenly achieving a

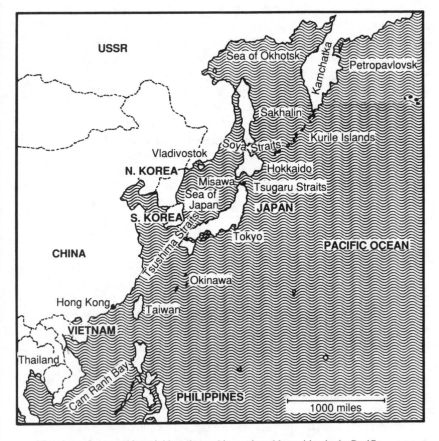

Map shows Japan and its neighbors located in a vulnerable position in the Pacific Ocean.

genuine strategic advantage—perhaps through some technological breakthrough in anti-ballistic missile defense (ABM) or SDI—does anyone believe they would be able to resist temptation?

Oil vulnerability

Another temptation to rearmament stems from the nation's painful dependence on imported oil. No industrialized nation was hit harder by OPEC's quadrupling of the price of oil in the 1970s than Japan. Today, nearly two-thirds of Japan's supplies come from the Persian Gulf. As in the 1930s, Japan is being forced to consider what must be done to secure vital supplies of raw materials.

In recent years, the country has taken steps to extend its long-range bombing capability. Extra fuel tanks have been added to the Japanese fleet of American-built F-15 fighter-bombers, and airborne tankers that allow them to refuel in midair have been purchased. By 1988, the Japanese defense budget had topped $40 million—the third highest in the world, behind the United States and the Soviet Union. These measures indicate that a military solution to the problem of protecting scarce resources has hardly been ruled out.

Soviet threat

Another factor that contributes to the increasing Japanese sense of urgency about defense is the threat just off the country's own borders. The Soviet Union has nuclear-armed submarines based at Vladivostock, just 400 miles to the west. It also has 85 Backfire bombers on station in the Far East, as well as 170 SS20 nuclear-capable ballistic missiles—many of which are believed targeted on Japan.[4] The Soviets have also stationed a division of troops on the Kuril Islands. (The Kurils were occupied by the Soviets during World War II and never returned.) The southernmost island of the Kurils lies just 25 miles north of the Japanese island of Hokkaido.

If the Japanese ever had any doubts about Soviet intentions, their worst fears were confirmed by the shooting down of the Korean Airlines flight 007 over Sakhalin Island—which also lies within 25 miles of Hokkaido. Who can blame the Japanese if from time to time they feel a little nervous about being so close to the Soviet Union?

A number of opinion polls have shown both increasing awareness of the Soviet threat and the need for greater defense spending. The following questions were asked in polls conducted by Asahi Shinbun:[5]

Question: Are you worried that Japan might be attacked or threatened with military force by a foreign country?

143

Date	Yes	No	Other/No Reply
December 1966	32%	52%	16%
September 1969	36%	50%	14%
December 1977	33%	54%	13%
October 1978	30%	54%	16%
March 1981	42%	46%	12%

Question: If you answered yes, which country are you thinking of? (Multiple responses were permitted.)

Date	USSR	USA	China	Other
December 1968	15%	6%	5%	11%
September 1969	16%	3%	7%	13%
March 1981	33%	2%	0%	7%

In September 1983, Yomiuri Shinbun posed the following question to a cross-section of the Japanese public:[6]

Question: Do you think that Japan is making sufficient defense efforts?

Yes	45%
No	39%
Other/No Reply	15%

Notice that the majority of respondents appears to think Japan is *not* making sufficient defense efforts. At the time these polls were taken, the Soviet Union emerged as the major foreign threat to Japanese security. But if a wave of American protectionism leads to another depression in Japan, that could soon change.

As the *Washington Times* expressed in a recent issue:

While most Japanese remain committed to their status as the world's only officially pacifist nation, it should not be forgotten that the spirit of bushido still lurks in the depths of the Japanese psyche. It was not so long ago that the relentless drive which now sustains the world's most dynamic economy was channeled into an equally dynamic war machine. The fact that the genie has been back in the bottle for 40 years should not encourage complacency about the dangers of tampering with the cork.[7]

Japan is as lacking in natural resources today as it was in 1930. Nor is the country any less dependent on access to foreign markets. Mindless protectionism in the 1980s could do more than sabotage world economic growth and kill the U.S. stock market. It could also invite a fresh disaster on the scale of World War II.

144

1. M. Bronfenbrenner, "Japan and Two World Economic Depressions," quoted in R. Dore and R. Sinha, R., *Japan and World Depression—Then and Now,* p. 33.

2. Viscount Tani Takeki, Ikensho, 1887 edition translated by R. K. Reischauer, included in Meiji Bunka Zenshu, cited by Bronenbrenner, *op. cit.*

3. M. McIntosh, *Japan Rearmed.*

4. *ibid.,* Chapter 2.

5. Cited by J.A.A. Stockwin, "Japanese Public Opinion & Politics on Security & Defense," from R. Dore and R. Sinha, *op. cit.*

6. *ibid.*

7. Smith, *Washington Times,* April 1984, p. 2.

Chapter X

The Japanese Stock Market

A Catastrophe in Waiting

Panics, in some cases, have their uses...Their duration is always short; the mind soon grows through them and acquires a firmer habit than before. But their peculiar advantage is, that they are the touchstone of sincerity and hypocrisy, and bring things and men to light, which might otherwise have lain forever undiscovered.

—Thomas Paine

Unless you're old enough to remember 1929, the 1982-1987 rally on Wall Street was the greatest bull market of your lifetime. But it's nothing compared with the historic bull market in Japan.

Stocks on Wall Street advanced some 243% during the great bull market of the 1980s. But in Tokyo, stocks advanced a spectacular 326% during the same interval. Moreover, the Japanese yen also rose 76%—raising the total return to any American who invested in Japanese stocks during this period to a staggering 402%.

The NTT story

Not only have Japanese stocks staged a spectacular rally, but they have gone so high that, to Western eyes, they almost appear to have lost touch with reality. Consider, for example, Nippon Telephone & Telegraph (NTT), the recently privatized telephone utility. Immediately after its initial public offering, investors bid up shares in a buying frenzy unanticipated by even NTT's most ardent boosters within the Japanese government—which had merely hoped to be spared the embarrassment of a public failure in selling off a former state-owned utility company to private shareholders.

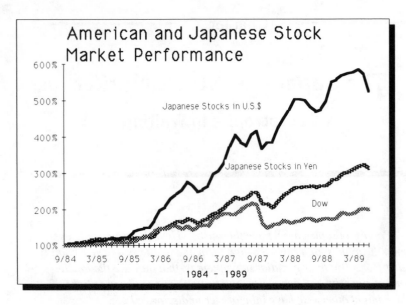

American and Japanese Stock Market Performance

1984 - 1989

Since then, NTT has surged to such heights that the value of this one company (as measured by the number of shares outstanding multiplied by the current price per share) was once worth more than the entire French and Australian stock markets combined!

Stock Market Value ($Billion)[1]

NTT	334
Germany (entire stock market)	236
France (entire stock market)	192
Italy (entire stock market)	153
Australia (entire stock market)	100
IBM	94
Exxon	61
General Electric	47

Prices like this—which seem to be far removed from any rational standard of value—are increasingly typical of the Japanese stock market. And if history is any guide, a market as overpriced as this is ripe for a fall. In due course, we'll examine both the likelihood of a crash and its probable effects on the U.S. stock market.

We also will uncover one especially potent and hidden threat—not only to Japan, but to the rest of the world as well—that is almost never mentioned in investment literature.

But first, let's try to understand what has propelled Japanese

148

stocks to these dizzying heights in the first place.

As always in the world of economics, we will find that there is more than one answer. But by far the most important factor behind the record-shattering advances in Tokyo is the Japanese capital surplus we discussed in the last section.

In large measure, Japanese capital surplus is a product of the

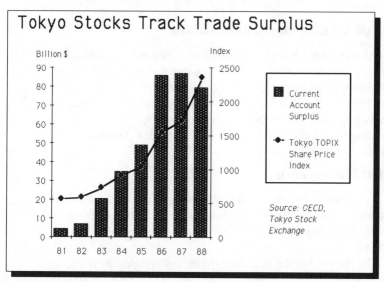

trade surplus. Japan consistently earns more abroad than it spends, and this extra cash has to be invested somewhere. Increasingly, it has gone into the stock market. As the preceding graph suggests, a major factor behind the phenomenal bull market in Tokyo is too many yen chasing too few stocks.

Corporate investors

Japan has enjoyed a trade surplus for decades. Previously, the proceeds from export sales were routinely invested in additional export capacity—plant and equipment to produce still more goods for export. Recently, however, a number of factors have combined to lower the expected return on further investment in export industries.

For one thing, Japan's export markets have become increasingly saturated. In addition, Japanese products have come under competitive pressure from comparable but lower-priced goods from Hong Kong, Singapore, Taiwan, and South Korea. Domestic manufacturers in Japanese export markets have complained of unfair competition and have agitated with some success for restrictions on imports.

In addition, the steadily rising value of the yen has made Japanese-manufactured products more expensive—and hence more difficult to sell. And finally, two giant waves of capital investment in the mid- and late 1970s have left most Japanese manufacturers with more than enough capacity to supply the declining export volumes of the 1980s.

Search for investment alternatives

As they have cut back investment in additional capacity, Japanese corporate executives have begun to search for something else to do with the proceeds from export sales—which suddenly have begun to mount up. Much of this extra capital has gone into the stock market. Some companies, such as Nissan, have become major stock market speculators and have tried to achieve trading gains sufficient to offset their losses abroad.

Individual investors

Corporate and institutional investors, however, hardly have the Japanese market to themselves. More and more individual investors have been shifting assets out of savings accounts and into the stock market.

The reasons for this are related to the high propensity of the Japanese to save. For decades, the Japanese tax code encouraged savings by exempting interest earnings on deposits up to $20,000 per person. Despite the tax break, nobody got rich off interest earnings. That is because interest rate cuts by the Bank of Japan reduced the yields on one-year deposits to less than 0.3% in the late 1980s.

As a result, those in search of higher returns had little alternative but to turn to the stock market. This trend accelerated in 1988, when the Japanese government ended the preferential tax treatment of savings deposits.

As noted in the previous chapter, large amounts of cash also are flowing into Japanese pension funds, which in turn must find suitable investments. Much of this money is ending up in Japanese stocks as well.

Fewer new issues

This expanding appetite for stocks is occurring at a time when new issues are approaching a historic low. Cash-rich Japanese corporations certainly don't need to raise still more capital by issuing new stock. New-share issues by Japanese corporations, which amounted to 2.1% of market capitalization in 1981, fell to 0.3% by 1985.[2] New issues have increased somewhat since then, but demand still outstrips supply by large margins. And as long as that is the case, the bull market in Tokyo is likely to continue.

No takeovers allowed

In a less rigid environment, cash-rich companies in declining industries would make irresistible takeover targets, or at least they would in the United States. But in Japan, roughly two-thirds of all outstanding shares are tied up in a tangled mass of cross-company holdings. As a result, the vast majority of shares are simply unavailable for purchase. This artificial limitation on the supply of tradeable securities is another factor behind the high stock prices in Tokyo.

Corporate cross-ownership of stock is a traditional Japanese way of cementing friendly, stable, long-term business relationships. But it is not the only obstacle to takeover activity. The Japanese Commercial Code prohibits mergers without the *unanimous* consent of all directors of both companies. Furthermore, the sale of a company connotes a certain degree of ignominy in face-conscious Japan—it is comparable to auctioning off treasured heirlooms or children. Nowhere is this clearer than in the very term used to describe corporate takeovers, *nottori*. The Japanese use the same word to describe an airline hijacking.

It is no surprise that there has been only one leveraged buyout in Japanese history. And since World War II, there have been only two tender offers—both friendly.

One effect of the near impossibility of corporate takeovers is to limit management's exposure to the wrath of disillusioned stockholders. Having more than half your company's stock in friendly hands is like having your entire family on the board of directors!

Corporate capital-gains tax

Finally, there is little hope that high stock prices will jar loose any of these cross-held shares. Most cross-company holdings have been carried on the books for many years at the original purchase price. With the Japanese corporate capital-gains tax rate at 53%, any sales of these shares would generate prohibitive tax liabilities for their owners. (Firms such as Nissan, which lately have been using corporate cash to speculate in the stock market, do so indirectly via the so-called *tokkin* funds. These funds are structured to allow corporate

151

speculators to escape taxes entirely on any capital gains they might achieve. Needless to say, these funds have been growing at a furious pace.)

No way to go short

Yet another factor in the relentlessly upward course of the Japanese market is the antiquated structure of Japan's eight stock exchanges. In the United States, a market at these heights would bring out short sellers in force and thus create a little pressure on the downside. But in Japan, short sales are not possible.

Neither are put options available, which are another way to play the downside. (You can buy options on Sony in New York but not in Tokyo.) Until recently, the only available Japanese stock-index futures contract traded in Singapore.

In June 1987, the Osaka Stock Exchange finally launched the first stock-index futures contract inside Japan. But like everything else in Japanese investment markets, it suffers from artificial limitations. Unlike most stock-index futures, which are settled in cash, this one requires physical delivery of share certificates—which tends to make it a cumbersome and illiquid vehicle.

Only in 1988 did Western-style index futures become available. Osaka now boasts a contract based on the Nikkei Dow. In Tokyo, a contract now is available on a capitalization-weighted index of the stocks traded on the first section of the Tokyo Stock Exchange.

Of course, the introduction of these contracts is no guarantee that they will succeed. The Japanese government often seems to issue investment regulations as if it could legislate bear markets out of existence. But if these contracts are permitted to assume a significant role in allowing Japanese investors to go short, it could help speed a downward readjustment in share prices.

The limited supply of stocks, the pressure of surplus capital and excess liquidity, and the inability to go short are the principal reasons the great bull market in Japan has been able to defy the pessimists for so long. The Japanese bull market also has defied a number of the established canons of stock market analysis. Three orthodox standards of value suggest that Japanese stocks are long overdue for a substantial decline. Let's evaluate each of them in turn.

Book values

One of the traditional tools for choosing stocks is the current stock price divided by the book value per share (P/Bs). Book value refers to the value of a company as it is reported on the company's books (or in its financial statements). It is what accountants figure out every quarter when they add up what the company owes and subtract this number from total assets.

When a stock's market price is many times higher than its book value, it is said to be overpriced and ripe for a fall. Conversely, when a stock is selling at a fraction of the value of its underlying assets, it may be an attractive candidate for purchase.

Prior to the crash of 1987, U.S. stocks were selling for 227%. At the market's peak before the crash of 1929, U.S. stocks had been bid up to 420% of book value. At the market's bottom in 1932—which would have been an excellent time to buy—stocks were selling at only 49% of book value.[3] In Japan, stocks are selling for upward of 500% of book value—well above the levels that foreshadowed both of the worst stock market crashes of this century.

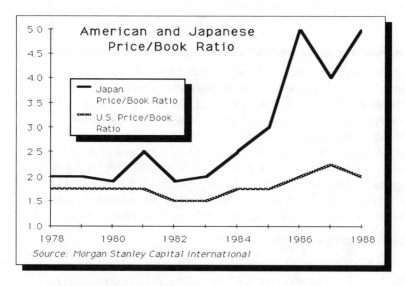

Source: Morgan Stanley Capital International

Average dividend yields

Average dividend yield is another orthodox measure of stock market value. You can find the dividend yields for individual securities reported every day in the stock market section of the *Wall Street Journal*—or the *Asian Wall Street Journal*, as the case may be. It is calculated by dividing last year's dividends per share by the current stock price.

153

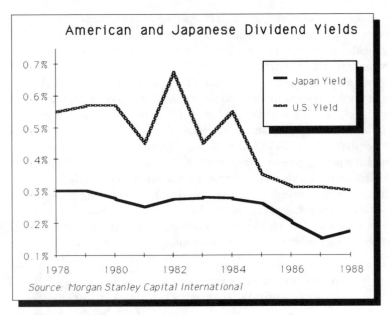

American and Japanese Dividend Yields

Source: Morgan Stanley Capital International

As stock prices rise, dividend yields decline, and vice versa. By observing fluctuations in yields over many market cycles, it is possible to make an educated guess about what the market's future trend is likely to be. For example, immediately prior to the crash of 1987, dividend yields on U.S. stocks averaged only 2.9%. At the market's peak in 1929, they were only 2.96%. Three years later at the bottom, stocks were so low that yields had risen to 12.45%.[4] In Japan, dividend yields have been declining for years. In 1965, they were 5%. By 1980, they had fallen to 2%. And today they are less than 1%—far past the levels that signaled the onset of the crash of 1929.

Price-earnings ratios

Probably the best known and most widely followed tool of stock selection is the venerable price-earnings ratio (P/E). P/Es are usually calculated by dividing the current stock price by the company's earnings per share for the last 12 months. (Some analysts calculate P/Es by dividing the current stock price by their estimate of next year's earnings.)

When a company's stock rises too high for it to generate a given stream of earnings, it is thought to be overpriced and ripe for a decline. (Conversely, when P/Es are very low, this is often taken as signal to buy.) P/Es averaged at 20 at the peak of the U.S. market in

154

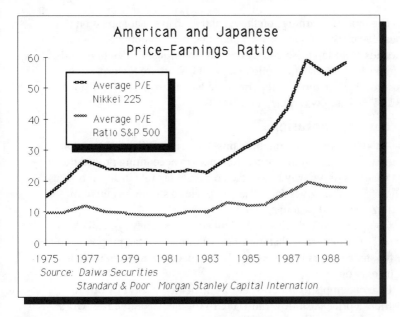

American and Japanese
Price-Earnings Ratio

Average P/E
Nikkei 225

Average P/E
Ratio S&P 500

Source: Daiwa Securities
Standard & Poor Morgan Stanley Capital Internation

1987—in 1929, they peaked at 29.8. At the market's bottom in 1932, they averaged only about 9.7.[5]

The accompanying graph shows the recent behavior of P/Es in Japan.

Measured in terms of P/Es, stocks in Japan are more than twice as high as those that preceded the worst stock market crash in U.S. history. By all three measures of value, stocks in Tokyo are long overdue for a fall.

Revising the yardsticks of value

That the fall has not yet occurred in Japan, despite the crash of 1987 that devastated markets around the world, means one of two things. Either this analysis basically is correct, and the proverbial—if much delayed—day of reckoning in Japan can still be counted to arrive in due course; or the analysis is incorrect and the Japanese market is not as high as it seems. If we accept the second alternative, we must then revise our standards of stock market value.

A number of efforts to do this have been underway for some time. One study done prior to the crash claimed that P/Es were not a reliable measure of value in Japan because widespread cross-ownership of shares meant most Japanese companies really were part investment trusts.

155

The reported earnings on these captive shares that appear on a typical Japanese company's financial statement amount only to dividends. And Japanese companies pay notoriously small dividends. Attempts by Mr. Andrew Smithers, of S.G. Warburg Securities, to adjust for this "distortion" reportedly reduced Japanese P/Es from 58 to 34.[6] This study was done in mid-1987.

Accounting confusion

Another claim often made against the use of P/E ratios to value Japanese securities stems from differences in accounting procedures. First of all, as previously noted, the corporate tax rate in Japan runs as high as 53%. That gives Japanese companies a strong incentive to minimize reported earnings.

Companies also do this in the United States. They typically keep two sets of books—one that minimizes earnings for tax purposes, and one for shareholders that does not. In Japan, companies count their profits only once.

Other attempts to circumvent this difficulty involve efforts to substitute a price/cash flow ratio (P/CF) for the venerable P/E. One study done in the summer of 1988—when the P/Es in Japan and the United States were 57 and 14 respectively—came up with P/CFs of 15 for Japan and seven for the United States.[7]

Now a market twice as high as the United States might still seem rather ripe for a fall. The study went on to perform another bit of analytic legerdemain. The major alternative to stocks, it was argued, is the bond market—in both the United States and Japan. So the true standard of value must involve more than merely substituting P/CFs for P/Es. It must also entail comparing P/CFs to bond yields in both countries.

To convert a P/CF to a yield figure, you simply take its reciprocal. On this basis, Japan's P/CF implies a yield of 1/15 of 4%, and the U.S. market's P/CF implies a yield of 14%.

At the time the study was done, 10-year government bonds were yielding 4% in Japan and 8.3% in the United States.

Dividing the P/CF implied yields by the bond yields gives the following result. On a cash flow basis, U.S. stocks yield 1.5% as much as government bonds. In Japan, they yield 1.68%.

Innovation or analytic heresy?

Let's take a moment to summarize. At a time when P/Es in Japan were more than four times as high as in the United States, analysis on the basis of P/CFs managed to reduce the disparity to 2 to 1. Introducing bond yields reduced that disparity to only 1.12 to 1.

156

But why stop here? Further manipulation by a sufficiently clever analyst, could undoubtedly show that Japanese stocks actually are underpriced!

Where does all this leave us? Well, there certainly are real and significant differences in the way profits are counted in Japan. However, there are differences in every country. Certainly an indispensable part of security analysis is trying to account for these differences. On the other hand, I would not be eager to discard time-tested standards of value merely because the Japanese crash has yet to occur. Once you start tinkering, it is hard to know when to stop. And, as we have seen, with sufficient tinkering, you can claim to have proved almost anything.

It may be that the Japanese stock market is not as high as it appears at first glance. But, by any reasonable measure, it is a lot higher than any of the world's other major markets. And I believe that is a signal any rational investor can ill afford to ignore. Japan also is in the 13th year of a bull market. And bull markets don't last forever.

In the 1960s, a group of stocks known as the "nifty fifty" stocks were very much in vogue despite P/Es that were, by historical standards, extraordinarily high. The effort to justify the purchase of what otherwise looked like rather overpriced stocks called forth an outpouring of analytic revisionism not unlike what we see today in regard to Japan.

What happened to the nifty fifty? They were killed in the bear markets of 1969-1970 and 1973-1974. In due course, Japan's turn will come.

An orderly decline or a rout?

Of course, no one knows for sure when the next bear market will occur. Perhaps it has already started.

After all, the bear market in the United States started the day after Aug. 25, 1987—when the Dow set its last all-time high. Nobody knew it was a bear market until October.

When dramatic declines do come to the Land of the Rising Sun, there is reason to worry that its financial institutions may not have sufficient elasticity to accommodate the strain. Will the creaky mechanisms of the Tokyo Stock Exchange (TSE) be able to bend like a palm tree in a tropical storm? Or will they snap like a reed in a gale?

As late as 1986, more than half of the transactions on the TSE were still being settled by physical delivery of securities. Imagine, if you will, the world's biggest stock market dependent on a army of men racing around on bicycles, to deliver pieces of paper at the right time.

David Miller of Jardine Fleming, a Hong Kong–based institutional investor in Japan, complains that 50% of the trades executed on the TSE fail to clear on the first attempt.[8] Not only do those long delays in clearing trades cost major traders such as Jardine Fleming thousands of dollars, but they raise a more serious question as well.

The volume of trading in Japan is admittedly large—as many as 3 billion shares have changed hands in a single day. But if the market's systems are creaking under the strain on the way up, what will happen on the way down—especially if a couple of Japan's largest brokerage houses get caught holding stock that they can't unload?

The last time that happened was in 1964. The Bank of Japan stepped in to bail out the brokerage houses. But that doesn't guarantee similar action in the 1980s. And even if it did, rescue procedures inevitably take some time to execute, and there is no guarantee that investors will not be caught with long positions of rapidly declining stock—stock that they can't unload for days—because of the failure of a major Japanese brokerage firm.

Crash rescue

Government action did help save the Japanese stock market from the worst effects of the crash of 1987. Share prices in Tokyo declined a modest 15% as opposed to 23% in New York. But it was scarcely done in such a way that inspires much confidence about the future.

Among the steps taken by the Ministry of Finance was a sudden loosening of margin requirements to prevent a flood of margin calls. The word then went out to banks and brokerage houses to use this extra margin to start buying stocks when the market hit certain trigger points.[9]

Government officials also rewrote some accounting rules on the spot—rules that would have required the tokkin funds, used by corporations as vehicles of stock market speculation, to report the magnitude of their losses to shareholders. For example, it allowed investment managers to carry stocks on their books at their historical cost—not current market value enabling them to to conceal October trading losses from shareholders. In at least one instance, the ministry allowed a fund to remove big losers from its portfolio without recognizing the loss.[10]

This kind of seat-of-the-pants rule-making may have relieved some of the selling pressure that large institutional investors would

158

have otherwise experienced. But no accounting gimmickry can keep losses from being losses—whether recognized or not.

Similar measures were tried in the United States in late 1929 and early 1930. In an effort to support the stock of their companies, executives formed investment trusts known as "blind pools." They raised money from shareholders and spent it in a mostly futile effort to support the prices of the stocks on which their personal wealth depended. They also resorted to all manner of chicanery to keep shareholders from finding out that they had been taken.

In the aftermath of the crash of 1987, the Japanese government was widely congratulated for its timely efforts to contain the damage. Methods like these, however, inspire little confidence for the future. The Japanese may have lucked out in 1987, but I think it would be unwise to count on it happening when the next crisis occurs.

Triggers of decline

Of course, the difference between a decline and a rout is largely the speed with which events occur. A number of things could push the Japanese stock market into a decline. Some are easier to anticipate than others. One or two of them could easily happen swiftly and unexpectedly enough to cause a crash.

One possible trigger is a sharp decline in the nation's extra-ordinary trade surplus—the engine that created the Japanese capital surplus in the first place. Macroeconomic shifts of this magnitude, however, usually take months to occur. And this should give Japanese investors plenty of time to adjust.

Another trigger might be a sudden spurt in the Japanese economy. If the business climate suddenly improved, managers of cash-rich Japanese companies might be convinced to take their surplus cash out of the stock market and put it back into new plants and factories. This, too, is something likely to require at least several months to accomplish.

Something like this began to occur in 1988, as the Japanese economy began to make an extraordinary transition from an export-led to a consumer demand-driven economy. After recovering the ground lost in the fall of 1987, the stock market went on to new highs. But the pace of advance was less frenetic than before. Share prices also began to suffer the dramatic one- and two-day reversals that often are characteristic of a market top.

Political events

How about another quadrupling of the price of oil? Japan must

159

import 100% of its oil. Moreover, the 42% decline in oil prices since 1986 is estimated to lower Japanese costs of production by some $40 billion a year. A reversal could drain cash out of the country at a comparable rate.

However, even if the Organization of Petroleum Exporting Countries (OPEC) somehow recaptured its old mastery of the oil market, this surely would not happen overnight. And even if it did, a new quadrupling of the price of oil would not have the same devastating impact that it did the first time. Policies designed to make oil-consuming nations less dependent on OPEC still remain in force around the world. Japan, for example, has made an enthusiastic and continuing commitment to the expansion of nuclear power.

Protectionism

Of course, the United States might do something that catches the Japanese market by surprise. Stocks plunged in Tokyo the day after Congress passed the protectionist textile bill in early 1987. (Fortunately, the bill was later vetoed by the president.) However, new protectionist measures continue to be introduced, and trade policy is certain to be an issue in the upcoming U.S. presidential campaign.

Protectionism, of course, is almost always a bad idea. Contrary to what its proponents claim, it does not help unemployment. It merely preserves present jobs at the expense of future jobs. And the damage it does is immense. The first casualty is trade. The second is the stock market.

As a result of a spate of protectionist measures enacted in the 1930s, foreign commerce plunged around the world. U.S. trade with the rest of the world fell 69% between 1929 and 1932. In the United Kingdom, France, Germany, and Japan, foreign trade declined between 54% and 71%.

This precipitous decline in commerce was a major factor in the worst stock market catastrophe on record. Between 1929 and 1932 the Dow Jones Industrial Average declined a staggering 89%. Much the same thing occurred in stock markets around the world.

Sudden enactment of protectionist legislation is certainly one thing that could take markets—both in Japan and elsewhere—by surprise. But there is another threat that I believe is even more serious. It is a threat you never read about in the financial press. And it is by its very nature unpredictable. What I have in mind is a natural disaster.

The Japanese islands lie in a horseshoe-shaped region of geological instability called the Circum-Pacific rim of fire. There are about

150 volcanoes among the Japanese islands, 40 of them active. Eruptions and earthquakes are common occurrences.

The Oshima eruption

In July 1986, for example, the 12,000 residents of Oshima Island—barely 100 miles south of Tokyo—began to notice a series of tremors. As late as Oct. 30, 1986, the authorities published an assessment of the situation that indicated no particular cause for concern. Seismologists inspected the slopes of Mount Mihara, Oshima's sleeping volcano, and found no evidence of bulges—a common harbinger of impending eruption. Two weeks later—on Nov. 15—Mount Mihara began to erupt on a scale not seen in 200 years.

Five new craters suddenly appeared, and molten lava poured down the slopes in the direction of the island's main settlements. The entire population of the island was hastily evacuated. On Nov. 22, explosions rocked bookcases and knocked pictures off walls in Tokyo.

Two minutes to noon

An average of four seismic disturbances occur somewhere in Japan every day. The last earthquake of truly devastating proportions, however, occurred about 64 years ago. At two minutes to noon on the morning of Sept. 1, 1923, an earthquake measuring in excess of 7.4 on the Richter Scale occurred in the Kanto region of southern Japan.

About 150,000 people lost their lives as Tokyo and Yokohama were both reduced to rubble. So were many smaller towns along the coast. Of those 150,000 dead, only about 50,000 were direct victims of the quake. The rest perished in the firestorm that followed.

Fires almost always occur in the aftermath of major earthquakes, especially because of the traditional Japanese fondness for paper and wood as building materials. In Tokyo alone, the combination of quake and fire reduced 7 square miles to rubble.[11] That's more than twice the area destroyed by the London, Chicago, and San Francisco fires combined!

In Yokohama, a 3-square-mile area was destroyed. Among the smaller towns, destruction ranged from 90% on Odawara—near the epicenter of the quake—to 10% in the coastal town of Ito—where a small tidal wave washed over the town and put out the fires before a conflagration could occur.

The official report of the Japanese Home Office (compiled by Viscount Goto and Rentaro Mizuno) estimated the total damage at 5 billion yen.[12] According to the *Japan Year Book 1923,* that amounted to 7% of the nation's total wealth. After adjusting for 64 years of inflation (and occasional deflation), that is approximately equivalent to 4.6 trillion yen today—or, in terms of U.S. currency, about $31 billion.

Potential for greater damage

If such an earthquake occurred today, the damage could be even greater. While fewer urban dwellings are being built of wood, gas utility lines now crisscross every town of any size at all. Widespread rupture of these lines would provide much more combustible material than was available 64 years ago.

In addition, since the oil crises of the 1970s, the Japanese have been building nuclear power plants at a rapid rate. Severe earthquake damage to the country's 33 operating reactors could cause a catastrophe many times worse than that suffered by the Russians at Chernobyl.

Yet another factor must be considered in any discussion of a great earthquake in Japan today: the extraordinary price of land in and around the Japanese capital. According to the Geneva-based consulting group Business International, Tokyo is the world's most expensive city in which to live. (Osaka is the second most expensive city.) Land prices in downtown Tokyo have been rising at the rate of more than 50% a year. Japan is about the size of California. At current prices and exchange rates, the value of all the land in Japan exceeds the value of all the land in the United States!

Let me tell you something else. All that high-priced property in the world's most expensive city is insured. What would happen if suddenly Japanese insurance companies had to pay off on the most expensive disaster claims ever filed? (Some Tokyo properties are insured by non-Japanese companies. I'm told, for example, that the two major worries at Lloyds of London are the possibilities of earthquakes in Japan and California.)

Effect on the U.S. stock market

In 1923, it took nearly a week for news of the Japanese earthquake to reach New York. In 1987, the effect would be instantaneous—leaving no time for investors to adjust. To raise cash, Japanese insurance companies would have to dump assets wholesale. Because a large portion of the nation would simply vanish in a disaster of this magnitude, Japanese institutional investors—which include the Bank of Japan—would be forced to liquidate their U.S. holdings.

The Japanese also could be expected to sell off their direct investments in the United States (for example, their real estate and factories). But these generally illiquid investments would take some time to dispose of. That's not true of stocks and bonds, however. And securities markets surely would plummet under the force of Japanese selling.

So would the U.S. dollar. Once Japanese investors cashed in their chips, they would have to convert them out of dollars and into yen. A fearsome round of dollar selling would inevitably ensue.

As capital fled the country, the full weight of the federal budget deficit would fall on the meager and depleted pool of U.S. savings, driving interest rates upward in a sickening spike. At that moment the Board of Governors of the U.S. Federal Reserve Board would be faced with an awful dilemma.

They could permit spiraling interest rates to shove the economy into a depression worse than the one in the 1930s. Or they could flood the system with freshly printed money to keep interest rates from rising to ruinous levels. In so doing, they would sow the seeds of another devastating period of inflation.

What is the likelihood of this terrible scenario actually coming to pass? The truth is, no one knows. Before he died, however, the eminent Japanese seismologist Kawasumi Hiroshi published a theory. It postulated that disturbances in the earth's crust of the kind that caused the great earthquake of 1923 occur every 69 years. That would make the next one due in 1992.

---

1. *Financial Times,* July 15, 1987, Section 3, p. 4.

2. R. Cottrell, "Before the Fall," *Far Eastern Economic Review,* Aug. 7, 1986, p. 50.

3. B.A. Wigmore, *The Crash and Its Aftermath—A History of Securities Markets in the United States 1929-1933,* p. 570-584.

4. *ibid.*

5. *ibid.*

6. I. Rodger, "Japan Market Theory Contested," *Financial Times,* Aug. 28, 1987, Section 2.

7. J. Curran, "Tokyo's Stock Market: Stronger than You Think," *Fortune,* April 11, 1988, p. 76-80.

8. C. Rapoport, "Tokyo's Stock Exchange," *Financial Times,* June 17, 1986, p. 21.

9. Curran, *op cit*.

10. *ibid*.

11. N.F. Busch, *Two Minutes to Noon*, p. 147.

12. "The Reconstruction of Tokyo," Tokyo Municipal Office.

Section III

Preparing for
Financial Upheaval

Rough Sailing on Uncharted Seas
Riding the Rough Waves Ahead

Years from now, the crash of 1987 will be remembered not only for bringing the spectacular bull market of the 1980s to a close. It will be remembered as the event that marked the beginning of a new age of financial upheavals—upheavals born of the loss of American self-sufficiency in energy and capital.

The bear market of 1973-74—which, until recently, was the worst stock market decline since 1929—was in large measure a result of the OPEC oil shocks discussed in Chapter 6. Similarly, withdrawal of foreign capital during those tumultuous two weeks in October 1987 was a factor in the crash of 1987.

Will further oil-related calamities send energy and precious metals prices climbing back toward their 1980 peaks? Or does the relative decline of OPEC promise a decade of inflation-free prosperity? What are the chances the crash of 1987 will turn out to be an early warning of the approach of a 1930s-style depression? Above all, what sort of investment strategy promises the best chance of financial survival in light of what we have learned about oil and war and the rise of Japan?

Chapter 13 is devoted to answering the last question. I shall attempt to address the first four in the pages that follow.

Oil and war revisited

At the end of World War II, two out of every three barrels of oil the world produced were produced by the United States. Those days, however, are long past. However, the forecasts put out in the 1970s by the Club of Rome and other official and semi-official purveyors of doom and gloom also have turned out wide of the mark.

On Jan. 21, 1976, the *Wall Street Journal* carried a full-page advertisement featuring a photograph of a distressed-looking infant. The headline of the advertisement read, "By the time he's out of 8th grade, America will be out of oil and gas."

About the same time, a public service commercial showed a young mother driving down a highway with her child when she suddenly runs out of gas. As she coasts toward the shoulder, she notices that she is the only car on what used to be a busy interstate thoroughfare. A somber voice-over informs us that she has just used up the last gallon of gas on earth. The scene shifts to a busy factory where the lights flicker and go out. The same voice tells us that all energy sources have now been depleted.

In 1917, the U.S. Interior Department concluded that only 27 years of oil remained. By 1920, only four years were left, according to U.S. Geological Survey. But only four years later, the same agency estimated that a six-year supply remained. In 1975, a popular estimate was that less than 12 years' worth of oil remained in the earth.

Fallacy of linear extrapolation

For forecasters, one of the most dangerous temptations is the impulse to simply extend whatever trend seems to be in progress as a straight line into the future. Very frequently this leads to absurd results. (For example, anyone who saw George Steinbrenner, the mercurical owner of the New York Yankees, fire several team managers within a matter of months, might be tempted to forecast that by the year 2020, 30% of the adult population of New York would have had a turn at managing the Yankees. Or maybe that Billy Martin would have been hired and fired more than a hundred times!)

Since the 1970s, however, proven reserves have increased more than 50%—enough to last 40 years at present rates of consumption.[1] In 1988 alone, proven reserves increased by 190 billion barrels.[2]

In part, this happy result is due to a freer market in oil. Because of the oil shocks of the 1970s, we are inclined to think that controlled markets started with OPEC. But they did not. Long before OPEC emerged as a significant force, there were the Rockefeller interests, the Texas Railroad Commission, and the Seven Sisters—all of which conspired in one way or another to fix prices.

Along with the decline of OPEC, however, has come a sharp increase in the volume of free market transactions. The volume of oil traded on the spot and futures markets, for example, has increased from 2 million or 3 million barrels a day to more than 200 million in just four years.

While OPEC can safely be counted on to remain an important influence on energy prices, the cartel is likely to remain under pressure. Since the early 1980s, non-OPEC production has soared more than 30%. As we learned in Chapter 6, the main reason OPEC lasted as long as it did was mostly because the Saudis were willing to shut in production to help keep it afloat.

That is less and less the case today. Now OPEC has trouble maintaining its benchmark price—even with nearly half of its production shut in. Because so much of their capacity has been kept idle, the Saudis have been unable to balance their budget for six years in a row. Through 1987, they financed the shortfall by drawing down their overseas assets—approximately half of which have now been consumed. (The crash of 1987 reportedly wiped out another $3 billion.)[3]

To finance 1988's deficit, the Saudis finally had to borrow money. It was the kingdom's first bond issue in two decades. As long as the Saudis eschew the role of swing producer, OPEC will be nothing more than a mere shadow of its former self. And it is increasingly clear that that is a role the Saudis can scarcely afford to fill.

The bad news in all this is that most of the world's new reserves are not in the United States, but in the Middle East, which already has the lion's share. Inside the United States, both production and proven reserves have continued the decline they began when the oil price broke back in 1986.

Increasing import dependence

Even more disturbing, U.S. consumption of foreign oil is on the increase again. The United States is now dependent on foreign sources for more than 40% of current consumption. By 1990, it will be 50%. And that means we are well on our way to becoming as vulnerable to an interruption in supplies as we were back in 1973.

Today, the U.S. strategic petroleum reserve holds only enough oil to supply two or three months' imports. Furthermore, there is some doubt whether the oil already in storage could be retrieved in timely fashion. Pumping capacity reportedly can accommodate not much more than 3 million barrels a day.[4] Whether even this much can be efficiently transported to thirsty refineries, however, remains to be fully tested.

Even with the discovery of oil in Alaska, Mexico, and the North Sea, the Middle East still supplies more than a third of the free world's oil. Roughly a third of that output moves through two major pipelines.

The Petroline pipeline runs west across Saudi Arabia's Persian

Gulf oil fields to the Red Sea. The Kirkuk-Ceyhan line runs north through Iraq and then west through Turkey to the Mediterranean. Both lines are vulnerable to a well-planned assault by regular forces or terrorists. A determined attack could cut Middle East output by 30% in a matter of hours. And, as we saw in Chapter 6, the Middle East is likely to remain a violent and war-torn region of the world for many years to come.

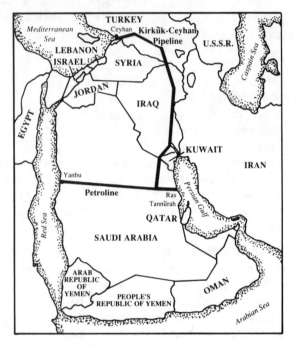

Mideast oil pipelines.

As OPEC's influence has waned, a number of oil producing countries have taken steps to lessen their dependence on the generally declining price of crude. The Saudis, for example, helped pioneer so-called netback deals in which the price of oil is linked to the price of the refined products into which it is eventually made. Another way to diversify away from the vagaries of the market in crude oil is to invest in refining and distribution facilities. If you own a string of refineries and gas stations, you have a guaranteed buyer for the output of your wells.

Foreign ownership

As a result, oil-producing countries have been energetically buying up oil-industry assets around the world. Between 1980 and 1986, foreign investment in the U.S. oil industry more than doubled. This trend accelerated as falling oil prices, as well as political and economic uncertainty spurred a massive restructuring of the U.S. oil industry. In 1988, for example, as much as 10% of industry assets— including reserves—went on the selling block.[5]

Both Kuwait and Venezuela have been major buyers of U.S. production and exploration properties. Other countries from Abu Dhabai to Saudi Arabia to Mexico have been buying oil assets downstream from their oil fields.

Some may see increasing foreign ownership of a strategic U.S. industry as a threat. Clearly, it will complicate U.S. policy in the next energy crisis. On the other hand, this is the sort of thing that cuts two ways.

As ownership of oil industry assets becomes increasingly intermingled, it becomes much more difficult for any country to act independently. If this limits U.S. options, it also should make the Arabs think twice about any future oil embargo. After all, they will increasingly have their own assets at risk in these downstream markets. This may make future oil-related military conflicts some-what less likely than they would otherwise be. On the other hand, it virtually guarantees the United States cannot help being in the middle of whatever conflict does erupt.

What do we conclude from all this? First, U.S. dependence on foreign energy sources will soon climb beyond what it was during the darkest days of the energy crisis. As a result, we may be more vulnerable to the next oil shock than we were to upheavals of the 1970s.

In the absence of another outbreak of oil-related conflict, OPEC's influence will continue to decline. And that implies oil prices are not likely to rise much above their long-term, inflation-adjusted value of about $15 per barrel.[6] Efforts to repair war damage in Iran and Iraq may result in both sides seeking to increase sales somewhat, but not so much as to set off a wholesale price war.

Iran, in particular, is a relatively mature producer. Unlike the Saudis, who have well in excess of a century's worth of proven reserves—and therefore have an interest in keeping prices low enough to discourage investment in alternative sources—it is in the Iranian's interest that prices remain as high as possible. That will ensure that they get the most out of diminishing reserves that remain in the ground. So even if a cessation of hostilities leads to a race to rebuild, oil prices are unlikely to remain much below their long-term inflation-adjusted value for more than a relatively short time.

In conclusion, the increasing internationalization of oil industry ownership will tend to have two opposing effects. On the one hand, it will raise the economic cost of engaging in military adventures. But in the explosive world of Mideast politics, economic considerations rarely rank above political or religious issues. And that means the next oil-related explosion could easily be more disruptive than any we've seen in the past.

* * * *

Foreign capital and the stock market

If the number of post-mortems of the crast of '87 is any guide, 1987 will soon replace 1929 as the most analyzed year in stock market history. For most of 1987, the Japanese, as discussed in Chapter 8, poured some $5 billion a month into U.S. securities. In October 1987, not only did new money stop coming in, but some $1 billion of Japanese capital fled the country.[7]

Six months after the crash, the investigation headed by Nicholas Brady, later to become Secretary of the Treasury, confirmed that foreign selling was indeed one of the major factors in the worst debacle in stock market history. On April 22, 1988, the page 18 headline in the *Wall Street Journal* read: "Task Force's Brady Says Japanese Sales of U.S. Bonds Touched Off Oct. 19 Crash."

Of course, it was scarcely the only factor. Rising interest rates also were an influence, as was a sudden worsening of the U.S. trade deficit. But the point I wish to make is that American dependence on the inflow of foreign capital makes U.S. markets increasingly vulnerable to events and decisions made far beyond our shores. To the extent that interest rates must be kept high enough to insure adequate supplies of foreign capital, one could argue that monetary policy was not really set in Washington at all, but in Tokyo, and in the capitals of other creditor nations.

The precise nature of this dependency, to be sure, is subject to considerable debate. According to the Commerce Department's reckoning, the United States became a net debtor nation in 1985. (For example, as of Jan. 1, 1989, U.S. assets owned by foreigners totaled

$1.786 trillion while U.S.-owned assets abroad totaled only $1.254 trillion. The difference between these two numbers is one approximation of the net debt of the United States.)[8]

But there is also much scholarly argument about how the government does its bookkeeping. One criticism is that these assets are measured according to their historical rather than their current market value. Another debate concerns whether the debts and assets of U.S. overseas subsidiaries should be counted as U.S. or foreign.

Another technical question concerns the balance of investment income. Some have argued that the United States is not truly a debtor nation as long the U.S. earns more on its overseas assets than foreigners earn on their U.S. assets. According to this measure the United States only went into the red in 1988.

The point I wish to make does not depend on which of these technical arguments is correct. As noted earlier, whenever the government spends more than it takes in, there are only two alternatives for making up the difference. It can borrow the money, or it can print it. The Reagan and Bush administrations have preferred to borrow. And as a result, the national debt has approximately doubled since 1980.[9]

Foreign creditors

Since 1980, between 15% and 20% of the total marketable public debt in the United States has been foreign-owned. It is therefore no surprise that the U.S. Treasury worries about how well attended the next government auction may be by the Japanese.

Spokesmen for the Bush administration have tried to put the best face on things by claiming that the inflow of foreign capital was less a result of the United States being unable to balance its budget than a perception among foreigners that the United States offered better investment opportunities than the rest of the world. Whatever the reason, 20% ownership of the total supply of government bonds is more than sufficient to have market-busting power.

Now I hasten to add that we are much better off with the inflow of foreign capital than without it—the crash of 1987 notwithstanding. The problem in the United States is not too much investment—but too little. How many times have you heard the familiar lament that Americans are too willing to consume today rather than invest for tomorrow?

Furthermore, interference in the cross-border flows of money and merchandise almost always create more problems than they solve.

Chapter 9 tells the story of how protectionism in the 1930s toppled civilian rule in Japan and paved the way for the rise of the militarists who eventually led the nation into World War II.

Capital controls and protectionism are two sides of the same coin. You can't limit trade in goods and services without also obstructing the flow of money to pay for those goods and services. Conversely, you can't impose controls on the free movement of capital without obstructing the sale of the goods and services that would have otherwise been purchased with that capital.

Unfortunately, both protectionism and capital controls are political issues with considerable impact inside the United States. Protecting foreign industry against foreign trade has become a regular election-year theme. So have capital controls.

Capital controls have taken several familiar forms. First is the effort to limit foreign ownership of U.S. assets. In 1988, for example, the mayor of Honolulu proposed outright limits on Japanese purchases of residential real estate in his city. Others have proposed limits on foreign ownership of so-called strategic industries. In 1989, several bills were introduced in the Congress that would promulgate disclosure requirements for foreign-owned assets inside the United States. Capital controls also appear in the guise of efforts to outlaw investment in South Africa or to restrict the movement of funds suspected to be associated with the drug trade.

(Notice that you don't have to be for apartheid or drug use to be against capital controls. All you have to be is concerned about freedom of international investment.)

Tides of history

Increasing American vulnerability to interruptions in the flow of capital and trade probably is an inevitable consequence of the relative economic decline of the United States. As the pace of development quickens in the rest of the world, the United States inevitably accounts for proportionately less of the world's gross national product. And nowhere has economic growth been more robust than in Asia.

In 1960, the gross domestic product of the Asian Pacific countries accounted for 7.8% of the world's total. By 1982, that had risen to 16%. By the year 2000, these countries will account for fully half the world's total output of goods and services.

In China, growth rates in industry and agriculture have averaged 10% and 3% since the 1950s. Under the capitalist reforms of recent years, however, those numbers have risen to 12% and 8%.[10]

In the early 1950s, Japanese GNP was a third of Britain's and a twentieth of the United States'. Thirty years later it was twice Britain's and half of the United States'. In the absence of war or natural disaster, it is likely to continue to grow 2% a year faster than any other major economy—except China.[11]

With only 3% of the world's population and 0.3% of the world's habitable land, Japan is already the home of the world's largest stock market. Measured in terms of GNP per capita, it is also the richest nation in the world. Earlier this century, the world's economic center of gravity moved from Europe to North America. Now it has continued westward across the Pacific.

To be sure, these great currents of world history move slowly— so slowly that most people don't even notice until a hiccup in world capital flows helps push a stock market over the edge somewhere. That, of course, gets everybody's attention. No doubt the next upheaval, such as the last, will also take most investors by surprise. But they scarcely can complain about being washed away when the tide has been plainly rising for a long time.

* * * *

Investment upheavals and long-wave theories

In October 1929, the upheaval that took investors by surprise ushered in both the worst bear market and the worst depression in modern times. Today, the full significance of the upheaval of October 1987 still remains to be fully understood.

When it comes to stock market crashes, the nearest relative to the crash of 1987 is the crash of 1929. In truth, a simple plot of the Dow Jones Industrial Average for the two periods reveals some striking similarities. In fact, the resemblance is so remarkable that it inspired a minor boom in apocalyptic literature about the stock market—even before the crash.

Numerous authors dusted off various long-wave theories that purport to show that crashes and/or depression tend to occur at 50- or 60-year intervals. The best known of the long-wave theories is the Kondratieff.

Nikolai Kondratieff was a Russian economist who, in the 1920s, published a theory that capitalist economies move in broad cycles of 45 to 60 years. While his theories, and those of others who have built upon his work, make interesting reading, it is hard to derive any definite conclusions as to when the next crash will occur.

For one thing, there is disagreement among the followers of

173

Kondratieff on exactly when the first cycle began. (If you don't know when your cycle starts, you have a hard time predicting when the next downturn should occur. However, Kondratieff does say that a farm crisis is one sign of impending downturn. That's one of the reasons for the popularity of his work in the 1980s.)

Another problem is that the number of cycles is too infrequent to permit testing for statistical reliability. Indeed Kondratieff himself conceded that "the period that was studied, covering a maximum of 140 years, is too short to permit definitive conclusions...."[12]

Finally, numerous studies have shown that while long-term fluctuations in prices appear to give some support to the long-wave hypothesis, other important economic time series do not.[13] Long-wave theories, for example, do not appear to be able to predict fluctuations in industrial production or changes in GNP—the true measure of recession and depression.

Batra's waves

Another long-wave theory that does make specific predictions belongs to Dr. Ravi Batra, an economics professor from Southern Methodist University.[14] Professor Batra claims to have identified a 30-year cycle of inflation, money-supply growth, and degrees of government intervention in the economy.

His charts appear to show that money-supply growth and vigorous government regulation tend to coincide with inflationary peaks. That inflation is caused by overexpansion of the money supply is one of the well-established tenets of monetarist theory. More interesting is his claim that because government regulations tend to increase the cost of doing business, periods of energetic regulation also coincide with periods of high prices.

One interesting aspect of this is that it claims to illuminate one of the great economic puzzles of the present day. Although the money supply has been growing at a rapid rate in the late 1980s, inflation—much to the puzzlement of orthodox monetarists—remains low. Batra claims the reason for this is because we are in an era of deregulation. Government withdrawal from active intervention in the economy lowers the cost of doing business and in this way offsets the effects of rapid money growth.

Batra expects inflation and money-supply growth to hit their next cyclical low in 1990, at which time the country will find itself in the grips of a deflationary depression to rival the 1930s. In fact, Batra goes as far as to suggest a direct correspondence between the 1980s and the 1920s. According to this reasoning, the 1929 stock market crash was supposed to recur in 1989—not 1987.

Lure of simplicity

One of the undeniably appealing aspects of long-wave theories is that they make possible simple interpretations of what might otherwise be complex, bewildering, even frightening phenomena. (An exception to this is the Elliott Wave Theory, developed by Ralph N. Elliott, an accountant who, it is said, lost some of his savings in the stock market crash of 1929. Elliott waves are so complicated that making sense of them is rather like Talmudic exegesis—presumably it requires years of study, and sometimes even then it escapes the ken of mere mortals. It is noteworthy, however, that the leading interpreter of the Elliott Wave, Robert Prechter, predicted the Dow would hit a high of 3,686 sometime in 1988. Only later was there supposed to come a cataclysmic 1929-style crash. Interestingly enough, this appears to approximately coincide with Batra's forecast depression of 1990.)

On the other hand, long-wave theories often explain very little. Kondratieff, for example, never gives a satisfactory explanation why capitalism should undergo a convulsion every 50 years. Neither does Batra adequately explain why his cycles should be 30 years in length. (He rather lamely suggests that 30 years is approximately the amount of time required for a new generation to forget the errors committed by its predecessors.)

Imaginary waves

One of the privileges of authorship is a forum for one's own opinions. I have an idea why long-wave theories are so frequently silent both on the specific question of what determines cycle length and the more general nature of the causes underlying wave phenomena. My idea is this: There are no underlying causes. As phenomena, most long waves are far more psychological than economic.

Totally random processes are capable of generating a series of results that, in retrospect, may appear to be cyclical. In fact, they are not. A random series is, by definition, patternless. If this all seems a trifle unconvincing, I invite you to try the following experiment.

What we will do is use a random process to generate an imaginary price history. Take three fair coins and toss them all at once. Each toss will determine the next day's closing price. Let's say we start with an opening price of 100. Now throw the coins. If two of the three turn up heads, the closing price will be one point above the previous day's close. If two of the three coins turn up tails, the new closing price will be one point lower. If all three turn up the same, the price will be unchanged.

Do this for 100 trials and plot the results on a piece of graph paper. Chances are what you will wind up with is something that looks very much like a chart of stock prices. Moreover, if you look closely, you may also see something that looks like rising and falling cycles of price movements. You should, however, resist the temptation to conclude that an analysis of these apparent cycles would enable you to predict the outcome of future tosses of the coins. If you are tossing fair coins, the outcome is, by definition, random.

Patterns run awry

Pattern recognition is a highly developed faculty of the human species. No doubt it proved its survival value again and again during our long evolutionary history. In some of us, perhaps, the tendency to see patterns is so strong that sometimes we see them even when they aren't there.

If you think no economist or stock market analyst could be fooled into mistaking a random series for the real thing (or imagining patterns and waves where none exist), I would like to call your attention to an ingenious experiment conducted by Arditti and McCollough and reported in the *Financial Analysts Journal*.[15]

Among those who make their living forecasting the stock market, the so-called technical analysts generally are among the most devoted to wave theories. Specifically, technical analysts generally devote themselves to painstaking study of price histories in an attempt to divine patterns that will help them forecast future price movements.

To test their ability to distinguish real waves from the merely imaginary variety, the experimenters asked a panel of analysts to examine a bunch of anonymous stock charts. Some were real stock charts, but others were drawn by a computer following a random process not unlike the one used in the coin-toss experiment. Their task was simple: Identify the real charts.

Want to guess what happened? They all flunked! These results suggest that people whose business it is to see waves will see them whether they are there or not. For this reason, I am inclined to regard most of the long-wave theories as interesting but generally uninformative curiosities.

Apocalyptic dimension

Another reason to be skeptical of long-wave theories—and, for that matter, much of what has been written about parallels to 1929—is their frankly apocalyptic character. It is human nature to fear the worst—particularly if you're rich. A residual streak of Puritanism in our national character seems to convince us that we court divine retribution whenever we enjoy ourselves too much. If the present economic recovery has lasted an extraordinary length of time, then an especially deep depression must lie around the corner. If the stock market sets too many new records, then malignant forces must be building up somewhere for a titanic eruption.

Not surprising, there always seems to be someone around to exploit these fears. Somewhere, in virtually every age, you can find the doomsday preacher. And chances are he's probably making a pretty good living at it. Even when disaster fails to occur on schedule, the prophet of gloom and doom is rarely disconcerted. Usually, he just goes back and recalculates. And then—lo and behold—he discovers that the date of the true apocalypse is still some months or years hence.[16]

While long-wave theories and gloom-and-doom scare-mongering make lively reading, I find that they really aren't much help in trying to answer the questions with which we began this chapter. Moreover, the fact that we have yet to suffer any economic calamities that can be directly traced to the crash of 1987 has helped to create an impression that there is really nothing much to be worried about. In fact, nothing could be farther from the truth.

A more fruitful line of inquiry would be to examine the factors that clearly have the potential to usher in the dark night of investment and economic collapse. Some of these, we have already discussed. In the first part of this chapter, for example, we noted that the United States is now as dependent on foreign supplies of oil as it was in the early days of the first oil crisis almost two decades ago. The oil shocks of the 1970s ushered in the worst economic decline since the Great Depression. Clearly the next oil crisis could be at least as devastating as the first.

We also noted the potentially disastrous effect of a sudden withdrawal of foreign capital on U.S. markets. In Chapter 10, we noted the potentially dire consequences of a stock market crash in Japan—or even an earthquake in Tokyo. In each case, the loss of American self-sufficiency in energy and capital has made us more vulnerable to shocks from abroad than at any time since the end of World War II.

There is, however, another potentially devastating factor that we have not yet discussed, a factor intimately connected with the rise and fall of oil. It has been widely written about, but not widely understood—the debt crisis.

The kiss of debt

The problem with most of what has been written about the debt crisis is that what it calls attention to is not really the problem. For example, writers ranging from the economist Henry Kaufman[17] to newsletter publisher and stock market maven Adrian Day[18] have argued that prosperity soon will be crushed beneath an ever-increasing burden of debt. They point out that debt—measured as a portion of GNP—is at something of a modern-day peak.

What this approach fails to note, however, is the crucial distinction between debt and debt service. After all, what separates solvency from bankruptcy is not how much you owe, it's whether or not you're able to make your payments. Suppose you borrow $66,000 to buy a $100,000 house. That means you put up a 33% down payment—a conservative arrangement by any home-buying standards. But unless your house has just been constructed, it doesn't show up in GNP figures at all. (Remember, GNP measures only the value of goods and services produced during the current period.) As a result, your $66,000 mortgage ends up counted as part of the "crushing burden of debt," despite the fact that it is more than adequately supported by its underlying asset.

Even the federal government—which, we probably all can agree, spends and borrows too much—is far from being an insolvent borrower. Some estimates place the value of property owned by the federal government as high as $5 trillion or $6 trillion. Even with a $2 trillion to $3 trillion national debt, the nation is scarcely any more highly leveraged than our conservative home-buyer above.

The problem with all this concern about the absolute magnitude of debt is that it tends to focus criticism on the wrong issues—such as the extra debt issued in connection with leveraged buy-outs and other forms of corporate mergers and takeovers. John Kenneth Galbraith, for example, complains that mergers and acquisitions merely increase the overall mountain of debt without contributing anything to economic growth or in any way enhancing market values.[19]

Takeover virtues

First of all, I would like to say a word or two in favor of takeovers. While it is indeed true that many of them are financed with borrowed money, they are scarcely without benefits. One of the major beneficiaries is the long-suffering shareholder of target companies.

178

Frequently, you find that the stock of these companies has been trading at depressed levels for a very long time. Sometimes this is because the company has fallen on hard times, and corporate restructuring offers the promise of better, or at least different, lines of business.

Sometimes the company is burdened by incompetent or inefficient management. In some sense, to be taken over is the market's punishment for having done a poor job of running your company. Personally, I find it gratifying to watch the new managers of a recently acquired firm throw out the executive jets, the hunting lodges, and other conspicuous perks accumulated by previous management. In cases such as this, the mere prospect of throwing the rascals out is often sufficient to raise the price of the company's shares.

A recent survey on mergers and tender offers reveals takeover activity substantially benefitted the stockholders of acquired firms. Even failed take-over attempts had, on balance, a salutary effect.

Percentage Change in the Stock of Target Firms[20]

Takeover Technique	Successful	Unsuccessful
Tender Offers	+30%	-3%
Mergers	+20%	-3%
Proxy Contests	+8%	+8%

In general, takeover activity helps bring the ownership concerns of shareholders closer to the day-to-day operating concerns of corporate management. It also helps speed corporate adjustment to rapidly changing business and financial conditions. And this can only be healthy for the economy in the long run.

The real debt crisis

The real problem with debt is not how much there is relative to the GNP, or even how total indebtedness is increased by federal borrowing or merger mania in the stock market. Rather it is the extraordinary number of bad loans on the books of U.S. banks and savings and loans. Widespread bank failures in the 1930s were a major cause of the depression that followed the stock market catastrophe of 1929. Anything that threatens the stability of the banking system today carries with it the possibility of a new catastrophe of similar magnitude.

Today, one of the principle dangers to the banking system lies in the billions of outstanding loans that will never be repaid. Many of these loans were to the Third World. Others were oil, gas, and real estate loans made to companies in energy-producing regions in the United States. Nearly all of them, however, were driven by the soaring price of oil in the 1970s and early 1980s—and by the naive assumption that oil prices would probably keep going up forever.

Oil-powered lending

When OPEC quadrupled the price of oil in October 1973—and then doubled it again a couple of months later—OPEC's revenues suddenly increased by $80 billion or about 10% of total world trade. Even the most profligate spenders in the Arab world scarcely could manage to spend more than a couple of these billions on expensive imported goods.

What could not be spent had to go somewhere. But in the Middle East's largest producing nation, Saudi Arabia, banking had long been inhibited by the Koranic prohibition of usury. As a result, banking practices were both primitive and full of lengthy circumlocutions all designed to recast interest payments as commissions and service charges.

Because Arab banks were undeveloped or non-existent, OPEC's surplus capital flowed to Western banking centers in Zurich, London, and New York. Approximately $11.2 billion in short-term deposits arrived at what were at the time the six biggest U.S. banks—Bank of America, Chemical, Citibank, Chase Manhattan, Manufacturers Hanover, and Morgan Guaranty.

Suddenly OPEC money accounted for more than 6% of total deposits, about half of which could be withdrawn on 30 days notice or less. A further $3.2 billion went to the next largest 15 banks. [21]

Banks are primarily in business to lend money. They acquire funds from depositors, on which they pay interest, and relend it at higher rates. The spread between their cost of funds and the rate they charge for loans is their profit.

Stuffed with Arab money, the banks had to figure out what to do with all of it. Loath to let surplus cash lie idle, they began to beat the bushes for new borrowers. Who they found were the impoverished nations of the Third World, where unloading loans was like selling whiskey to the Indians.

As a former Latin American financial minister observed: "I

remember how the bankers tried to corner me at conferences to offer me loans. They wouldn't leave me alone. And if you're trying to balance your budget, it's terribly tempting to borrow the money instead of raising taxes. It puts off the agony." [22]

From the point of view of short-term profits, poor countries made excellent prospects. Because most of them were poor credit risks, they could be charged very high interest rates. But that was not all. Most of these deals were loaded with various front-end fees. Ostensibly to cover the costs of processing and administration, these fees were based on a percentage of the entire loan and were payable in their entirety at the outset.

While the loan itself might take decades to be repaid, the front-end fees associated with it all showed up on the current quarter's financial statement. Raking off 1% or 2% on a few billion-dollar loans could go a long way toward producing hefty increase in reported earnings—and generous executive bonuses at year end.

In the rush to unload all that cash, a curious herd mentality emerged in commercial lending. The prevailing attitude seemed to be: If it's good enough for some New York bank, it's good enough for me. Although most banks making sovereign country loans had professional country risk experts on their staffs, their analyses often were regarded as mere formalities.

When asked by a reporter why he thought professional risk analysts were unnecessary, a Morgan executive came straight to the point: "Politics is like sex. You don't need training to get the job done." [23]

Of course, some recipients of OPEC's recycled cash, such as Mexico, had significant oil reserves. In the days when it looked as if oil was never going to stop going up in price, oil in the ground looked like excellent collateral.

The domestic energy boom

In the 1970s, the naive belief that high oil prices would last forever also encouraged an enormous expansion of bank loans to energy companies in oil-producing areas of the United States. Not only was there an enormous push to develop sources of oil outside of OPEC, but at $35 to $40 a barrel, lots of previously marginal wells suddenly became very profitable.

Contributing to the wild and woolly drilling frenzy was a series of tax breaks for investors in oil and gas. As one Oklahoma oil man put it: "These people aren't in here to look for oil, only to keep their money away from Uncle Sam. And when they find out that they can actually lose it, they start squealing like pigs stuck under a fence." [24]

Typical of the reckless, oil-powered banking buccaneers was William G. Patterson, Executive Vice-President of Oklahoma's Penn Square Bank. Under his tenure, energy loans accounted for 80% of the bank's loan portfolio.

Whenever Patterson received a request for a loan so big that it would take Penn Square over its legal lending limit—which was often—he simply sold parts of it off to other banks. Among them were Continental Illinois and Chase Manhattan and a host of smaller banks.

These banks regarded Penn Square as their agent in the booming oil industry, and they didn't mind paying Penn Square a finder's fee for a piece of the action. Since the big banks relied on Patterson to ensure the creditworthiness of the borrowers, their overhead on a share of a Penn Square loan was very low indeed. And low costs meant higher profits.

The problem was that Patterson never did any credit checks. He just said the magic words: oil and gas. After Penn Square collapsed, federal investigators were appalled to discover that in only a few cases did he even bother with routine credit reports. And in many instances, all his files contained was a name and an address.

Nor were the banks the only players in this lending free-for-all. Although they did not have billions in OPEC deposits to move, savings and loans—especially in energy producing areas of the country—plunged head over heels into deals that were more intended to produce front-end fees rather than long-term profits.

Of course, the oil-powered party came to an abrupt halt when the Saudis started driving the price of oil back down. In Chapter 6, we saw how the pinch of falling oil revenues threatened Iran's ability to finance the war with Iraq. Falling revenues also impaired the ability of debtors who relied on oil revenues to make their interest payments. In time, a wave of defaults, near-defaults, and defaults that were called something else at the time swept over the international banking system.

Apocalypse delayed

Two early shocks should have warned both the banks and the banking regulators that the U.S. financial system was perilously close to collapse. One June 24, 1982, federal regulators discovered that bad loans had exhausted all of Penn Square's capital. And two months later—on Friday the thirteenth, no less—Mexican Finance Minister

182

Herzog arrived in Washington, DC, to announce that his country could no longer make its interest payments.

In both cases, a crack team of U.S. crisis managers swung into action to keep the house of cards from tumbling. In the aftermath of the Penn Square debacle, the Federal Deposit Insurance Corp. (FDIC) duly paid off all the insured depositors. But little was done to repair the damage at other banks who had bought millions of dollars of impaired loans from Penn Square. And after the bad news from Mexico, Federal Reserve Chairman Paul Volcker and Treasury Secretary Donald Regan spent a long weekend hammering out a package of more than $3.5 billion in new loans.

Of course, these measures merely had the effect of putting off the day of reckoning even further. But in government and in banking, apocalypse tomorrow is always better than apocalypse today.

In the aftermath of the Mexican default, the major European banks that had been aggressive lenders to the Third World elected to face the fruits of folly. West German, British, Dutch, and Scandinavian banks all set aside additional reserves to cover both real and anticipated losses on loans to less developed countries.

This was not the case in the United States, however. As late as 1983—even as the number of sovereign country borrowers unable to make their payments rose from 10 to 15—George J. Clark, executive Vice President of Citibank, insisted that an increase in loan loss reserves was not necessary "because the likelihood that the developing world would not service is obligations is low." [25]

Less than two years after the Mexican default, the bell tolled for Continental Illinois. Like the widespread bank closings that ushered in the Great Depression, it all began with a rumor that led to a run on what was the seventh largest bank in the United States.

No one knows for sure how the fatal rumor got started. But what made it plausible was that everyone knew Continental had been in trouble ever since its Penn Square loans went bad.

Nervous dawn over Chicago

During the first weekend of May 1984, a syndicated columnist Robert Novak commented on a TV talk show that it might take the failure of a major bank such as Continental Illinois to persuade the Federal Reserve to loosen up the money supply. Early on Monday morning, the Commodity News Service carried a rumor that a Japanese bank was interested in buying Continental. While it was still the middle of the night in the United States, the story was picked up by a Japanese wire service.

183

Here, a critical thing happened. The translator on duty rendered "rumor" into Japanese as "disclosure." And "disclosure" of an acquisition could only mean one thing—serious trouble at America's seventh-largest bank. Within hours, $1 billion in Asian money fled the bank. And as dawn moved westward toward the Atlantic, Europeans began joining the stampede.

At 11:39 a.m. Eastern time, the Reuters News Service carried a story to the effect that both Asian and European banks were suddenly demanding much higher interest rates on loans to Continental. The story also reported rumors that the bank was considering filing for bankruptcy.

Alerted to the impending crisis, the U.S. Comptroller of the Currency quickly issued the following statement: "The Comptroller's office is not aware of any significant changes in the bank's operations, as reflected in its published financial statements that would serve as a basis for these rumors."

Few professional investors were reassured by this tepid vote of confidence, however. As the day began in Chicago, word leaked out that the Chicago Board of Trade Clearing Corp., a well-known, long-time Continental customer, had withdrawn $50 million. The rush was on.

By Friday, Continental applied at the Federal Reserve's discount window for an emergency loan of $3.6 billion. In Washington, DC, a meeting was hastily called among the Federal Reserve, the Comptroller of the Currency, and the FDIC on how to handle the crisis. Before the crisis could spread to other banks, they acted.

The FDIC put in $4.5 billion in new capital and assumed liability for Continental's bad loans. The Federal Reserve promised to lend whatever was necessary to keep the bank afloat until the mess could be sorted out. In due course, emergency loans to Continental topped $8 billion.

In some respects, this may have been a poor decision. Not only did it spare a huge, inefficient enterprise the usual ignominy of business failure, but a bailout at taxpayer expense also set a precedent for an unsettling double standard—namely, that only small banks have to suffer the adverse consequences of their own poor business judgment. Big banks presumably can count on being rescued by the government. But even if all these things are true, no one can deny that the bailout of Continental Illinois effectively stopped a potential banking panic from spreading throughout the system.

On the other hand, the Federal Reserve's misguided policy

actions in the 1930s actually made the banking crisis more acute. By simply standing by and allowing banks to fail by the hundreds, it allowed the panic to cause a catastrophic contraction in the money supply as banking customers scrambled to withdraw their deposits. (In a fractional reserve banking system, cash withdrawals reduce money supply.)

Monetarists argue that this collapse in the money supply was the principal cause of the Great Depression. According to the Keynsians, it was the loss of confidence caused by the crisis and subsequent cutbacks in business investments that pushed the economy over the edge. Whichever theory you prefer, the fact remains, inappropriate action on the part of the government helped make sure that what started out as a financial crisis precipitated the worst economic collapse in American history.

Can the government prevent such a debacle in the future? The answer is a somewhat less than reassuring maybe. Unsurprisingly, it depends on many things. One of them is the possibility of recession.

Fleeing a banking crisis

In the three decades ending in 1980, U.S. commercial banks wrote off a total of $28 billion in bad loans. Compare that with the $52 billion written off in 1986 and 1987 ($32 billion for domestic loans, $20 billion for Third World debt). Now, there was no recession in 1986 and 1987. In a typical recession, loans go bad at a rate usually two or three times higher they do during an expansion.[26]

The FDIC has something in the neighborhood of $18 billion in assets—far less than what it would probably take to engineer a major nationwide bailout of troubled banks, particulary in an economic downturn.

The government agency charged with insuring the safety of deposit-taking financial institutions, the Federal Savings & Loan Insurance Corp. (FSLIC) has been technically bankrupt for some time. In 1989, Veribanc Inc., the Woburn, MA-based banking research organization, counted 315 savings and loans (S&Ls) that were technically insolvent according to the government's own regulatory standards.

As a group, these thrifts are losing between $2 billion and $4 billion a quarter.[27] That amounts to more than $1 million per hour. Day in and day out. Evenings and weekends included. Every hour these thrifts remain open, the hole that the government already can't afford to fill only gets deeper. And if the public ever gets the idea that government might not be able to honor its commitment to deposit insurance, we could see a total collapse of the U.S. financial system. This is the real debt crisis.

To be sure, there also have been some positive developments with regard to the debt crisis. The recent decision by a number of major banks to increase their loan loss reserves helps bring a welcome dose of reality back in their balance sheets.

Ultimate junk bonds

Another is the developing interbank market for Third World loans. The financial weekly, *Barrons*, reports the market prices for commercial bank loans to Third World countries—the ultimate junk bonds. Many are worth only a few cents on the dollar. The existence of this market raises the possibility that some banks might be able to get out from under some of their bad loans by selling them to someone else willing to assume the risk.

The development of this market is part of a larger trend toward increasing securitization of bank loans. What this means is that more and more loans are not being made by banks at all but are being issued directly by borrowers in the form of debt securities or bonds. Increasingly, borrowers are finding that they can raise money on more favorable returns in the bond market than they can by sitting down with their friendly banker.

Whether or not this is an entirely good thing is open to debate. Proponents argue that securitization spreads the risk throughout the market rather than concentrating it in the banking system.

Skeptics, however, point out that a troubled debtor might be able to negotiate easier terms with the bank, something that would be virtually impossible to do with millions of bondholders. The many debt reschedulings that have taken place in recent years, for example, have surely spared the international financial system outright defaults that certainly would have occurred had there been no banks to negotiate with.

Securitization may have a further destabilizing effect. Only the most credit-worth borrowers will be able to successfully issue debt securities in the bond market. That leaves the banks lending more and more to less credit-worthy borrowers who have no place else to turn. In this way, securitization may indirectly increase the likelihood of default by bank borrowers.

Another promising development for the debt crisis is that the federal government has finally begun to recognize the seriousness—if not the magnitude—of the savings and loan disaster. According to the General Accounting Office, President Bush's plan will cost $285 billion over 30 years. (That's well over $1,000 for every living American.) And that assumes no further setbacks—such as a recession or the end of the real estate boom in California, which accounts for about one-third of all thrift assets.

The banking system is vulnerable in other ways as well. Any external shock to the international financial system—an earthquake in Tokyo, a collapse of a major bank would go straight to the heart of the dollar-based banking system: where checks, wire transfers, and other securities transactions are cleared and settled.

Billion-dollar clearing crisis

There are two clearing systems in the United States. One, Fedwire, is operated and guaranteed by the Federal Reserve. The other, the Clearing House Interbank Payments System (CHIPS), is run on faith. Between the two of them, they clear more than $1.1 trillion every business day.

At CHIPS, payments are regulary made before cash is received. The system closes daily at 4:30 p.m. Eastern Standard Time. Between then and settlement an hour later, huge overdrafts frequently occur. Ofther they amount to more that $80 billion.[28] So far, no bank has ever failed to settle. If one did, system rules call for deleting all its payments and receipts and resetting the computers. If the system still fails to net out, member banks would be left facing a dilemma. They could decide to preserve the system by honoring all commitments regardless of the risk that one or more of them might be left holding the bag. Or they could look to their own exposure and let the whole clearing system come crashing down. My guess is that none would want to have to justify how they risked both depositors' and stockholders' money in any gallant gestures to keep a flawed system afloat.

Image what would happen if a trillion dollars of checks in the clearing pipeline suddenly got trapped in a kind of financial limbo. And in the case of CHIPS, there is no guarantee things could be cleared up quickly or easily. A bank's failure would quickly spawn a thicket of legal claims and counterclaims that the courts might take years to hack through. As a result, banks' assets could end up frozen for a long time. Checks could likely become non-negotiable. Commerce could grind to a halt. It is easy to see how a crisis of this magnitude could quickly culminate in an economic depression from which it would take years to heal.

Three phases of collapse

Before anything that starts out as a crisis of confidence ends up in the dark night of economic depression, however, it goes through three distinct phases. The first is local panic, as people scramble to reduce their exposure to whatever institution is believed to be in trouble.

In the second phase, the crisis broadens, as financial panic spreads to other institutions. If, for example, one bank fails, people may lose confidence in all banks, and a run on otherwise perfectly sound institutions may develop. Note that this phenomenon is not unique to banks. In Chapter 12, we examine the possibility of a run on open-end mutual funds.

The third phase occurs when financial disaster spills over and paralyzes the real economy. Growth halts, business contracts, people lose their jobs, and the long slide toward depression begins. The transition from one phase to the next, however, is not inevitable. As history has shown, government action sometimes can arrest the process. Unfortunately, it also can make it worse.

An example of timely intervention occurred early in 1986, when a computer failure prevented the Bank of New York from settling its accounts. The Federal Reserve advanced $22.6 billion until the machines could be restarted. In 1982, similar action prevented the collapse of CHIPS.

At that time, the clearing agent for the bankrupt Brazilian government, Banco de Brasil, cleared through CHIPS. As a stopgap measure, the Fed quietly supported efforts of a group of 14 banks headed by Bankers Trust Co. to provide short-term loans until Brazil's debt could be formally rescheduled. Every night Banco de Brasil came up short, the group of 14 lent it as much as $400 million so that it could settle its accounts. Some nights Banco de Brasil suddenly came up with funds no one knew it had, money that proba-bly came directly from the Fed.

What do we conclude from this? The U.S. banking system is fragile, and will remain so for the foreseeable future. What you should do as an investor, in light of this fact, is the subject of Chapter 13. As a depositor, however, there are several steps that you should consider.

The first is to make absolutely certain you do not have any deposits that are not federally insured. Not all thrifts, for example, are. Ten states (California, Colorado, Iowa, Kansas, Maryland, Massachu-setts, North Carolina, Ohio, Pennsylvania, and Utah) permit private insurance schemes of one kind or another.

Remember that the limit of deposit insurance by either the FDIC or the FSLIC is $100,000 per account owner. If you have checking and savings accounts, they both count against the $100,000 limit. (However, if a husband and wife have individual checking accounts plus a joint account at the same bank, all three accounts have different legal owners. So each one is individually insured up to the $100,000 limit.)

In light of the condition of both the FSLIC and the FDIC, you are well-advised to reduce your balance to the minimum required for your regular household or business transactions. Even when federal regulators takeover a failed institution and pay off its depositors, it is not uncommon for the process to take weeks or more. So why risk being denied access to your funds?

In general, money market accounts are a safe alternative to bank deposits. No depositor has ever lost money in a money market fund—a record unmatched by either banks or savings and loans.

List of problem banks and thrifts

The federal government, in its effort to monitor the banking industry, regularly compiles a list of banks and thrifts that are precariously close to insolvency. Unfortunately, this official list of problem banks is never released to the public. The official concern is that release of such information alone could start a run on the weaker banks, which might be sufficient to push them over the edge.

However, you can find out what kind of shape your bank is in. Veribanc, Inc., *Box 2963, Woburn, MA 01888; (617)245-8370,* assesses the solvency of individual banks and savings and loans by careful analysis of data obtained from various federal regulatory agencies. Detailed reports on individual banks are available on request at a modest cost.

So where does all this leave us? Skeptical of long-wave theories and gloom-and-doom merchants, and full of respect for the folly of governments—which can transform even the most modest crisis into an enduring calamity. Barring any further disasters, I think we will probably endure a bear market no worse than the average decline and duration. I also believe the odds favor a recession before the end of 1989. But in the absence of serious mismanagement on the part of government, I think we will muddle through the difficult times ahead without falling into another depression.

---

1. J. Cook, "We're Not Going to Freeze in the Dark," *Forbes*, June 27, 1988, p. 106.

2. J. Tanner, "World Oil Reserves Rose 27%," *Wall Street Journal*, Feb. 9, 1988.

3. "Saudi Arabia: A Loan Again," *The Economist*, Jan. 16, 1988, p. 59.

4. J. Cook, "The Third Oil Crisis," *Forbes*, Dec. 14, 1987, p. 37-40.

5. "U.S. Oil Industry Restructuring Puts 10% of Reserves on Block," *Investor's Daily*, Aug. 24, 1988, p. 23.

6. A study done for *Forbes* by the American Petroleum Institute, The Dept. of Commerce, and Washington Analysis Corp. puts the long-term inflation-adjusted price of oil at $15 a barrel—measured in 1987 dollars. See J. Cook, "We're Not Going to Freeze in the Dark," *Forbes*, June 27, 1988, p. 105-112.

7. "Summary of Federal Debt," *Treasury Bulletin*, June 1989, p. 29.

8. *Wall Street Journal*, June 30, 1989, p. 2.

9. "Summary of Federal Debt," *op. cit.*

10. P. Kennedy, *The Rise and Fall of the Great Powers: Economic Change and Military Conflict from 1500 to 2000*, p. 451.

11. *ibid.*, p. 467.

12. N. Kondratieff, *The Long Cycle*.

13. M.N. Cleary and G.D. Hobbs, "The 50 Year Cycle: A Look at the Empirical Evidence," in C. Freeman, *Long Waves in The World Economy*.

14. R. Batra, *The Depression of 1990*.

15. F.D. Auditti and W.A. McColough, "Can Analysts Distinguish Between Real and Randomly Generated Stock Prices," *Financial Analysts Journal*, November to December 1978.

16. For an excellent anthropological study of apocalyptic behavior, see Leon Festinger, *When Prophecy Fails*.

17. H. Kaufman, *Interest Rates, The Markets, and the New Financial World*.

18. A. Day, *"The Coming Crisis,"* Agora Inc., Baltimore, 1987.

19. J.K. Galbraith, "The 1929 Parallel," *The Atlantic*, January 1987, p. 65.

20. E.I. Altman and M.G. Sabuahmayan, *Recent Advances in Corporate Finance*.

21. Sampson, *The Money Lenders: Bankers and a World in Turmoil*, Viking, New York, 1981.

22. *ibid.* p. 145.

23. *Wall Street Journal*, Feb. 18, 1983.

24. *Wall Street Journal*, Aug. 27, 1982.

25. P. Lernoux, *In Banks We Trust*, Doubleday, New York, 1984, p. 246.

26. *Dessauer's Journal*, Aug. 24, 1988, p. 1.

27. Press release from Veribanc Inc., January 1989.

Chapter XII

The Coming Mutual Fund Debacle

Understanding the Five Major Threats to Your Mutual Fund Investment and How to Avoid Being Caught Up in the Carnage

If making money is a slow process, losing it is quickly done.
—Ihara Saikaku

In the crash of 1929 and in the bear market of 1973-74, mutual fund investors were hurt worse than just about any other class of stock market investor. Much the same thing also happened during the two-year period ending in December after the crash of 1987.

Ironically, one of the original aims of the modern mutual fund industry was to lower investment risk through diversification. By pooling the capital of many like-minded investors, mutual funds could offer individuals a share of a portfolio larger and better diversified than they could ever hope to amass on their own. But mere diversification is yesterday's mutual fund product. Today's crop of speculative new funds—the industry funds, the sector funds, the funds that invest only in certain geographical areas—are all selling something else and have abandoned mere diversification to distinguish themselves from the competition.

At one time, mutual funds may properly have been regarded as safe "buy-'em-and-forget-'em" investments. But that time is long gone—if indeed it ever existed. The crash of 1987 may be behind us, but the danger lingers. Now, more than ever, it is important to know how to steer clear of the quicksand.

For the sake of clarification, I will identify five threats to mutual fund profits that are widely unrecognized by the investing public. Two of them are never mentioned in any mutual fund prospectus,

193

despite the Securities and Exchange Commission's (SEC) efforts to require "full and fair" disclosure of investment risk. I will also detail what you can do to protect yourself and your investments. But first, a little background and history.

Bull market in mutual funds

If you don't remember 1929, the bull market that ended in October 1987 was the greatest of your lifetime. However, with all the attention focused on the stock market, it was easy to lose sight of the fact that the mutual fund industry was in a bull market all its own. In the mid-1980s mutual fund assets grew faster than at any other time in recorded stock market history.

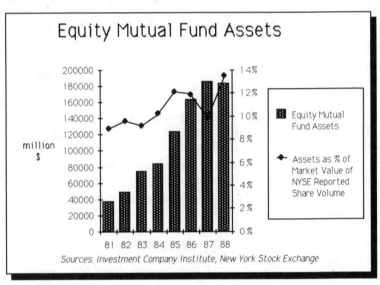

The formation of new mutual funds also hit a near-ßrecord pace. During the first three-and-a-half decades following World War II, the increase in the number of funds was very modest. All that changed, however, with the surging inflation and sky-high interest rates of the Carter years.

At the beginning of the Carter presidency, the major savings vehicle for most Americans was the passbook savings account. But the rate of return on passbook accounts was fixed by law at 5.25%. With inflation roaring along at 15%, passbook savers weren't saving at all. In real terms, they were losing 10% a year! It was an unenviable situation. Fortunately, the mutual fund industry came to the

194

rescue. In the early 1980s, money market funds appeared. By pooling the assets of hundreds of small investors, they allowed each to earn the going rate of return in the nation's money market.

In a few years, money-market mutual funds were selling like hotcakes. Hundreds of new funds were created to meet investor demand. And the growth in the number of funds began its long acceleration through the present day.

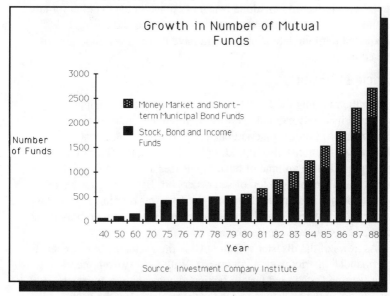

The debacle of 1929

By any reckoning, 1929 was an epic year for investment funds as well as the stock market. It all began inauspiciously enough. The Dow opened at 300 on the morning of Jan. 2 and rose 17 points on the first trading day of the year. The market remained essentially confined to a fairly narrow trading range between 300 and 320 until summer. But in late June the deceptive lull suddenly came to an end.

In the midst of what should have been the summer doldrums, when brokers go on vacation and investors go to the beach, the market suddenly exploded. Soon every morning paper was full of stories on the previous day's record close. As the weeks passed, brokers discovered they couldn't afford to leave their desks. The back-office staffs of major brokerage firms routinely worked far into the night to keep up with the record volume of trades.

195

Investors discovered that lazy days in the summer sun could scarcely compare with the excitement of following the market. The words of noted stock market observer Robert Nicholson aptly describe the character of those incredible months before the crash: "It was a time when every barber shop had a ticker...and a flapper with a broker was the cat's meow."[1]

In September a flood of new issues hit the market. The volume of new shares in that month alone was more than double the total for any previous year in stock market history. It set a record that stood unequaled until the late 1960s. (I will have more to say about this in due course.)

Black Thursday

On the morning of Oct. 24, the New York Stock Exchange mustered its newly expanded corps of employees to handle the heavy margin and sell orders that had been placed overnight. Extra telephones had been installed at trading booths along the floor to handle the expected huge volume of business. Prices at the opening bell were steady, but then the backlog of sell orders hit. By 10:30 a.m., there was pandemonium on the floor, and the tape was running 16 minutes late. Prices dropped $5 and $10 at a clip, and there were no bids at all for many less actively traded issues.

As news of the disaster spread outside the exchange, the streets of the financial district were in an uproar. With reports from the trading floor lagging farther and farther behind events, anxious investors descended on the exchange to see for themselves. For the vast majority of investors, it was the beginning of a financial nightmare.

The headline in the *New York Times* the following Monday read, "Stock Prices Slump $14,000,000 in Nationwide Stampede to Unload." Three weeks later, the Dow stood at 198.69—down 49% from its 1929 high. However, the worst was still to come. In July of 1932, the Dow hit 41.22.

Carnage among the funds

No company or industry was spared the devastation of the crash or the stomach-churning decline that followed in the next several years. Financial stocks suffered the worst, and among them, investment trusts were hardest hit.

Leading Investment Trusts 1929-1932[2]

Trust	Market Price as % of Book Value at 1929 High	1929 Low as % of 1929 High	Market Price as % of Book Value at 1932 Low	1932 Low as % of 1929 High
Goldman Sachs	295	2	17	1
Lehman Corp.	149	46	53	23
Tri-Continental	356	18	na	3
United Corp.	205	25	11	3
United Founders	245	33	42	na

The funds of the 1920s and 1930s were closed-end funds. Unlike open-end funds, which appeared later, a closed-end fund does not stand by ready to redeem shares on investor demand. Instead, a fixed number of shares is created. Thereafter, shares in the fund trade on an exchange just like any other stock.

Fifty-percent casualty rate

Approximately 1,200 investment companies were created in the 1920s and early 1930s. By 1936, approximately 600 had disappeared as a result of dissolution, merger, or bankruptcy—a failure rate of 50%. This, however, was not the first time that investment companies took investors to the cleaners. U.S. investment companies had been modeled after their English predecessors. Following the Barish crash of 1890, the average British fund investor lost 75 cents of every dollar invested.

While a bear market imposes losses on all stockholders, too often fund investors seem to get hurt worse than anyone else. This is an investment risk you will never read about in any investment company prospectus.

Let's examine why this has been the case. One reason for the fund debacle of 1929 was that fund managers embraced an ancient temptation: reckless use of leverage. Leverage is the first of the five threats to your mutual fund investments.

Greasing the skids with borrowed money

Most investors today are familiar with the practice of buying stocks on margin. That simply means you borrow money from your broker to buy stocks for your portfolio. Let's take a quick look at a hypothetical example to see how this exaggerates both gains and losses.

197

Suppose you are interested in 100 shares of an alpine grain producer, Ethereal Cereals, which currently sells for $20 a share. A 100-share investment would cost you $2,000. If the stock moves $1, the change in the value of your portfolio is $100 (100 shares x $1). On a $2,000 investment, that amounts to a 5% ($100/$2,000) gain or loss.

Now suppose you buy the stock on margin. Let's say you put up $1,000 and borrow $1,000 from your broker. If the stock moves $1, you still have a $100 change in the value of your portfolio. But on the basis of only a $1,000 initial investment, that means a gain or loss of 10% ($100/$1,000).

Increase your margin, double your fun

In this case, borrowing half your initial investment effectively doubled your rate of return. But if the stock had moved down, it also would have doubled the rate of your loss. Many investment companies of 1929 did exactly the same thing. They raised money from the public to buy stocks, and then they borrowed money to buy more. In 1929, United Founders was in hock for $10 million. Goldman Sachs owed $24 million.

Leverage was also achieved in other ways. Goldman, Sachs & Company, for example, created its first investment company, Goldman Sachs Trading Corp., in 1928. During the height of the new-issues craze in July 1929, the company created a second investment company, the Shenandoah Corp. Goldman Sachs Trading Corp. (along with Central States Electric Co.) sponsored the new issue and retained 80% of its common stock.

No one ever accused the Goldman Sachs managers of being insufficiently aggressive. Having discovered a good thing, they tried it again a month later. In August 1929, they created a third investment trust, Blue Ridge Corp. This time, Shenandoah retained 80% of the common stock issued.

Incest among the trusts

Here is a case in which one investment company issued stock in a second, which in turn issued stock in a third. Blue Ridge raised approximately $100 million in both common and preference stock. Guess what stocks these shrewd financial wizards bought with the public's funds. One of their largest holdings was Central States Electric, co-sponsor of the previous new issue!

The net result of these practices was to create a corporate pyramid as highly leveraged as if it had all been bought with borrowed money

198

(which in a sense it had been!). In 1929, the president of Goldman Sachs, Waddill Catchings, wrote a book called *The Road to Plenty*, in which he explained to the public his method for achieving and preserving prosperity. Anyone who took his advice soon found out that this particular road was a two-way street.

The lure of larceny

Another reason for the 1929 investment company debacle was widespread disregard for the law. Fund managers frequently "borrowed" fund assets for their personal use. After the 1937 bankruptcy of the Continental Securities Co., several officers were tried for larceny—they had plundered $3.25 million from the investment company portfolio.

Other fraudulent practices included using the fund's money as a vehicle for stock market manipulation and dumping (buying the leftover stock from failed public offerings at inflated prices). In effect, the fund was used as a dumping ground for issues that could not be sold to anyone else.

Temptations of fraud

Alarmed by the growing number of complaints received by his fraud division, the attorney general of New York, John J. Bennet Jr., ordered an investigation of investment companies within his jurisdiction. In a report to the state legislature, he revealed that half the 100 companies examined had engaged in dumping.[3]

Further public indignation fell on the aggressive promoters of investment trusts, many of whom made fortunes despite the funds' dismal performances. According to an SEC investigation of investment trusts ordered under the Utility Holding Acts of 1935, one of the original promoters of the United Founders Investment Trust pocketed $30 million in 1929 alone. Larceny, fraud, and questionable promotion tactics constitute the second major threat to your mutual fund investments.

Birth of regulation

In due course, congressional investigations led to new securities legislation. The Securities Act of 1933 established the SEC. It also required "full and fair" disclosure of all information relevant to newly issued securities. The Revenue Act of 1936 established the special tax status of investment companies that distribute 90% of their dividends and capital gains to shareholders.

199

Seven years later, the Investment Company Act of 1940 codified standards for formation, capital structure, management, and underwriting of "regulated investment companies." This is the legislation that, along with its several amendments, established the modern mutual fund industry.

How much has changed since 1929?

To be sure, a half-century's worth of securities legislation has left its mark upon the mutual fund industry. Since World War II, most new investment companies have been organized as open-end. In fact, the term mutual fund has become practically synonymous with open-end funds. Only in the last few years have their closed-end cousins started to emerge from relative obscurity.

Funds still find ways to leverage their returns. Some are permitted to buy on margin, others indulge in the newest highly leveraged instruments of the present era: futures and options. The important difference today is not that leverage is less widely used than it was in 1929. Rather, it is that the use of leverage is more openly disclosed.

Whether or not a fund may use these techniques must now be clearly stated in the prospectus. At least theoretically, any changes to the investment rules as declared in the prospectus require the approval of a majority of the fund's shareholders. Clearly this is a step forward. But it means that the burden is on the individual investor to take responsibility for keeping up with what fund managers are doing.

Lower incidence of fraud

By just about any measure, the incidence of fraud is lower now than it was in 1929. This is not because mutual fund managers are more virtuous than they used to be, but only because stringent disclosure requirements have made it much more difficult to commit fraudulent acts. For a clearer picture of just how much things have changed since 1929 (and how much they have not!), let's look at another more recent cycle of stock market boom and bust.

Debacle of 1968–1974

One common characteristic of speculative stock market bubbles is a simple vision of instant wealth. In 1929, everyone was going to get rich on steel company and utility stocks. In 1961, everyone was going to get rich on electronics stocks. Like 1929, 1961 saw a flood of new issues.

It all started innocently enough when a number of technology issues began to do spectacularly well. Investors who bought shares in Control Data when it was first issued in 1958 watched their holdings appreciate 120% by 1961. Shares in Litton Industries, to cite another example, increased fiftyfold during nearly the same period.

Intoxicated by the prospect of profit on such a scale, investors began to seize anything that sounded electronic or scientific. Soon a flock of new issues appeared to satisfy the public's demand for companies with names ending in "onics" or "tron." Underwriting new securities suddenly became a land-office business. "Why go broke? Go public," became the joke along the corridors of Wall Street.

New-issue orgy

A company named Dynatronics issued its first stock offering at $7 a share. Within days it was trading at $25. Simulmatics, a company with a *negative* net worth of $21,000, went public at $2 and rose almost instantly to $9. The boom in electronics and technology companies cooled off in late 1961. But by 1967, it was back again in force. This time the highflyers included a number of now familiar names—IBM, Texas Instruments, Xerox, and Polaroid.

Mutual fund managers were now ready to get in on the act. By 1976, a generation of mutual fund managers had appeared with no real memory of 1929. Dubbed "gunslingers" by the financial press, these were members of a new breed of financial swashbucklers—men such as Fred Carr, Gerald Tsai, Fred Mates, and Fred Alger.

Go-go funds

Tsai was one of the earliest pioneers of what later became known as the go-go style of mutual fund investing. Go-go investing simply meant an aggressive, short-term-oriented trading strategy. At the time, this kind of fast, in-and-out trading was new to mutual funds. Using these methods, Tsai increased the Fidelity Growth Fund 65% in 1968.

Sensing that he was on to a good thing, Tsai quit Fidelity to go into business for himself. In 1967 he started the Manhattan Fund, which more than doubled the 20% rise in market averages that year. Despite this superb record, within less than a year more money was flowing out of the Manhattan Fund than was coming in.

No great test of skill

The reason was simple. It required no particular feat of analytic genius to pick stock market winners in the climate of the late 1960s. Virtually any company with an exciting story to tell and a technical-sounding name was enthusiastically bid up by investors. At a loss to account for the tenfold increase in his company's stock since the last annual meeting, the chief executive of one such firm simply observed, "God has been good to Solitron Devices."[4]

Managers of rival funds quickly caught on and were soon beating Tsai at his own game. Fred Carr's Enterprise Fund was up 116% in 1967. Fred Mates' Mates Fund was up an astounding 158%. Why should anyone be satisfied with the Manhattan Fund's paltry 40% when gains such as those were available?

Passion for short-term performance

Amid the speculative fervor of the times, big money flowed to mutual fund managers who could post higher quarterly performance figures than their rivals. Before long, many were unable to resist the temptation of financial chicanery.

One favorite tactic was to cash in on new issues. Because go-go investing meant turning over every stock in the portfolio several times a year, the gunslingers generated enormous brokerage commissions. Some clever fund managers dangled their sizable commission business before the underwriters of new issues.

A typical arrangement worked something like this. In exchange for the fund's commission business, the underwriter would agree to sell large blocks of hot new issues to the fund at the issue price. As soon as the initial public offering was completed, many of these new issues immediately went to substantial premiums in the secondary market— thus generating instant profits for the fund.

Market price manipulation

Another tactic was to pour money into thinly traded issues. In many cases, the weight of the fund's buying power alone was sufficient to raise the stock 20%, 30%, or more. These holdings were then listed on the fund's books at the most recent—and higher—market price. This is the third threat to your mutual fund investments.

Profits such as these amounted to little more than accounting fiction. If the fund attempted to actually realize the trading gains listed on its quarterly report, it would find almost no one else to sell to. This is because the fund's selling would drive the price down as fast or faster than buying the stock had pushed it up.

Letter stock roulette

Finally, there was a whole new game going on with restricted securities, or so-called letter stock purchased directly from the company by a major investor according to the terms of a private agreement. Because such stock is never publicly offered, it allows both buyer and seller to circumvent the disclosure of all new public issues required by the SEC. This is the fourth threat to your mutual fund investments.

A typical arrangement works like this. A company in need of some quick capital issues letter stock to a mutual fund at a substantial discount (usually 30% to 50%) to the market value of the firm's comparable publicly traded securities. The fund agrees to hold the stock for some minimum period—usually two or three years.

This amounts to a very cozy arrangement. The company gets fresh capital on better terms than it could get from banks or bondholders. The mutual fund gets a discounted security, which it immediately revalues on its books at the market price for the firm's comparable publicly traded securities. Another source of instant profit!

World Series of restricted securities

Testimony before the U.S. House of Representatives Committee on Interstate and Foreign Commerce detailed Fred Carr's mastery of this particular technique:

On March 27, 1967, the Enterprise Fund paid $316,000 for Bell Electronics convertible debentures. Its March 31 report listed the value of those debentures at $444,744—a 40% gain in four days.

On May 1, the fund bought 100,000 shares of Texas American Oil Co. at $5.52 per share. The fund's June 30 report up-valued the shares 38%, to $7.63 each.

On June 28, Enterprise paid $743,000 for 50,000 shares of Wellington Electronics and up-valued them to $1,263,938 in its June 30 report—an appreciation of 59%, one-third of a million dollars, in 48 hours.

On Dec. 22, the fund bought 80,000 shares of AITS for $2,081,000 and put a value of $2,718,000 on those shares in its Dec. 31 report six business days later—an increase of 30.6%.

On Dec. 22, Enterprise bought 21,000 shares of Larsen Industries for $2,101,000 and valued them five days later at $2,473,000—an 18% increase.[5]

Every time a quarterly report came due, Mr. Carr added a little something extra to boost his performance figures. It's no wonder the Enterprise Fund had a good year—at least according to the numbers!

In 1969 the SEC filed charges against Fred Mates for representing to shareholders that the Mates Fund would not deal in restricted securities, when in fact the fund had substantial letter-stock holdings in its portfolio.

What happened to the highflyers when the bulls ran out of steam and the market turned south? Well, the Enterprise Fund went from a net asset value of $11.88 in 1968 to $3.84 in 1974—a decline of 68%. The Mates Investment Fund went from a net asset value of $15.51 in 1968 to $1.12 in 1974—a 93% decline.

In fact, a quick look at the table on page 161 reveals that the glory of 1968 was short-lived indeed. Only three of the top 20 funds in 1968 managed to finish in the top 20 again in any of the following five years. Only one of the 20—the Templeton Growth Fund— managed to post an increase in net asset value (NAV).

The gunslingers quickly fell on hard times as their performances slipped. The original go-go star, Gerald Tsai, left the mutual fund business for more fertile pursuits. Today he heads the American Can Co. After conceding the SEC charges against him, Fred Mates left the securities business to open a singles bar in Manhattan! Only Fred Alger is still in the mutual fund business today. If you read the financial press, you've undoubtedly seen his advertisements.

Fund investors clobbered again

Consecutive annual declines of 15% and 26% in the stock market[6] made the bear market of 1973-74 the worst two-year period since 1930-31. And just like 50 years ago, mutual fund investors got hurt worse than just about anyone else.

The Investment Company Institute (ICI), the Washington, DC–based trade association, has compiled industry-wide performance figures from 1970 to the present. According to the ICI's weighted equity mutual fund index, the average fund lost 19.2% between 1970 and 1974. That's significantly worse than the 14.6% decline in the stock market as a whole.

Performance this poor did not go unnoticed by the investment public. After years of pouring more money into mutual funds, the public abruptly began pulling its money out. ICI figures reveal that the money started pouring out of mutual funds in 1972 and continued without interruption for a record seven consecutive years.

Fund	1968 Rank	1969 Rank	1970 Rank	1971 Rank	1972 Rank	1973 Rank	1974 Rank	1968 NAV	1974 NAV	Change in NAV
Mates Investment	1	312	424	512	465	531	400	15.51	1.12	-93%
Neuwirth Fund	2	263	360	104	477	397	232	15.29	6.24	-59%
Gibralter Growth	3	172	456	481	na	na	na	17.27	na	na
Insurance Investors	4	77	106	317	417	224	na	7.45	na	na
Pennsylvania Mutual	5	333	459	480	486	519	521	11.92	1.09	-91%
Puerto Rican Invest.	6	30	308	387	435	na	na	19.32	na	na
Crown Western-Dallas	7	283	438	207	244	330	133	13.86	4.66	-66%
Franklin Dynatech	8	342	363	112	120	453	453	14.47	4.56	-68%
First Participating	9	49	283	106	27	220	310	19.25	13.47	-30%
Connecticut Western	105	202	na	na	na	na		127.27	na	na
Enterprise Fund	11	334	397	133	364	250	416	11.88	3.84	-68%
Ivy Fund	12	357	293	233	161	312	443	12.37	4.58	-63%
Century Shares	13	120	55	62	62	127	428	13.09	8.48	-35%
Mutual Shares	14	284	272	152	452	62	4	22.18	15.44	-30%
Putnam Equities	15	376	384	45	54	354	211	17.05	6.42	-62%
Fin. Indust. Income	16	244	222	277	231	35	90	8.40	4.73	-44%
Consumers Invest.	17	354	na	na	na	na	na	6.21	na	na
Columbia Growth	18	33	322	27	370	332	253	14.23	9.05	-36%
Templeton Growth	19	1	241	163	1	81	84	4.00	6.23	56%
Schuster Fund	20	129	231	253	425	445	434	12.29	4.86	-60%

Fear of redemption

One long-time market observer, noted money manager Charles Allmon, has suggested that the mutual fund industry was responsible for making the bear market of 1973-74 deeper and more prolonged than it would have been otherwise.

The first premise of this school of thought is that investors are often stampeded by emotions—usually fear or greed. After the crash of 1987, there can be little doubt that this at least occasionally occurs in a fairly dramatic fashion.

Because open-end mutual funds now compose such a large segment of the market, they cannot hope to escape any sudden wave of selling. Open-end funds, remember, are required by law to redeem shares on demand. So unless fund managers anticipate a wave of redemptions and keep large amounts of cash on hand to meet them,

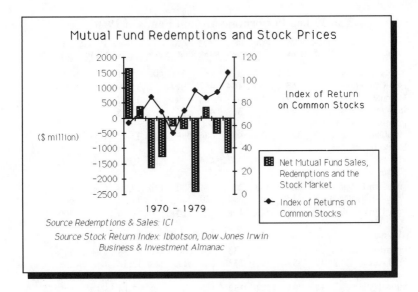

Mutual Fund Redemptions and Stock Prices

($ million)

Index of Return on Common Stocks

Net Mutual Fund Sales, Redemptions and the Stock Market

Index of Returns on Common Stocks

1970 - 1979

Source Redemptions & Sales: ICI

Source Stock Return Index: Ibbotson, Dow Jones Irwin Business & Investment Almanac

they are soon forced to sell off some of their holdings to raise the necessary funds.

Whenever the stock market takes a major tumble, a run on the funds can easily develop, as investors scramble to get their money out. This leads to a round of forced selling, as hard-pressed fund managers scramble to raise cash to pay off panicky shareholders. Net asset values inevitably take a further beating as fund managers have to sell into a declining market.

Forced liquidation

More importantly, this forced liquidation now has the power to knock stock prices down even more, thereby worsening investor panic and increasing the demand for redemptions. A self-intensifying rush to convert securities into cash is, of course, the definition of a stock market crash. This is the fifth and final threat to the mutual fund investor.

The price-bashing power of mutual fund sales has increased along with the number of funds and the increase in the assets under management. As far back as 1967, SEC Commissioner Hugh F. Owens noted two instances in which fund selling had contributed to extraordinary declines in individual securities.[8] In both instances, stocks that had suddenly fallen out of favor with the funds declined 8% and 16% in a single trading session. In the first instance, mutual funds accounted for 44.7% of the selling volume; in the second instance, they accounted for 43.5%.

In 1987, the price-bashing power of mutual fund redemptions was first felt in the bond market. Early in the spring, U.S. interest rates reversed their long-term downtrend and turned up for the first time in more than four years. And the first to get burned were investors in fixed-income or bond funds. (Remember, as interest rates rise, the value of bonds declines, and vice versa.)

At the time, a lot of bond-fund investors were folks who remembered with great fondness the double-digit yields they had earned on their money-market funds in the late 1970s and early 1980s. Of course, those yields evaporated as interest rates declined. Sensing a sales opportunity, brokers and mutual fund promoters began touting their higher-yielding bond funds as "safe" alternatives to the now disappointing money-market yields.

As long as interest rates kept going down, of course, these investors did fine. But they were living in a fool's paradise. When rates suddenly began rising in March 1987, they saw the net asset values of their funds start to plunge. And then they all wanted to sell at the same time.

When angry shareholders started calling their funds and demanding their money, a number of fund managers had no choice but to start liquidating their portfolios to raise cash. Most bonds are traded over the counter in markets that are rather thin even in less chaotic times. When the avalanche of selling hit, there was nowhere to hide. The spread between bid and ask prices hit new highs. For some issues there were no bids at all.

As it turned out, the spring debacle in fixed-income funds was only a preview of the fall catastrophe in the stock market. There, panic selling—fueled in part by mutual fund redemptions—pushed the stock market into the steepest decline on record.

Defending against financial catastrophe

I hope by now I have been able to convince you that mutual fund investments are not as safe as commonly thought. If there is a lesson to be learned from the last 60 years of mutual fund history, it is that failure to look beyond mere appearances can easily lead to financial ruin. Let's re-examine each of the five threats to mutual fund investments to see what you can do to head off any unhappy surprises.

Leverage

As mentioned earlier, a fund's use of margin, or leveraged instruments such as futures and options, must be disclosed in the fund's prospectus. Be sure to read all the fine print before you invest. In addition to the prospectus, the fund's statement of additional information should also be required reading.

Once you understand what the fund's investment rules are, be alert for any effort on the part of management to change them. This may mean going to the annual meeting to speak against any changes that increase the risk to shareholders. It certainly means taking the time to read your proxy materials carefully and voting accordingly. If all else fails, you can always sell your shares.

Fraud

Without a doubt, regulation and surveillance by the SEC has decreased the incidence of mutual fund fraud. Nonetheless, there is never any shortage of rogues and rascals out to make a quick killing for themselves with your money. And occasionally one will slip through the cracks.

A few years ago, for example, the portfolio manager of the United Services Advisors' Prospector Fund was charged with taking bribes from a couple of Vancouver promoters in exchange for loading the portfolio with worthless securities. Although it left the mutual fund industry untouched, the wave of arrests following the Ivan Boesky and Dennis Levine insider-trading scandal provides ample evidence that a sufficiently clever operator can almost always find a way to circumvent securities regulations.

Perhaps the best defense against mutual fund fraud is to deal only with well-established, reputable investment companies. Or as the title of a frequently requested SEC publication urges: "Investigate Before You Invest." There are also two other publications that should be of interest to mutual fund investors concerned about fraud. They are *Consumers Should Know* and *What Every Investor Should Know: A Handbook from the U.S. Securities and Exchange Commission*. Both are available from the SEC Office of Consumer Affairs and Information Services, *Washington, DC 20549; (202)272-7440*. You may also be able to find them at your local SEC regional office.

Thinly traded issues

Whether or not a fund is trying to inflate its paper profits by dealing in thinly traded securities is an especially difficult matter to evaluate. Sometimes the investment rules stated in the prospectus limit the fund's investment in any one company to a certain percentage of that company's market capitalization. Such a provision may make price manipulation of thinly traded securities more difficult, but it is scarcely any guarantee.

There is no law that prohibits a fund from buying obscure or thinly traded stocks. Furthermore, there are whole classes of funds with legitimate interests in such stocks. Small-company funds and emerging-growth funds, for example, regularly comb the universe of obscure stocks in their search for the next IBM or the next McDonald's. If you're in such a fund, I'm afraid you'll just have to trust the investment manager in this matter. Make sure the fund is reputable and well-established and limit your investment to 20% or less of your total portfolio. That way, even if you make a bad choice, you will still survive.

Restricted issues and letter stock

There is no law against a fund's participation in restricted issues. But there is a law against failing to disclose the practice in the prospectus. So read the fine print and be alert.

Redemptions and bear markets

The last and perhaps most insidious threat to your mutual fund investment is the possibility that mutual fund redemptions might set off another self-intensifying wave of liquidations.

Of course, one way to avoid such a debacle is to sell your shares before the next bear market hits. But as everyone who was taken by surprise by the crash of 1987 can attest, this is easier said than done.

You can, however, do a couple of things on your own. One is to stay abreast of mutual fund redemptions. These figures are reported monthly in *Barron's*. They also appear in *Trends in Mutual Fund Activity* (Investment Company Institute, *1600 M Street N.W., Washington, DC 20036;* $36 per year).

The mutual fund industry as a whole hasn't had a year of net redemptions since 1979. But sooner or later, this explosive period of expansion in mutual fund assets will come to an end. When you start to see more money flowing out than is flowing in, it's time to be on your guard. A sustained period of net redemptions will eventually force fund managers to begin liquidating their portfolios.

Closed-end protection

One way to reduce the danger of being caught up in a mutual fund bear market is to avoid open-end funds entirely and to limit yourself to closed-end funds. Closed-end funds, remember, have no obligation to redeem shares on demand and therefore are immune to the danger of forced liquidation. The universe of closed-end funds is much smaller than that of open-end funds, and selection is somewhat limited. But this is starting to change. More and more closed-end funds are now being launched as investors become increasingly aware of the risks associated with conventional open-end funds.

Before you go plunging into closed-end funds in a big way, however, let me add a word of caution.

Never buy a closed-end fund at an initial public offering. Usually the underwriter takes his fee out of the money raised from the public in such an offering. That means that only a portion of the money you put up is actually ever invested. If you wait until the fund starts trading in the secondary market—and then buy it—you avoid having to contribute to the underwriter's profits.

If you wait a little longer, you may get an even better deal. History shows that almost all closed-end funds sell at a discount to net asset value sometime in the first year after they are issued. (Unlike open-end funds, closed-end funds may trade at prices either above or below net asset value.)

By buying them at a discount, you can effectively purchase shares at 85 cents or 90 cents on the dollar (assuming a 15% or 10% discount to net asset value). That's a lot better than the $1.10 or $1.15 you'd pay for a dollar's worth of stock if you bought at the initial public offering.

False security and toll-free busy signals

Many mutual fund families offer telephone-switching facilities that include a toll-free number and the promise that you can cash in your chips on a moment's notice. Beware of the false sense of security that sometimes comes with telephone switch privileges. Some of the worst horror stories from the crash of 1987 concerned toll-free numbers that suddenly turned into toll-free busy signals.

The sheer human dimension of the stock market tragedy that unfolded in October 1987 came home to me in the hundreds of telephone conversations I had with readers. One called me late at night three or four days after the crash and told me how he had stayed home from work to telephone sell orders to his mutual funds. All day he had sat by the phone, dialing. And not once did he get through.

Meanwhile, the market was falling farther with every passing minute. "It was like being caught in a burning building," he said, "with no way out."

There are a couple of things you can do to avoid a catastrophe such as this the next time the market goes into a tailspin. One is to let a broker handle your mutual fund trades. Most brokers are accustomed to handling load fund transactions for their clients. More recently, Charles Schwab Discount Brokers has begun handling no-load fund transactions.

Chances are, your broker can get through to your mutual funds even if you can't. But there may still be a catch: During the panic that followed Black Monday, a lot of people had trouble even getting through to their brokers.

To guard against this possibility, I recommend you find out the location of your broker's nearest office. If you can't get through on the phone, you can always show up in person. Another possibility is to arrange for your broker to accept instructions by telegram.

You also can take a similar approach in dealing directly with your fund. Find out the location of the nearest office. Some of the larger fund families maintain branch offices in several major cities. Assemble in advance all the necessary documents (including signature guarantees and whatever else your fund may require) to liquidate your holdings. Then you can deliver them yourself. Or if all else fails, you can dispatch them by overnight express mail.

Of course, the ideal solution would be to arrange redemption by telegram. If your fund offers such privileges, be sure to make arrangements in advance.

Remember, a crash is a crash because very few people are able to see it coming, and once it hits even fewer are able to react quickly enough to escape without damage. But with proper planning, attention to detail, and a healthy regard for the risks, you need not be among those caught up in the next mutual fund debacle.

1. Robert Nicholson, speech delivered before a meeting of Investment Seminars International Inc. in Fort Lauderdale, FL, January 1984.

2. B.A. Wigmore, *The Crash and Its Aftermath: A History of Securities Markets in the United States 1929-1933.*

3. D. Palance, *Mutual Funds...Legal Pickpockets?*, p. 53.

4. Quoted by D.A. Dreman, "Psychology and Markets" in *Readings in Investment Management.*

5. Testimony before the House Committee on Interstate and Foreign Commerce, quoted by J.L. Springer, *The Mutual Fund Trap,* p. 141.

6. Declines calculated on the basis of the "Total Return on Common Stocks Series," part of the Index of Year-End Cumulative Wealth 1925-1986 compiled by R.G. Ibbotson and R.A. Singuefield, *Dow Jones-Irwin Business and Investment Almanac 1987.*

7. Lipper Analytical Division, Lipper Analytical Services Inc., quoted by B.G. Malkiel, *A Random Walk Down Wall Street,* p. 166-167.

8. Speech by SEC Commissioner Hugh F. Owens delivered before a group of investment bankers in 1967, quoted by D. Palance, *op. cit.,* 132.

Chapter XIII

Riding the Last Wave

Investment Success in a World of Accelerating Events

What a country calls its vital economic interests are not the things which enable its citizens to live, but the things which enable it to make war. Gasoline is much more likely than wheat to be a cause of international conflict.

—Simone Weil, *L'Enracinement*

Two great themes have dominated the first 12 chapters of this book—the loss of American self-sufficiency in energy and in capital. Together, they constitute the twin threats to your safety and prosperity. I should hasten to add, however, that when upheavals threaten, opportunities abound for those farsighted enough to anticipate what takes everyone else by surprise.

Almost every political or economic development, no matter how desirable, is bad news for someone. Imagine, for example, that someone invented a machine that prevented hurricanes. Over the years, countless lives would be saved, and untold millions of dollars worth of property damage would be averted. Nonetheless, such a development would be very bad news for companies specializing in insurance against flood and weather damage.

By the same token, few catastrophes have been so severe that no one survived, or somehow even managed to make a profit. The secret to successful investing is knowing how to find the good news—even when you must search beneath the surface of rather grim and forbidding waters. The time has come to do exactly that.

213

Oil and war

We live in a world of accelerating events. And nowhere is the accelerating pace of events more evident than in the day-to-day fluctuations of the price of oil. Much of today's investment-related oil trading takes place via one of a host of crude oil and petroleum-product futures and options contracts that have been created in the last few years. Short-term advice on how to trade in these notoriously volatile markets, however, is beyond the scope of this book. And in any case, even the best advice is soon overtaken by events.

There are, however, certain insights that may be of some value in longer-term trading on oil-related developments. One of the conclusions of Chapter 11 was that OPEC would probably be unable to sustain oil prices much above an inflation-adjusted $15 a barrel. Another was that American dependence on foreign oil was on the rise. Two companies that are well-positioned to benefit from both developments are British Petroleum (BP-NYSE) and Royal Dutch Shell (RD-NYSE).

First of all, both companies enjoy a robust cash flow and should remain profitable even if oil prices settle in the low teens. Both companies have large reserves outside the Middle East, and therefore any interruption of Mideast supplies would tend to increase demand for their products. British Petroleum, for example, is the largest North Sea producer.

But the real kicker is this: Both companies have claims on a piece of Alaskan wilderness that may contain deposits on a scale second only to Prudhoe Bay. The catch is that this land is part of the Alaska Wildlife Refuge, and it will require an act of Congress to authorize drilling rights.

Legislation to this effect already has been introduced only to die in committee, or in the second chamber after having passed the first. Moreover, Congress is sure to take its time in the aftermath of Exxon's catastrophic oil spill in the spring of 1989. But the nation's steadily climbing bill for imported oil is likely to improve the chances in subsequent legislative sessions. So would any effort to shore up an American oil industry increasingly squeezed by lower oil prices. In fact, there is good reason to believe that U.S. companies will benefit under a Bush administration dominated by Texans.

One of my Washington sources tells me that George Bush and James Baker tried to push through a tax on imported oil as cabinet members of the Reagan administration as early as 1986.

That was when concern about sharply falling oil prices finally

214

reached the highest levels of the American government. Both Bush and Baker have political roots deep in Texas where the oil industry, relentlessly squeezed by falling prices, faced its worst crisis in decades. And both were inclined to regard a healthy domestic oil industry as a national security issue.

Bush, a former oil company executive, made much of his personal fortune in the Texas petroleum industry. And when former President Reagan asked him to oversee a White House task force on the banking crisis, he also saw firsthand the trouble falling oil prices were causing for the nation's financial system. A large fraction of the nation's failing banks tend to be concentrated in oil-producing regions of the country.

In an effort to alleviate these twin crises, it is believed that Bush and Baker went to the president sometime in 1986 to plead the case for an oil import tax. Such a tax, they argued, would help save the strategic oil industry from near-collapse, and take some of the pressure off the banking system—all in one fell swoop.

But Reagan, to his credit, was adamant on the subject of tax increases—and rejected the proposal out of hand.

As we noted in Chapter 6, the major force for lower world oil prices—both in 1986 and today—is Saudi Arabia. With several centuries worth of proven reserves, the Saudis' interests are best served by keeping the price of oil low enough to discourage the development of alternative sources.

That view, however, was not shared by the rest of OPEC. Iran—under both the Shah and the Ayatollah—has historically been an advocate of high oil prices. With relatively few reserves, the Iranians have always wanted the highest possible price to maximize revenues while the oil lasts. In fact, it was precisely this disagreement that tore OPEC asunder in late 1985.

Inspired maneuver

If Bush and Baker couldn't get an oil-import tax past the president, the next best thing was to find a way to put pressure on Saudi Arabia. As a former director of the CIA, Bush was keenly aware of what could be accomplished by skillful covert action. And speculation along these lines led to an inspired maneuver.

Suppose Bush were to propose secret negotiations with Iran for the release of American hostages. The Iranians, increasingly on the defensive in the Gulf War, were known to be desperately short of ammunition and spare parts for their American-built weapons. And

215

Reagan was known to be extremely concerned about the release of American hostages.

Furthermore, any break in the long-running hostage drama would have the additional advantage of conferring political gains on the Republican Party. And if Iranian access to fresh supplies of American weapons also made the Saudis a little nervous—so much the better.

In fact, the Saudis were always acutely aware of the ebb and flow of Iranian military power. In Chapter 6, we detailed the chilling massacre at Mecca—Islam's holiest shrine—which was led by Iranian pilgrims. And that was only the most visible of many Iranian efforts to foment rebellion among the Shi'ite minority in Saudi Arabia. And as the Gulf War unfolded, Tehran periodically threatened to attack the Saudis directly if they did not end their aid to Iraq.

It is, of course, impossible to be precise about how effective this maneuver turned out to be. Certainly the Saudis suddenly became very attuned to American interests. Remember how agreeable they were when solicited to contribute funds for the Nicaraguan Contras. And oil prices did indeed recover—they remained in the $20 range until truce talks between Iran and Iraq finally brought the war to a halt.

From a political point of view, the hostage issue turned out to be a perfect cover. When the news finally leaked out, National Security Council staffer Col. Oliver North was a perfect—if unwitting—point man. By making patriotism and Central America the issues, he made certain that the question of oil prices would never come up during the ensuing investigations. And it never did.

Well-kept silence

Of course, we may never know all the details. Besides Bush and Baker, the one man most likely to have understood the full implications of the arms-for-hostages deals, CIA Director William Casey, died without writing any memoirs. Israeli arms dealer Nir, who is also believed to have played a key role, died in a mysterious Mexican plane crash in late 1988.

Bush has been conspicuously silent about his conversations with Reagan on the arms-for-hostages issue. And it will be decades before sensitive White House documents of the Reagan administration are declassified.

Nonetheless, a couple of things are clear. First, oil prices are weakening again. Moreover, the case that the American oil industry ought to be preserved in the interests of national security grows more persuasive as U.S. dependence on foreign oil grows. Meanwhile, the savings and loan crisis continues to grow steadily worse.

In light of all these considerations, there is little reason to suppose that President Bush and his Secretary of State, Jim Baker, have lost interest in either an import fee or other measures to aid the American oil industry. Most likely to be enacted are a tax credit for oil and gas exploration and some sort of energy user tax—for example, an oil import fee or a boost in the gasoline tax, or both.

Notice that an oil import fee stands at the confluence of four of the nation's most pressing issues. It might take some of the pressure off the banking system precisely in the areas of the country where it is most in trouble. By discouraging imports, it also would contribute to an improvement in the trade deficit. The revenue it produced could be used to reduce the federal budget deficit. And finally, it could also be justified as a measure to reduce the increasing dependence of the United States on foreign oil—a national security issue.

Efforts to aid the American oil industry will also help British Petroleum. Although it is an English company, it also is a major American producer. But a more diversified way to cash in on these developments is the Financial Programs Energy Portfolio sector fund. Approximately 45% of its assets are in domestic oil companies.

This is a no-load fund, and the minimum initial investment is only $150. (To obtain further information or to request a prospectus, contact Financial Programs Inc., *P.O. Box 2040, Denver, CO 80201; (800)525-8085* or *(303)779-1233.*)

$2 a barrel solution

Of course, the most obvious solution to the problem of American energy dependence is simply to increase domestic oil production. Unfortunately, that is easier said than done.

According to the Energy Information Agency and Robert W. Fisher, a director of the Independent Petroleum Association of America, the United States has something on the order of 25 to 30 billion barrels of recoverable, proven reserves. Moreover, Fisher counts an additional 327 billion barrels of oil reserves inside the continental United States.

That's more than twice the amount of oil ever pumped in the long history of U.S. oil production—and more than enough to rival the oil sheiks themselves. The problem is that this oil is unrecoverable by conventional means.

Actually, most oil is "unrecoverable." In the United States, standard extraction techniques usually manage to get only about 20%

or 30% of the oil actually in the ground before the rate of flow becomes so slow that the well becomes uneconomic to operate. In some cases, the oil is so heavy or is so loaded with paraffin that it clogs the equipment.

Conventional enhanced recovery techniques include pumping chemicals or steam into the ground to force more oil out. One problem with these methods is that they often produce large amounts of environmentally messy waste products—such as waste water from condensed steam. And in the aftermath of the Exxon *Valdez* debacle, the country is in no mood to put up with oil company pollution.

Furthermore, conventional enhanced recovery techniques are expensive. The heating costs for steam injection, for example, run $10 to $15 dollars per barrel produced. As a result, they are often uneconomic at today's price levels.

Recently, however, two promising electrothermal technologies have been developed that appear to have solved these problems. They involve using the metal tubing in oil wells to radiate heat underground in a process not unlike what goes on in your kitchen toaster. The idea is to warm things up so that the heavy crude becomes thin enough to seep out of underground formations that formerly held it captive.

Not only do electrothermal technologies avoid environmentally hazardous waste products, but they are capable of producing sustained production at a heating cost of only $2 to $3 a barrel.

One of the companies at the forefront of these technologies is the Fort-Worth-based International Royalty & Oil Co. (IROC), a penny stock traded in the over-the-counter pink sheets. ORS Corporation (ORS-OTC), which uses a different heating technique—more like a microwave oven than a toaster—is located in Denver and is effectively controlled by TransAlta, Canada's largest investor-owned utility.

Both technologies feature low capital costs, can be applied on a single-well basis regardless of depth, and can be used in conjunction with more conventional enhanced recovery techniques in especially difficult formations. In addition, both have been successfully demonstrated in pilot projects.

I believe electrothermal technologies will become increasingly important elements in meeting the energy needs of the United States. Sooner or later there's bound to be another explosion in the Mideast. And when the next oil shock arrives, these technologies are certain to become a very hot item.

Accordingly, a few shares of IROC and ORS would make an

excellent long-term speculation on what appears to be an virtually an energy inevitability.

Chemical defense

As we saw in Chapter 6, one of the legacies of the Persian Gulf war is the re-emergence of chemical weapons on world battlefields. Not only did the Iraqis pioneer the first large-scale use of chemical weapons since World War I, but open violation of all existing international treaties resulted in scarcely any adverse political consequences.

And with the Gulf War wound down, the Iraqis are free to turn their new weapons against their traditional enemy—Israel. Nor are they alone. The Syrians are also known to be developing chemical warfare capability.

Under present conditions, even the threat of chemical attack—which forces soldiers to wear bulky, poorly ventilated chemical warfare suits—is sufficient to significantly degrade the battlefield performance of an opposing army. Accordingly, it is likely that a fair amount of money will soon be spent on upgrading conventional defenses against chemical attack.

One solution to this problem may be a special ion-exchange resin developed by Rohm & Haas (ROH-NYSE). This resin has a special property that enables it to grasp and immobilize molecules of various chemical poisons with which it comes into contact.

Conventional chemical warfare suits create a barrier by encasing the soldier in rubber or plastic—which is both hot and clumsy. In contrast, this new resin (or others like it) might be used to impregnate a soldier's conventional battle dress to make it chemical resistant.

At present, this product is not a significant contributor to annual revenues at Rohm & Haas. But it could become one as the drive to improve chemical defenses gathers steam.

Oil and gold

Another profit opportunity exists in precious metals. As we noted in Chapter 6, whenever the threat of war intensifies, people with assets to protect move them to safety wherever they can. For some, this means moving assets to the United States. (That is why the U.S. dollar does not always decline on rising oil prices like the currency of other oil-consuming nations. Flight capital creates a demand for greenbacks, and therefore tends to push the dollar up in times of acute crisis.)

Other people convert assets to gold, the traditional hedge against political turmoil and economic upheaval. This makes gold prices—and, to some extent, other precious-metals prices—something of a barometer of world tension.

There are many easy ways to invest in gold. Merrill Lynch, for example, has for years offered a "gold sharebuilder account." This is very much like a regular brokerage account—only your balance is in ounces instead of shares. Similar accounts are offered by the other major brokerages and even a few banks. Any of these accounts will save you the insurance and assay costs that you would inevitably incur if you traded bullion directly. (Many accounts, however, offer you the option of withdrawing your holdings in the form of actual bullion, should you desire to do so.)

Precious-metals mutual funds offer another easy way to profit from increases in the gold price. ASA, a closed-end fund listed on the New York Stock Exchange, is made up entirely of the common stocks of South African precious-metals mining companies. If you prefer to avoid any connection at all with the moral stigma of apartheid, you might consider USAA Gold, a no-load, open-end precious metals fund with no South African holdings. For further information or to request a prospectus, contact USAA Gold, *9800 Fredricksburg Road, San Antonio, TX 78288; (512)498-8000* or *(800)531-8000.*

(Shares in open-end funds may be purchased directly from the fund itself. Closed-end funds are listed on an exchange and purchased just as any other stock. Consult your broker for details.)

Of course, there is always some danger that these financial institutions may not survive. If, for example, the United States suffered a military defeat similar to Germany at the end of World War II, probably very little would remain of the assets once held by brokerages, banks, and mutual funds. In such a situation, it would be far better to have your precious-metals holdings in the form of gold or silver coins. I recommend the Austrian Crown, the Canadian Maple Leaf, or the Canadian Silver Maple Leaf. All are small, easy to carry or conceal, and readily negotiable.

The rise of Asia

One of the arguments of Chapter 11 was that world's economic center of gravity is moving westward from North America across the Pacific. Japan already has surpassed the United States in terms of GNP per capita, and Tokyo is the new home of the world's largest stock market.

The turn of island trading states as leaders upon the world stage, however, has been generally brief. Frequently they have been surpassed by a continental power—with correspondingly greater population and resources—that merely copies their methods.

So just as the island power of Britain was overtaken by the continental power of the emerging United States in the last century, so Japan will probably be eclipsed in the next century by Asia's emerging continental power, China. Certainly, the industrialization of China will offer one of the major opportunities for building the great fortunes of the future.

But you don't have to wait until the next century to start. Major investments already are under way in what promises to be Asia's largest and most profitable markets. China has recruited hundreds of foreign companies to help build roads, a modern electric power and telephone system, and otherwise help in the mammoth task of bringing the country's antiquated infrastructure up to 20th-century standards.

Today, China has privately owned companies that are as free to make a fortune as they are to go broke. Fledgling stock markets have even been established in Shanghai and Beijing.

In the aftermath of the bloody crackdown on the peaceful demonstrators in mid-1989, it is fashionable to expect economic reform will be one of the first casualties of a Stalinist-type crackdown by Chinese communist authorities. Not only will this *not* be the case, but extreme reactions such as that which occurred in Hong Kong—where the market crashed twice in seven days—create a phenomenal profit opportunity for adventurous investors.

If you had invested heavily in U.S. stocks immediately following the crash of 1987, you already would be vastly richer today. Between May and June 1989, the Hong Kong stock market crashed twice. It's not often one has the chance to buy in at the bottom of three crashes in two years.

Investors with the courage to buy Hong Kong shares when fears are running high and civil order may hang in the balance across the border can expect to enjoy the same benefits as those who bought at the bottom of the U.S. stock market crashes of 1929 and 1987. Only in this case, they will be the Rockefellers and the Carnegies of the 21st century.

After a careful analysis of the situation in China, I have come to the conclusion that the odds favor victory for economic reformists in the power struggle now going on behind the scenes in Beijing. Economic reform, however, will not necessarily lead to Western-style democracy. While it is true that freer markets tend to make totalitarianism less manageable, they scarcely guarantee an end to authoritarian government.

A common mistake in the West has been to regard senior leader Deng Xiaoping as a kind of Chinese Thomas Paine whose long-term goals included not just economic development—but an end to communist rule as well.

What is going on in China is not a great outpouring of frustrated democratic idealism, but a bitter struggle between competing interests. Moreover, it is a struggle that will be ultimately won by those who will be able to extend market reforms—not by those who seek to reverse them.

Legacy of upheaval

The economic decentralization that has already occurred has certainly served to encourage a degree of political fragmentation. But this is nothing new. The periodic breakup of centralized authority into warring factions is an ancient theme of Chinese history. "The empire, long divided, must unite; long united, must divide" is the opening line of one of China's most famous historical epics.

I would not be surprised to see political instability persist in China for an extended period of time. After all, the power struggles that gave rise to Cultural Revolution lasted nearly a decade. During this time, expect to see local and regional officials increasingly at odds with the central party bureaucracy in Beijing.

Economic reforms, however, will survive. One reason is that once people have tasted prosperity—as well as the political influence that prosperity brings—it is impossible to turn back the clock.

Unless the economy keeps growing faster than the population, living standards can never improve, and China will never be able to join the ranks of the industrialized world. And unless food production keeps growing faster than the number of new mouths to feed, China's leaders will once again be forced to choose between widespread starvation and becoming dependent on foreign sources of food.

That's why economic reform will continue. Not because China's leaders like free markets, or because market reforms sometimes give rise to democratic impulses. It will continue because they are compelled by some pretty grim arithmetic.

The United States in the third-largest investor in China. Dozens of American companies have joint ventures of one kind or another. General Electric sells locomotives, for example, and both Pepsi and Coca-Cola have established bottling operations in China. But for an individual interested in cashing in on China, the problem with these companies—and most other American joint ventures—is that China operations count for less than 1% of revenues and profits.

The second-largest investor in China is Japan. But if you read Chapter 10, you may be pretty bearish on Japanese stocks. The largest investor, however, is Hong Kong. It is not hard to find reasonably priced companies for which China comprises a major market.

My first recommendation for cashing in on China is Hopewell Holdings. You might think of Hopewell as a Hong Kong version of the familiar real estate investment trust (REIT). An investment holding and property company, it has interests in investment and development, construction, project management, real estate, and building management on both sides of the China border. In 1987, about 38% of revenues came from China operations.

The company's first China project was the 1,200-room China Hotel in Guangzhou (Canton). Other projects include the Shajiao coal-fired Electric Power station and the Guangzhou-Shenzhen-Zhuhai superhighway. You can buy Hopewell in the United States in the form of an American Depository Receipt (ADR).

ADRs are certificates issued by a bank, and they trade as proxies for the underlying shares. One advantage of ADRs is that you can buy them through your regular stockbroker. Another is that your dividends come in U.S. dollars rather than in foreign currency.

In view of what you now know about the precariousness of many American banks, let me add a word or two about the relative safety of ADRs. ADRs are issued by banks in a fiduciary capacity. That means you are legally protected in the event that the bank goes broke. If that should happen, ADR holders *do not* end up in a long line of unsecured creditors along with everyone else the bank owes. Nor can the underlying shares of foreign stock be seized by any other creditor as part of the bank's assets. If the bank that issues your ADR goes broke, you might have to put up with some delays in processing ADR business. But you don't have to worry about losing your investment. About the worst that could happen is that you could end up the direct owner of some foreign share certificates.

Red chip funds

There are several mutual funds that specialize in China market-related investments. One is the Thornton Group's open-end Hong Kong & China Gateway Fund, *10th floor United Center, 95 Queensway, Hong Kong.* Another is the closed-end Baring China & Eastern Fund, *1901 Edinburgh Tower, 15 Queen's Road Central, Hong Kong,* which is listed on the London Stock Exchange.

Unless you are an institutional investor, however, you'll run into serious bureaucratic obstacles if you try to buy shares in either of these funds. That is because neither is registered inside the United States with the Securities and Exchange Commission. Even though it is perfectly legal for you to own shares, it is a violation of U.S. securities regulations for an unregistered company to send virtually any information to a U.S. address.

That makes it hard to communicate, unless you visit Hong Kong yourself—or establish an offshore correspondent address. (For a list of offshore mail forwarding services, see the classified section of the *International Herald Tribune*.) Another problem stems from recent changes in the U.S. tax code—they greatly complicate matters for anyone who has to declare income from a non-U.S. registered fund.

There is, however, one way around these complications. The London Stock Exchange lists a warrant on the Baring China & Eastern Fund. (A warrant is a call option with several years to expiration.)

If you buy the warrant—and not the fund itself—you never have any income to declare for tax purposes. And that avoids any tax complications associated with ownership of a non-U.S. registered fund. Each warrant gives you the right to buy one share of the China & Eastern fund for $1 anytime between Oct. 1, 1988, and Sept. 30, 1991.

You can find both the shares and the warrants quoted daily in the *Financial Times'* London Share Service under the heading of "Investment Trusts." (Remember that the price you see there is quoted in pounds sterling.)

Pearl Harbor II

If you still own Japanese stocks, it probably is time to take your profits. And be ready to sell your U.S. shares the instant you hear any reports about a major natural disaster in the Japanese home islands. For the reasons we've already explored, an earthquake in Japan is likely to shake stock markets as far away as the United States.

Another promising opportunity for profit is to invest in other rapidly growing Asian markets that are likely to benefit from any decline in Japan. First choices in this regard are Hong Kong, Singapore/Malaysia, and Thailand. A good way to invest in the latter is through the New York Stock Exchange–listed closed-end Malaysia and Thai Funds.

No pure Hong Kong fund exists in the United States. However, you can achieve excellent exposure to the Hong Kong economy by buying the shares of three blue-chip companies, all of which are available inside the United States as ADRs: Hong Kong & Shanghai Bank; Cheung Kong; and Jardine Matheson.

These three stocks will give you a stake in all three major areas of the Hong Kong economy. Hong Kong & Shanghai Bank is a leading financial services firm and owner of the U.S.–based Marine Midland Bank. Cheung Kong is a blue-chip property and real estate company, and Jardine Matheson is a major trading firm.

Japanese-American spread

There are, of course, alternative interpretations concerning the investment implications of the situation in Japan. Some analysts who have examined the data have concluded that Japan is blazing new investment trails—and that the United States eventually will follow. If they are correct, what you should look for is not so much a dramatic decline in Japanese stocks, but a dramatic increase in the U.S. stock market.

Fortunately, there is a way to play both these scenarios at once. What you should do is combine a long position in U.S. stocks with a short position in Japanese stocks. (Taking long positions is what old-fashioned buy-and-hold investors do. They buy a stock and wait for the price to go up. A short sale, on the other hand, is a way of profiting from *declining* prices. Your broker will be happy to explain the details.)

If you are long America and short Japan, you make money when either the U.S. market rises or the Japanese stock market falls. If both happen at once, you make money on both sides. This kind of double trade is called a spread—and generally is less risky than betting on either the American or Japanese side alone. With a spread like this, you are essentially betting on a narrowing of the difference in stock prices in Tokyo and New York.

I believe that a narrowing of this difference is a pretty safe bet. All over the world, the trend is toward increasing deregulation of financial markets. More and more stocks are listed on exchanges in more than one country. Trading links are being established that allow you to buy and sell in several world markets simultaneously. Markets are extending their hours so that time differences are less of an obstacle in cross-market trading. Sometime in the next decade—barring a major war or depression—I predict you will able to trade the world's major markets on a 24-hour-a-day basis.

All these trends point toward a lowering of the very barriers that allow big differences in price levels among major markets to persist. Narrowing those differences in prices is just what this spread is designed to allow you to capitalize on.

What securities to buy and sell

Assuming I've convinced you that this is a good idea, let us now turn to the matter of which securities you should buy and sell. An excellent means of taking a position in the U.S. market as a whole would be to buy the Vanguard Index Trust. This is a no-load index fund from the Vanguard family of mutual funds. (For further information or to request a prospectus, contact Vanguard Group, *Vanguard Financial Center, Valley Forge, PA 19482; (800) 662-SHIP.*)

The Vanguard Index Trust, as its name implies, simply buys the stocks that make up a broad U.S. stock market index—in this case, the Standard & Poor's 500 Index. As a result, it makes an ideal vehicle for taking a long position in the U.S. stock market as a whole.

Taking a short position in the Japanese market, however, is not so easy. As we saw in Chapter 10, short selling is not allowed in Japan. That means you have to look to Japanese funds or stocks listed in the United States. There are numerous U.S.–based international funds that invest in Asian or Pacific stocks. But the only pure play in the Japanese market is the Japan Fund, now part of the Scudder family of mutual funds.

The problem with the Japan Fund, however, is that it is an open-end fund. Except for a handful of funds issued by Fidelity, the Boston-based mutual fund giant, and traded by their in-house brokerage firm, no open-end funds can be sold short. If we can't use the Japan Fund, we will have to create our own portfolio to sell short. Fortunately, there is no particular problem in executing short sales of ADRs.

What follows is my suggestion for a diversified portfolio of Japanese stocks to use as a short position opposite the Vanguard Index Trust.

Stock	Cusip
Aida Engineering	008712200
Fuji Heavy Industries	359556206
Japan Steel Works	471100206
Kirin Brewery Co.	497350207

Mitsubishi Chemical Industries	606759207
Mitsubishi (Real) Estate Co.	606783207
Mitsui Bank	606833200
Nagoya Railroad Co.	629744202
Nomura Securities	655361301
Taisho Marine & Fire Insurance	874021207
Toyota Motor Corp.	892331307
Tsugami Corp.	898536206

Nikkei put warrants

Another way to profit directly from a decline in Tokyo is to buy the Nikkei put warrants listed on the Toronto stock exchange. Note that the price you will be quoted is in Canadian dollars. (Put options, like short sales, are a means of profiting from declining prices.)

Here's how these put warrants work. If the Nikkei Dow is below 32,174 (called the exercise level) in February 1992, when the warrants expire, you are in the money. By how much? That depends on the amount by which the strike price exceeds the level of the Nikkei Dow at expiration.[1]

But the truth is, you don't have to wait until expiration to take your profits. If the Japanese market took a tumble tomorrow, the warrants would immediately rise in price. So you could simply call your broker and ask him to sell your holdings. If Japanese share prices recovered and you wanted to speculate on a further decline, you could always buy in again at some later time.

But the major advantage of the Nikkei put warrant is that it offers highly leveraged returns on a very modest initial investment. You can buy a single contract for less than $300—far less than what it would take to put on the Japanese-American spread outlined above.

If you find that your regular broker can't trade them, contact Barry Murphy & Co. of Boston at *(800)288-1400*. For further information about the warrants themselves, contact the Toronto Stock Exchange, *2 First Canadian Place, Toronto, Ontario, Canada M5X 1JS; (416)947-4700*.

Two other markets that would likely benefit from a decline or a crash in Japan include Taiwan and South Korea. Closed-end country funds are available for each on the New York Stock Exchange. However, I recommend neither one of them for purchase at this time.

Before I explain why, let me quickly review some of the things that distinguish closed-end funds from their better known open-end brethren. Unlike open-end funds, closed-end funds are listed on an exchange. That means you can buy them through your regular broker as you would any other stock. (You also can sell closed-end funds short.) But there is another, more important difference. Unlike open-end funds, closed-end funds can trade at prices either above or below net asset value. (Net asset value simply is the current market value of the fund's holdings divided by the number of fund shares outstanding.)

Funds trading above net asset value is said to be trading at a premium. Funds below net asset value is said to be trading at a discount. Closed-end funds and their premiums and discounts appear every Monday in the *Wall Street Journal* and *Barron's*.

Shorting Asia's little dragons

Experience has shown that most closed-end funds tend to trade at a discount. Both the Taiwan and Korea Funds, however, often trade at enormous premiums. Buying a closed-end fund at a 50% premium, for example, means paying $1.50 for the privilege of owning a dollar's worth of assets in South Korea or Taiwan. Why would anybody do that? Because these two funds have a monopoly on access to these markets.

Unlike Hong Kong and Singapore/Malaysia, both Taiwan and South Korea are, except for their respective country funds, closed to investment by foreigners. There are, for example, no South Korean ADRs. As an American you can't even buy South Korean stocks through a Korean stockbroker. The *only* way for you to invest in South Korea is through the Korea Fund. This virtual monopoly on foreign investment is what sustains share prices of the Korea Fund so far above net asset value. It is the same story with the Taiwan Fund.

Paying monopoly prices surely is no bargain. Worse, both markets will someday open their doors to more direct foreign equity investments. When that happens, the monopoly will be broken, and the premiums on these two funds will be certain to disappear. In my opinion, that makes the Korea and Taiwan funds attractive candidates for short sales whenever you see them trading at a premium of 50% or more. However, I recommend this strategy only to patient investors. No one knows how long it might take for these barriers to direct foreign ownership of equity to be relaxed.

Danger of a banking collapse

There are several ways to profit from a banking crisis. One is to buy gold. This, however, must be done no later than the first phase of the crisis—when the crisis of confidence begins. (For more on the three phases of a banking crisis, see Chapter 12.) Gold, as we have noted, is something of an indicator of the market's level of tension. The time to sell, therefore, is during phase two of the crisis—when panic begins to spread to other institutions.

By the time the crisis gets to phase three—when financial crisis spills over into deflationary depression—gold is likely to be well on its way back down. In a deflationary depression, cash—not gold—is king. As prices fall, unspent cash increases in value every day. That means the people who hold cash will be best off, and those who owe money will be among the hardest hit.

Another way to profit from the banking crisis is to pick up a few shares in a company that has built a reputation for itself working with the FDIC to restructure troubled U.S. banks. Hallwood Group (HWG-NYSE) is such a stock.

Hallwood's team of restructuring specialists has been helping put bankrupt and near-bankrupt firms back on their feet for some time. Usually these restructuring plans include the sale of new stock. And Hallwood's compensation usually includes fees as well as an equity stake in the turnaround effort.

Past projects have left Hallwood with a 9% share of CGA Corp., a 11% share of Brock Hotels and a 37% share of Saxon Oil Development Partners. In recent years, Hallwood has become very involved in efforts to rescue failing banks. A share of the restructuring of Bank Texas Group Inc. netted the company $8.3 million in 1987. The company also has a stake in the restructuring plan for Alliance Bancorporation of Alaska.

In addition to a provider of specialized financial services, Hallwood also is a real estate company with rental properties in both the United States and Europe. Property management fees produce a third of its real estate income.

Contrarian S&L selection

Another way to profit from the banking crisis is to pick up shares of quality companies at depressed prices. One such company is Loyola Capital (LOYC-OTC), the holding company for the Baltimore-based Loyola Federal Savings & Loan.

Loyola's reputation as one of the most conservatively run of Maryland's thrifts served it well during the state's much publicized savings and loan catastrophe several years ago. While most S&Ls faced a net outflow of funds from panicky depositors, Loyola enjoyed a huge inflow from nervous investors seeking a safe haven for their funds.

When Loyola Capital went public in late 1986, shares were initially offered to depositors—who responded with such enthusiasm that the initial public offering was more than 50% oversubscribed.

With seven subsidiaries that include real estate development companies, an appraisal company, an insurance company, and a full-service stock brokerage operation, it is well-positioned to survive in a volatile interest rate environment. Nor is it overly dependent on the health of the local real estate market. Six or seven years hence, when the S&L crisis has passed, and the barriers to interstate acquisitions of thrifts begin to come down, Loyola will make a prime takeover candidate.

TED Spread

Yet a third way of profiting from the banking crisis is the well-known TED spread. The T stands for T-bills, ED for Eurodollars.

T-bills, of course, are short-term debt securities issued by the U.S. Treasury. And, in the TED spread, they are a proxy for the interest rates paid by the most creditworthy borrowers—in this case, the U.S. government.

The term, Eurodollars, refers to a pool of footloose capital be-

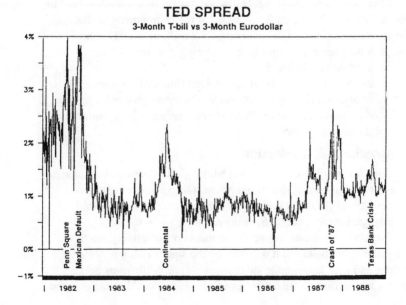

TED SPREAD
3-Month T-bill vs 3-Month Eurodollar

230

yond the regulatory jurisdiction and control of any nation. A Eurodollar loan, therefore, is not guaranteed by any national authority.

In times of crisis, the spread between T-bill interest rates and Eurodollar interest tends to widen. That's because Eurodollar lenders demand a higher return as compensation for the extra risk of making what amounts to largely unsecured loans. When the crisis passes, and people stop worrying about widespread bankruptcies and defaults, this risk premium shrinks, and the spread tends to narrow.

The easiest way to put on a TED spread is use the T-bill and Eurodollar futures contracts traded on the International Monetary Mart at the Chicago Mercantile Exchange. If you expect the banking crisis to worsen, you would be long T-bills and short Eurodollars. If you expected a crisis to abate, you would do the opposite.

This, however, is a strategy suitable only for experienced futures traders. If you're new to futures trading, start with something simpler.

(For a fuller treatment of the topic of banking crises, see my *Complete Report of Banking Safety and Privacy,* published by Agora Inc., 824 E. Baltimore St., Baltimore, MD 21202.)

Cashing in on capitalism

Yet another long-term investment opportunity lies in the new global popularity of capitalism. Stock markets are on the rise in less developed countries, as governments turn to foreign capital as a source of investment. The International Finance Corp., an arm of the World Bank, has been instrumental in encouraging this trend. It has even participated in the creation of several closed-end country funds.

It is an axiom of traditional security analysis that the investor often can make more money in small emerging growth stocks than he can in established blue-chip issues. The same logic can be applied to emerging countries as well.

An emerging country is any nation with a low- or middle-income economy. According to criteria defined by the World Bank, there presently are 95 such countries. Of those, only 42 are sufficiently stable to make suitable candidates for foreign investment. Those 42 countries, however, managed to achieve average annual economic growth of 2.85% during the decade ending in 1984. During the same period, the world's industrialized countries managed only a 2.4% growth rate. Like small stocks, small economies often outperform the rest.

Some 6,000 stocks (amounting to a total market capitalization of about $150 billion) are listed in these 42 countries. Some of them are bound to contain the IBMs and AT&Ts of tomorrow. Digging up reliable investment information on obscure companies in obscure markets, however, is an extraordinarily difficult task. Fortunately, somebody has done the work for you. One is the Templeton Emerging Markets Funds, a closed-end fund listed on the American Stock Exchange is an excellent long-term bet for the future. (For further information, contact Templeton Emerging Markets Fund, *700 Central Ave., St. Petersburg, FL 33701; (813)823-8712.*)

Hong Kong and Finland

Another way to cash in on the growing popularity of capitalism is to invest in those economies most likely to benefit from the increasingly capitalist methods being adopted by the world's two communist giants, the People's Republic of China and the Soviet Union.

Nearby Hong Kong is likely to be the principal beneficiary of China's experiment with capitalism. During a recent visit to the Far East, I toured one of the enterprise zones recently established in southeastern China. Already, Hong Kong companies and Hong Kong–based investors appear to have captured the lion's share of the business. As this trend continues, the Hong Kong economy stands to be the principal beneficiary of the increasingly profitable China trade.

I already have suggested a portfolio of Hong Kong stocks in connection with the discussion of Japan. However, these Hong Kong stocks also would make excellent prospects on their own merits.

Not to be outdone, the Soviet Union under Gorbachev has recently begun its own experiment with capitalism. Just as the Chinese have turned to Hong Kong for help in modernization of industry and economic development, the Soviets also are likely to turn to a nearby capitalist neighbor—Finland.[2]

As yet there are no mutual funds investing only in Finland. However, there are three Finnish stocks that are available in the form of ADRs.

ADR	Cusip
Finnish Sugar	317912202
Instrumentarium Corp.	457805208
Oy Wartsila AB	692087208

Finnish Sugar is a food, animal feed, and biotechnology company. Instrumentarium Corp. is a manufacturer of hospital and diagnostic equipment. And Wartsila is an industrial conglomerate

232

with close connections to Moscow. All three stand to benefit from Soviet President Gorbachev's effort to use Western technology to modernize the backward Soviet economy.

These, then, are my suggestions for riding the last wave to investment prosperity. Much more could be said, of course, but it would necessarily be of a more short-term nature, and therefore better suited to some other forum. (If you are interested in this kind of analysis on an on-going basis, I invite you to become a reader of my monthly newsletter. See details in the note from the publisher at the back of the book.)

Preparing for a dollar crisis

One of the great themes of this book has concerned how the loss of American self-sufficiency in capital puts the stock market at the mercy of events far beyond our shores. Nowhere is this clearer than in the relationship between the foreign exchange value of the dollar and the stock market.

After the Dow's August 1987 peak, the stock market began showing uncommon sensitivity to the dollar. Whenever the greenback drops too much, it often seems to drag the stock market down in its wake. Such a state of affairs makes non-dollar-denominated investments especially attractive.

If, for example, you own a security priced in West German Deutschemarks or Japanese yen while the dollar declines, the price of that security goes up even if it does nothing in nominal terms.

If you own a West German bond, you get the same amount of Deutschemarks in interest every reporting period. But as U.S. currency weakens, the same number of Deutschemarks buys a greater number of dollars each time. In effect, the falling dollar provides you with a dividend increase.

When weakness in the greenback tends to send Wall Street into a tailspin, a few investments such as these are like money in the bank. I have two suggestions designed to help you make the most of this phenomenon.

The first is the Global Yield Fund, a diversified, closed-end global bond fund listed on the New York Stock Exchange. For most of 1987, it posted a yield of 10% or better. After the crash of 1987, it posted a series of new highs. (Remember, you can purchase closed-end funds through your regular stockbroker just as you would any other stock.)

My final suggestion is the Huntington Global Cash Portfolio. This fund invests in short-term, non-dollar-denominated, money-market-

233

type instruments. You might think of it as a kind of non-dollar money market fund. This also is an open-end fund, and you will have to pay a small sales charge on your initial purchase. For further information or to request a prospectus, contact Huntington Advisors, *251 S. Lake St. #600, Pasadena, CA 91101; (800)826-0188* or *(213)681-3700.* (Huntington Advisors also offers single-currency funds denominated in Swiss francs, West German Deutschemarks, Japanese yen, British pounds sterling, Australian dollars, and Canadian dollars.)

Epilogue

"Money," said Scipion de Gramont...no doubt quoting someone else!..."is the blood and soul of men. He who has none wanders as one dead among the living."

I hope that after having come this far, I have left you fortified with some full-blooded investment ideas for making the most of the last wave of investment prosperity and the troubled times ahead. And even if I have not, I hope I have at least spun a compelling tale.

[1.] To calculate your profits at expiration, assume the Nikkei Dow closes at 26,174 in February 1992—that is, 6,000 yen below the exercise level of 32,174.

The first step is convert the amount by which you are "in the money"—in this case 6,000 yen—to Canadian dollars. Suppose C$1 buys 121 yen. Then 6,000 yen would buy C$49.59.

The next step is to multiply this amount by the exercise number, which is 11.68. (C$ 49.59 x 11.68 = C$ 579.17) That's what each warrant contract would be worth at expiration. Of course, if the Nikkei Dow is above the exercise price at expiration, the warrant expires worthless.

[2.] For an excellent treatment of this topic, see W. Rees-Mogg, J.D. Davidson, and J.B. Wittenberg, "How to Profit from the Crisis in Communism;" and J.D. Davidson and W. Rees-Mogg, *Blood in the Streets.*

See also *Kennedy,* The Decline of the West.

Bibliography

Addington, Larry. *The Patterns of War Since the 18th Century,* Indiana University Press, Bloomington, IN, 1984.

Ahrari, Mohammed E. *OPEC: The Falling Giant,* University Press of Kentucky, Lexington, KY, 1986.

Batra, R. *The Great Depression of 1990,* Simon & Schuster, New York, 1987.

Beres, Louis R. *Terrorism and Global Security: The Nuclear Threat,* Westview Press, London, 1987.

Brodie, Bernard and Fawn M. *From Crossbow to H-Bomb,* Indiana University Press, Bloomington, IN, 1973.

Brown, Harold. *Thinking About National Security: Defense and Foreign Policy in a Dangerous World,* Westview Press, Boulder, CO, 1983.

Bush, N.F. *Two Minutes to Noon,* Simon & Schuster, New York, 1962.

Clark, R.C. *Technological Terrorism,* Devin-Adair Co., Old Greenwich, CT, 1980.

Cooper, Chester L. *The Lion's Last Roar: Suez 1956,* Harper & Row, New York, 1971.

Czeschin, Robert. *The Complete Report of Banking Safety and Privacy,* Agora Inc., Baltimore, MD, 1989.

Davidson, James D. and Rees-Mogg, W. *Blood in the Streets,* Summit Books, New York, 1987.

Deese, David A. "Oil, War, and Grand Strategy," *Orbis*, Vol. 25, Fall 1981, Foreign Policy Research Institute.

Dore, R. and Sinha, R. *Japan and World Depression—Then and Now,* St. Martin's Press, New York, 1987.

Dunnigan, James F. and Bay, Austin, *A Quick & Dirty Guide to War: Briefings on Present and Potential Wars,* William Morrow, New York, 1986.

Fabozzi, F. A. *Readings in Investment Management,* Richard D. Irwin, Homewood, IL, 1963.

Festinger, L., Riechen, H. W., and Schachter, S. *When Prophecy Fails,* Harper & Row, New York, 1956.

Freedman, Lawrence Z. and Alexander, Yonah, eds. *Perspectives on Terrorism,* Scholarly Resources, Inc., Wilmington, DE, 1983.

Fullick, Roy and Powell, Geoffrey. *Suez: The Double War,* Hamish Hamilton, London, 1979.

Girardet, Edward R. *Afghanistan: The Soviet War,* St. Martin's Press, New York, 1985.

Goralski, R. and Freeburg, R. *Oil and War,* William Morrow and Co., New York, 1987.

Guderian, Heinz. *Panzer Leader,* E.P. Dutton, New York, 1952.

Herz, Martin F., ed. *Diplomats and Terrorists: What Works, What Doesn't, A Symposium,* Institute for the Study of Diplomacy, Edmund A. Walsh School of Foreign Service, Georgetown University, Washington, DC, 1982.

Herzog, Chaim. *Arab-Israeli Wars: War and Peace in the Middle East from the War of Independence through Lebanon,* Random House, New York, 1982.

Kaufman, Henry. *Interest Rates, the Markets, and the New Financial World,* Times Books, New York, 1986.

Kennedy, Paul. *The Rise and Fall of the Great Powers: Economic Change and Military Conflict from 1500 to 2000,* Random House, New York, 1987.

Kindel, Stephen. "Catching Terrorists," *Science Digest,* September 1986.

Kondratieff, Nickolai. *The Long Wave Cycle,* trans. Guy Daniels, Richardson & Synder, New York, 1984.

Laffin, H. *War Annual I,* Brassey's Defense Publishers, London, 1988.

Lewis, B. *The Assassins: A Radical Sect in Islam,* Weidenfeld and Nicolson, London, 1967.

Livingston, Neil C. *The War Against Terrorism,* Lexington Books, Lexington, MA, 1982.

Machiavelli, Niccolo and Detmold, D.E., trans. *The Prince,* Penguin Books, Middlesex, England, 1963.

Macksey, K. *Technology and War: The Impact of Science on Weapon Development and Modern Battle,* Prentice Hall, New York, 1986.

Maurice, C. and Smithson, C.W. *The Doomsday Myth: 10,000 Years of Economic Crisis,* Hoover Institution Press, Stanford University, Stanford, CA, 1984.

Martin, David C. and Walcott, John. *Best Laid Plans: The Inside Story of America's War Against Terrorism,* Harper & Row, New York, 1988.

McIntosh, M. *Japan Rearmed,* St. Martin's Press, New York, 1986.

Miller, Marshall Lee. "Soviet Military Developments—The Soviet General Staff's Secret Plans for Invading Iran," *Armed Forces Journal International,* January 1987.

Modderno, Francine. *Traveler's Health & Safety Handbook,* Agora Inc., Baltimore, 1986.

O'Ballance, Edgar. *Language of Violence: The Blood Politics of Terrorism,* Presidio Press, San Rafael, CA, 1979.

O'Connor, Harvey. *World Crisis in Oil,* Monthly Review Press, New York, 1962.

Odell, Peter R. *Oil and World Power,* 7th Edition, Richard Clay (The Chaucer Press) Ltd., Bungay, Suffolk, U.K., 1983.

O'Sullivan, Noel, ed. *Terrorism, Ideology, and Revolution,* Westview Press, Boulder, CO, 1986.

Palance, D. *Mutual Funds...Legal Pickpockets?,* Vantage Press, New York, 1963.

Pipes, D. *In the Path of God,* Basic Books, New York, 1983.

Rustow, Dankwart A. *Oil and Turmoil: America Faces OPEC and the Middle East,* W.W. Norton & Co., New York, 1982.

Schemmer, Benjamin F. "Was the U.S. Ready to Resort to Nikes for the Persian Gulf in 1980?" *Armed Forces Journal International,* September 1986.

Shansab, Nasir. *Soviet Expansion in the Third World: Afghanistan: A Case Study,* Bartleby Press, Silver Springs, MD, 1986.

Springer, J.L. *The Mutual Fund Trap,* Henry Regnery Co., Chicago, 1973.

Sterling, Claire. *The Terror Network: The Secret War of International Terrorism,* Holt, Rinehart and Winston, New York, 1981.

Stoff, Michael B. *Oil, War, and American Security: The Search for a National Policy on Foreign Oil, 1941-1947,* Yale University Press, New Haven, CT, 1980.

Talbot, Strobe, ed., trans. *Khrushchev Remembers,* Little, Brown & Co., Boston, 1970.

Thomas, Gordon and Morgan-Witts, Max. *Pontiff,* Doubleday & Co., New York, 1983.

Thucydides, trans. by Rex Warner. *History of the Peloponnesian War,* Penguin Books, Middlesex, England, 1956.

Tuchman, Barbara. *The Guns of August,* Bantam, New York, 1976.

Uchino, Tatsuro. *Japan's Postwar Economy: An Insider's View of its History and Future,* Kodansha International Ltd., Tokyo, 1978.

Venn, Fiona. *Oil Diplomacy in the 20th Century,* St. Martin's Press, New York, 1986.

Viner, Aron. *The Emerging Power of Japanese Money,* Dow Jones-Irwin, Homewood, IL, 1988.

Wigmore, B.A. *The Crash and Its Aftermath—A History of Securities Markets in the United States 1929-1933,* Greenwood Press, Westport, CT.

Wright, Peter and Greengrass, Paul. *Spycatcher,* Dell, New York, 1987.

Wright, Robin. *Sacred Rage: The Wrath of Militant Islam,* Simon & Schuster, New York, 1986.

238

Acknowledgments

Like most writers, I owe countless debts that I can never repay. Books are never a one-man show, and this one rests upon the labors of many. My sources appear in the dozens of footnotes that adorn the closing pages of this book, but my inspiration grew out of conversations with two great men: John Dessauer, publisher of *Dessauer's Journal of Financial Markets,* and James Davidson, editor of *Strategic Investment.* Both have contributed mightily, if unwittingly, to my education as both an investor and a writer.

I am especially grateful to Bill Bonner, president of Agora Books, who not only served as the guiding light of this project, but also paid my salary during the many months it was under way. I also would like to thank Washington, D.C.–based Mideast consultant Michael Miklaucic for his thoughtful comments on several previous drafts of this manuscript. I am also indebted to numerous others both inside and outside the United States for insightful comments and suggestions.

Others to whom I own special debts include Adrienne Locke, for many hours of research; Kathleen Peddicord and Brenda Greene for careful copy editing; Becky Mangus, Denise Plowman, Wilma Vinck, Sara Morris, and Elizabeth Cox for production; and Jane Lears for shepherding the entire enterprise on to its logical conclusion.

To all these people, I owe credit for what is worthy of merit in this slim volume. That which is not, I cheerfully acknowledge as mine alone.

About the Author

Robert Czeschin is the former editor of the prestigious *World Financial Review* and the *Mutual Fund Performance Journal.* He speaks frequently at investment conferences in the United States, Europe, and the Far East. Educated in Chicago, he earned a bachelor of arts in philosophy from the University of Chicago and a master's in business administration from the University of Illinois. Upon graduation, he was inducted into Beta Gamma Sigma, the honorary society for excellence in graduate business studies. He is presently editor of *Czeschin's Mutual Fund Outlook and Recommendations.*

A note from the publisher:

If this kind of analysis appeals to you—and you don't want to wait until Czeschin's next book—perhaps you'd like to join the readers of *Czeschin's Mutual Fund Outlook and Recommendations.* This monthly newsletter brings you up-to-the-minute market commentary as well as three separate model investment portfolios: the Income Portfolio, for the conservative investor who aims to maximize current income; the Long-term Growth Portfolio, for investors interested in long-term capital appreciation; and the Jaguar Portfolio, for fast-moving aggressive investors with a carnivorous appetite for profits.

As a reader of *The Last Wave*, you are entitled to a special low introductory rate of only $77 for 12 issues. Fill in the coupon and mail it today. You never know where the market will be by this time tomorrow.

Special Introductory Offer

[ ] **Yes!** Please begin my subscription to *Czeschin's Mutual Fund Outlook and Recommendations* for the low introductory rate of only $77.

[ ] Enclosed is my check for $77

Name _____

Address _____

City/State/Zip _____

Mail to:
Czeschin's Mutual Fund Outlook and Recommendations,
P.O. Box 1423
Baltimore, MD 21203-1423
USA

FREE! To readers of The Last Wave: "Mutual Fund Secrets," an eye-opening special report on little known techniques that you can use to nail down your share of investment profits—even in a bear market! Just mail this coupon today.

Enclosed with your special report will be a free copy of *Czeschin's Mutual Fund Outlook and Recommendations,* the only financial advisory that applies the investment insight of *The Last Wave* on an ongoing basis.